D0875472

ALFONSO REYES AND SPAIN

ALFONSO REYES
Madrid, 1923

Alfonso Reyes and Spain

HIS DIALOGUE WITH

Unamuno, Valle-Inclán,
Ortega y Gasset,
Jiménez, and
Gómez de la Serna

BY BARBARA BOCKUS APONTE

UNIVERSITY OF TEXAS PRESS, AUSTIN & LONDON

International Standard Book Number 0-292-70300-7
Library of Congress Catalog Card Number 78-37254
© 1972 by Barbara Bockus Aponte
All rights reserved
Type set by G&S Typesetters, Austin
Printed by The University of Texas Printing Division, Austin
Bound by Universal Bookbindery, Inc., San Antonio

To my father

CONTENTS

ACKNOWLEDGMENTS

The correspondence between Alfonso Reyes and his Spanish friends, which is the basis for this book, is presented through the kindness and generosity of the late Sra. Manuela Mota de Reyes, under whose wise and friendly guidance I conducted my research in the Alfonso Reyes library. I am also grateful to Dr. Alfonso Reyes, the son of doña Manuela and don Alfonso, and to their granddaughter, doña Alicia Reyes, who allowed me to use this material and whose continued interest stimulated me in my work.

I am also indebted to the following people for their permission to quote from the personal correspondence of the writers: doña María de Unamuno, Dr. Carlos del Valle-Inclán, doña Soledad Ortega, don Francisco Hernández-Pinzón Jiménez, and don Gaspar Gómez de la Serna.

From the very outset I have been fortunate to have the counsel and encouragement of Professor Ricardo Gullón of The University of Texas at Austin and hereby acknowledge my deep gratitude to him.

A Summer Research Award from Temple University, Philadelphia, enabled me to complete this project.

BARBARA B. APONTE

ALFONSO REYES AND SPAIN

The Background
to a Dialogue

IN 1913, AT THE HEIGHT of the Mexican Revolution, a thoughtful
young man of small stature and slightly rounded figure set out for
Europe in search of a future. The national upheaval had marked
him with personal tragedy: his leave-taking hinted at honorable
exile. He was not to return permanently to Mexico until 1938.
Alfonso Reyes had become, during these years, Spanish America's
foremost humanist and man of letters, whose many books and far-
flung friendships attested to his creative sojourns in the capitals of
Europe and America, and to the *simpatía* that was the mark of his
personality. At the time of his death in December 1959 he had
been honored throughout the Hispanic world for over fifty years
of devotion to the literary profession. Essayist and poet, literary
critic and theorist, classicist, author of short stories and poetic

drama, brilliant stylist, he is revealed by every facet of his protean genius as a scholar endowed with a love of grace and poetry, an erudite who writes, it was said, "with the facile elegance of a god arranging the universe."[1] The unique blend of profundity, lyricism, and sparkling ingenuity of thought that characterizes his prose earns him a place among the greatest essayists of the twentieth century.

The breadth of his interests and enthusiasms was extraordinary. His wit, his knowledge, and his love of beauty encompassed all men and all cultures with cordial and sensitive understanding. Mallarmé, Goethe, Vergil, Chesterton—each captured his imagination and inspired many of his essays. Classical Greek literature initiated him into humanistic endeavors, and in his later years he insistently probed the values of Greek culture. He revealed himself as an idealistic social philosopher in his preoccupation with the significance of Spanish America's history and with the delineation of its future goals. Mexico stands brilliantly illuminated in *Visión de Anáhuac* (1917), where the first encounter between the Aztec and the conquistador is painted with glistening, dynamic strokes. Myriad themes, an irrepressible stream of ideas deftly molded into a flowing form, all are united by the intimacy of Reyes' presence.

Whether he has one savor culinary delights, follow a medieval Spanish archpriest over snowy mountain passes, or envy the destiny of New York's 2,350 missing persons, whether his theme is philosophy or whimsy, it matters not: he persuasively draws the reader into a cordial dialogue. Such is the special enchantment of his style, a reflection, perhaps, of the proverbial graciousness and courtesy of the Mexican. Reyes never pontificated, nor overwhelmed one with his erudition, but wrote as though conversing with friends.[2] His essays have been aptly called an exercise in intimacy.[3]

---

[1] José Luis Martínez, ed., *El ensayo mexicano moderno*, I, 267.

[2] This idea is expressed by Federico de Onís in his Foreword to Alfonso Reyes, *The Position of America and Other Essays*, p. *x*.

[3] Amado Alonso, "Alfonso Reyes," *Sur* 6, no. 23 (1936): 122.

A strong lyric undercurrent—the imprint of the inner Reyes—
gives an unmistakable flavor to his essays, to his correspondence.
Reflected on every page is a conversational art rarely equaled in
Hispanic literature. The total identification between Reyes the
man and Reyes the writer enables the reader to enter into the
same highly personal literary world, alive with perceptions born
of seemingly inexhaustible knowledge, that drew so many visitors
from all over the world to Reyes' Mexico City home.

The Reyes of these later years rarely left the shelter of his
books, but behind him were the years of travel and a life lived as
a continual cultural experience. The books, rather than a weight
upon his soul as he had sometimes viewed them in his youth, were
the symbol of his freedom from narrowness, provinciality, and in-
tolerance. When had this universal outlook taken definitive root?
Principally during the years he spent in Spain, years fundamental
to his literary development, and whose description will be the
subject of this book.

Reyes arrived in Madrid in 1914, penniless and unsure of the
path he would take. Yet the ten-year period that followed was, he
said, "the central period of my life, the best that this earth has
given me since the childhood years spent with my parents."[4]
There can be no doubt about its focal position in Reyes' literary
career. At its conclusion he had achieved professional maturity
and wide acclaim as a writer. He had become a perfect example
of the true literary humanist whose enthusiasm and interests are
international in scope. Such was the rapidity of his literary development and the universality of his viewpoint that it might
surprise those unfamiliar with the two distinct cultural atmos-
pheres to which he was initially exposed: that of pre-revolutionary
Mexico and that of pre–Civil War Spain.

The Athenaeum Generation in Mexico

Mexico does not seem at first glance to be a suitable setting for
such a man as Reyes; the English-speaking writer and traveler has

[4] Letter to Enrique Diez-Canedo, August 6, 1931. All letters (unless otherwise noted) are in Alfonso Reyes' archives in Mexico City. In subsequent quo-

often depicted Mexico as an alien land, strangely exotic and primitive, outside of the mainstream of Western culture. Yet, at the turn of the century, Mexico was, if anything, too slavishly imitating European philosophies, literary fashions, and economic theories. When the Revolution of 1910 erupted, one hundred years after the War for Independence from Spain, it freed Mexico from a century of cultural and economic colonialism and created a modern nation, ready to claim its place in the Western world. The revolution was preceded by several years of intellectual as well as economic and social unrest. Reyes, newly arrived in the capital from his native Monterrey, soon found himself at the forefront of a small yet fervent group of young intellectuals who were in rebellion against the oppressive inflexibility of the official modes of thought. Though the years of its collective action were few (1906 to 1913), this group, later called the Athenaeum or Centennial Generation, achieved a cultural revolution as important for Mexico's future as the political one.[5]

As Mexico entered the twentieth century it enjoyed an international reputation for stability and technical progress due to the policies of General Porfirio Díaz' dictatorial regime. For the intellectuals of the upcoming generation, however, the price paid for thirty-some years of internal peace began to seem too high; it had meant immobility, stagnation, and an almost medieval rigidity of thought. As Reyes said, "Peace also grows old." The official Comtean philosophy governed every phase of national life. It gave moral justification for the rejection of theories of social or economic justice, and the Indian was forgotten or discounted as a national factor. On the cultural plane as well, Mexican reality was pushed aside: it was more "civilized" to imitate Europe, and especially Paris. The official programs of study excluded the humanities almost entirely. Only "practical" subjects were counte-

---

tations from all such letters the date of the letter, when known, will be given parenthetically in the text.

[5] María del Carmen Millán, "La generación del Ateneo y el ensayo mexicano," *Nueva Revista de Filología Hispánica* 15, no. 3–4 (1961): 628.

nanced. Reyes described the effect of these educational theories on Mexican culture by saying that

> it became the fashion, precisely among the middle class for whom that educational system had been conceived, to consider that there was a schism between the theoretical and the practical. The theoretical was a lie, a falsehood, and belonged to the metaphysical era, if not to the theological one. The practical was reality, the true truth. All of it an expression of a reaction against culture, of a love for the meanest ignorance, that which refuses to recognize itself and cherishes and delights in itself. When society loses confidence in culture, it retrocedes to barbarity with the swiftness of light.[6]

Reyes and his young companions sensed this social malaise. "We felt the intellectual oppression," wrote Pedro Henríquez Ureña, "along with the political and economic oppression of which a great part of the country was already aware. We saw that the official philosophy was too systematic, too definite, not to be in error."[7] They lost faith in positivism and in the pedagogical routine to which they were subjected. They gradually abandoned the former norms of thought in favor of a completely new moral and aesthetic outlook. Reminiscing a few years later in Spain, Reyes wrote:

> That generation of young men educated itself—as in Plutarch —among philosophic dialogues which the thunder of revolutions was to suffocate. What happened in Mexico in the Centennial year was like a shot in the deceiving silence of a polar landscape: the whole circle of glacial mountains collapsed, and they all came toppling down one after another. Each of us, hanging on to his board, has saved himself as best he could; and now the scattered friends, in Cuba or New York, Madrid or Paris, Lima or Buenos Aires—and others from within Mexico itself—renew the adventures of Aeneas, guarding in their breasts the gods of the fatherland.

[6] Alfonso Reyes, *Obras completas*, XII, 193. All subsequent quotations from Reyes' work (unless otherwise noted) will be from this edition, and volume and page numbers will be given parenthetically in the text.

[7] Pedro Henríquez Ureña, *Obra crítica*, p. 612.

Good-by to nights dedicated to genius, along the streets of admirable stillness, or in Antonio Caso's library, which was the
very temple of the Muses! Presiding over the conversations was
a bust of Goethe, from which we used to hang hat and overcoat,
converting it into a grotesque guest. And a clock, in the background, strikes the hours as it wishes; and when it importunes too
much, it is silenced: for in the house of the philosophers, as in
that of *The Wild Duck*, time does not pass. Caso hears and comments upon everything with fervid intensity; and when—at three
in the morning—Vasconcelos finishes reading us the meditations
of Buddha, Pedro Henríquez opposes the dissolving of the *tertulia*,
because—he alleges amidst the general uproar—"it is just beginning to become interesting." (III, 302)

Reyes would not lose the custom of the *tertulia* when he came to
Madrid, for no Spaniard would miss that weekly and sometimes
daily meeting with his friends, around a café table or in a private
home, where he could express his views on politics, on philosophy,
on women, on the topic of the hour. Reyes has re-created here the
intellectual ardor of his own group of friends and has introduced
the three members of the Centennial Generation who, along with
himself, were to achieve greatest prominence in the years ahead.
Antonio Caso, who became Mexico's foremost philosopher, led the
campaign against positivism and demolished it publicly in 1909
in a devastating series of lectures. Within a few years positivism
had passed into history, and a new philosophical humanism had
taken its place. Caso was to introduce the study of philosophy
again into the Mexican classroom and direct all his influence
toward the cultural emancipation of his country.[8] José Vasconcelos,
revolutionary, man of political action, prolific and much-read
author in the fields of philosophy, sociology, and history, who as
Secretary of Education organized Mexico's system of primary education and promoted very effective literacy campaigns, was a
visionary and passionately individualistic writer. Pedro Henríquez
Ureña, a Dominican of distinguished family forced to live away

---

[8] María Rosa Uría-Santos, "El Ateneo de la Juventud: Su influencia en la
vida intelectual de México," p. 78.

from his politically troubled island, was adopted by Mexico and, with Reyes, gave the movement its cultural direction.

Their goal of total cultural renovation led Reyes and Henríquez Ureña to delve into the classical sources of philosophy and the humanities and from them to derive not only aesthetic pleasure and intellectual teaching but also moral discipline.[9] Due chiefly to their influence, the Centennial Generation came to be characterized by

> the belief that things should be thoroughly understood, and learned at first hand as much as possible; the conviction that the activity of thinking as well as that of expressing thought necessitates a previous technique, usually laborious, difficult to acquire and dominate, absorbing, and without which no product of the intelligence is lasting; the persuasion that neither philosophy, nor art, nor letters is a mere pastime or noble way of escape from the daily aspect of life, but a profession like any other, to which it is necessary to devote oneself completely, if one is to work in it decently, or not devote oneself at all.[10]

These are the words of Martín Luis Guzmán, a companion of Reyes in Spain and novelist of the revolution, written while he was in exile in New York in 1916. These beliefs were largely responsible for Reyes' being accepted in the Spanish cultural environment, one noted for its seriousness of purpose, and were, as well, of unusual import in Latin America, where the idea of the literary vocation as a total commitment of self is of relatively recent origin.

One of the most decided contrasts between the preceding literary generation, which tended to isolate art from social involvement, and the Athenaeum Generation, was the latter's social and educational preoccupation (XII, 186). Their cultural reform campaigns produced a profound change in the spiritual climate of the capital. The new philosophical orientation and the rebirth of interest in classical humanities brought with them a renewed belief

---

[9] Henríquez Ureña, quoted in Juan Hernández Luna, ed., *Conferencias del Ateneo de la Juventud*, p. 162.

[10] Martín Luis Guzmán, *Obras completas*, I, 76.

in progress, in the perfectability of man, and in freedom of thought and investigation. In 1906 the young reformers sponsored the first public exhibition of Diego Rivera's paintings. The next year they organized the first of a series of public lectures. It is indicative of their humanistic spirit that their early lectures were always preceded by the performance of a musical composition and followed by the recitation of original poetry (including that of Reyes).

In 1909, on the eve of the Centennial celebration, Reyes and his friends founded the most famous literary organization of the period, the Ateneo de la Juventud (Athenaeum of Youth). Some of its members, Reyes the youngest of all, had barely reached twenty. Organized to give a formal home to the new ideas, the Athenaeum met semimonthly for several years and came to represent the social and cultural conscience of the time. Its first formal lecture series had a Latin American theme—Reyes spoke on a Mexican poet—and was symbolic of its search for the essence of Mexican nationality and of Americanism.

Soon after, the political revolution broke out in their midst, but instead of interrupting their labors, it increased them. The *ateneístas* concentrated then on two tasks: the penetration of the newly reorganized National University and the founding of a Popular University. By 1913, Caso, Reyes, Henríquez Ureña and other members of the group were serving without compensation on the faculty of the new School of Humanities and, in effect, took possession of it. The Popular University, the first of its kind in Mexico, was formed in 1912 to bring free instruction to the working classes and thus generalize the humanistic ideas believed necessary for the country's spiritual regeneration.

His participation in these campaigns and preoccupations explains Reyes' early maturity. The atmosphere of pre-revolutionary Mexico promoted the formation of what were to be his principal intellectual concerns, and they are reflected in his first book of essays, *Cuestiones estéticas* (Aesthetic questions), published in 1911. From these experiences also came a purity of intent and a belief in the goals of the spirit which never abandoned him. The spiritual heritage that Reyes carried with him to Spain lies here.

In February, 1913, don Alfonso's father, General Bernardo Reyes, was killed in a misguided and unsuccessful assault on the National Palace, and the tragedy was a turning point in his son's life. Seventeen years after his father's death Reyes wrote that masterpiece of elegiac prose which is his *Oración del 9 de febrero* (Prayer of the ninth of February), published posthumously in 1963. With classical elegance, he penetrates the depths of sorrow and love:

> No: it is not his actual presence that I miss the most, for it is so warm, so magnetic, so sweet and so tender for me, so rich in stimuli for my admiration and my fantasy, so satisfying to my concept of a style of life, so pleasing to my pride as a son, so beneficial to my sincere efforts as apprentice human being and apprentice Mexican (because I have known so few human beings and so few Mexicans!). I do not weep for the lack of his terrestrial company, because I have substituted for it a spell, or, if you prefer, a miracle. I weep for the injustice with which that noble life annulled itself; I suffer because, on considering my father's history, I have a presentiment of an obscure equivocation in the moral clockwork of our world; I despair before the consummated fact of the grave, before the thought that the generous balance of a rich and full life is not enough to compensate for and to fill the emptiness of a single second. My tears are for the tower of a man that collapsed; for the precious architecture—accomplished from the accumulation and the carving of exquisite materials, over many centuries of severe and scrupulous inheritance—that only one jolt of chance could undo; for the wine of seven consuls that had concentrated its sugars and its spirits for so long a time, and that an adventuresome hand came suddenly to overturn.
>
> And since the wine had to be overturned, let it be a sacrifice. I accept: let it be an efficacious libation for the land which has received it.[11]

[11] Reyes, *Oración del 9 de febrero*, pp. 8–9.

The recent memory of this tragedy, along with political differences within his family, made him feel he could no longer stay in
Mexico. With his wife and young son, Reyes left for France in
1913. "My image of Paris, in keeping with the mode of those days,
is cubist," he wrote a few years later (III, 103). His was the Paris
of the creators of "modern" art, of Gertrude Stein, and of the
Spanish painters Picasso and Juan Gris (whom Miss Stein called
the only true cubists).[12] In trips of later years Reyes would be able
to compare the excitement of post-war Paris and of the "lost generation" with that of Madrid, which would also be in the midst
of an extraordinary period of artistic experimentation and achievement. His residence in Paris in 1913 was brief, however, for at
the outbreak of the war he went south to Spain.

Madrid in 1914

Eighteen ninety-eight had marked a crossroads in Spanish history. With the loss of its last colonies, following a century of
violent political struggle and gradual moral decline, Spain was at
its lowest ebb. Yet this date is also symbolic of a reawakening of
Spanish culture after two twilit centuries: a national regeneration
became the preoccupation of a group of writers later to be classified under the term Generation of 1898. An enlightened critical
attitude toward Spanish traditionalism and toward all types of
dogma and criteria of authority produced a crisis of conscience
and, in consequence, a desire for reform, which would lead even-
tually to the formation of the Republic. This crisis was also a
literary one and brought about a revision of cultural values. Not
since its Golden Age in the sixteenth and seventeenth centuries
had Spain witnessed such a brilliant outburst of literary genius.

The leading Spanish intellectual figures at the turn of the century had cultural goals in some ways similar to those later espoused by the Mexican *ateneístas*. They were disciples of the
famous educator, Francisco Giner de los Ríos, whose Institución
Libre de Enseñanza (Free Institute of Teaching) sought to instill

---

12 Ricardo Gullón, *De Goya al arte abstracto*, p. 87.

high moral purpose and progressive, liberal ideals. Giner's moral influence pervaded Madrid intellectual life:

> Mourn me with work and hopes.
> Be good and no more, be what I have been
> Among you: soul.[13]

Thus Antonio Machado, one of Spain's greatest lyric poets, had him speak in a poem written after Giner's death in 1915. Giner was in great part responsible for the character of the "Athenian Madrid," as Reyes called it. In spite of an increasingly dismal political situation, cultural life flourished undaunted. The intellectuals had become, for all too short a time, the guiding spirit of the nation, and a feeling of freedom and optimism prevailed.

At the time of Reyes' arrival in Spain, the so-called Generation of 1898 did not appear as a united group, but the robust individualists newly classified under that title showed themselves more active than ever. In 1914 alone, Miguel de Unamuno, heterodoxical philosopher and anguished spokesman for man's struggle to believe himself immortal, published his experimental novel *Niebla* (*Mist*); Ramón del Valle-Inclán, novelist and playwright of great originality, his collection of short stories *Jardín umbrío* (Shady garden); and Azorín, exquisite prose writer and sensitive historian of daily minutiae, his *Discurso de La Cierva* (Discourse of La Cierva). And the following generation, equally active, was just coming to the forefront and beginning to publish definitive works. Nineteen fourteen saw the publication of José Ortega y Gasset's fundamental reinterpretation of the Cervantian genius, *Meditaciones del Quijote* (Reflections on the *Quijote*). Juan Ramón Jiménez published his poetic and nostalgic sketches, *Platero y yo* (*Platero and I*). And the ever-prolific precursor of Surrealism, Ramón Gómez de la Serna, produced three works in various genres: *Ex votos*, a collection of plays; *El rastro* (The flea market), sketches of Madrid; and *El doctor inverosímil* (The unlikely doctor), a novel. Soon to appear on the scene, but still adolescents in 1914, were the

[13] Antonio Machado, "A Don Francisco Giner de los Ríos," *Poesías completas*, p. 176.

vanguardist poets who, by the time Reyes left Madrid, had begun to establish their ascendency.

The literary world lived at a rapid pace: social gatherings (*tertulias*), literary and non-literary, political and non-political, took place not only in the Athenaeum but also in the well-known cafés Regina, Universal, Levante, and Castilla. It was an intellectual democracy in which almost all participated. Guillermo de Torre, the well-known critic, then a young poet with adventuresome literary spirit, wrote that "the city still maintained a certain intimate *fin de siècle* physiognomy: the only European capital—together with Lisbon—radically different from all the rest for its slow pace, its unity of atmosphere, its confiding sweetness."[14] The writers moved about in a Madrid still small and in a central area even smaller: from the Duque de Alba Street, where the newspaper *El Imparcial* had its offices, to Larra Street, where those of *El Sol* were located; from the Plaza Mayor to the Plaza de Toros, nearer to the center of the city than the present one. The city could be covered on foot, and indeed it was, since long strolls along its avenues and in its plazas were a frequent pastime. "What enchantment has Madrid," wrote Valle-Inclán's *tertulia* companion, the newspaperman Luis Bello, "in the mornings, under the bright hothouse sun, if we wish to search for it in the small gardens of Recoletos and the Prado."[15]

Occupying the pre-eminent position in the Madrid literary scene was what Pedro Henríquez Ureña called "the closed aristocracy of Spanish literature." This group was distinguished by the seriousness of its outlook, the severity of its discipline, and the refinement of its tastes. Henríquez Ureña described it, saying:

> In order to give an idea of what the class is like, it would be enough to mention some of its better-known members: Unamuno is its mystic philosopher; Juan Ramón Jiménez and Antonio Machado are its principal poets; Azorín is its critic; Enrique Díez-Canedo is its modern humanist. . . . In social pedagogy the class

[14] Guillermo de Torre, *La aventura estética de nuestra edad*, p. 110.
[15] Luis Bello, "Ensayo sobre Madrid," in Ángel del Río and M. J. Benardete, eds., *El concepto contemporáneo de España*, p. 358.

is related to the Institución Libre de Enseñanza, to the clear and fecund tradition of Giner. In the world of erudition, it is allied with the group headed by Menéndez Pidal, men of perfect discipline and pure knowledge. It did not have American ramifications. . . . Now the group includes American members such as Alfonso Reyes.[16]

It was within this select circle that Reyes was to make his friends.

However, this was all in the future. "My first view of Madrid . . . was a very painful one," Reyes confessed (II, 150). The nights spent in one shabby guest house after another weighed heavily on his spirit and left their imprint on the pages of *Cartones de Madrid* (Madrid sketches), 1917, a collection of impressionistic, almost cinematographic essays jotted down during nights of insomnia. These fleeting scenes exhibit for the first time that rapid, dynamic style which was to characterize Reyes' short poetic essays. Here it records moments of both beauty and grotesquery. He captures a glimpse of the women of Madrid: "Alcalá or Toledo Street. Coarse or delicate women. All beautiful. One after another, with maddening frequency. Inexhaustible rhythm, melody of eyes and hair, infinite march of feet. Dizziness, a general fleeing of desires, until you remain cold and perfect, like crystal itself" (II, 78–79). And he comments on its beggers: "The beggar and the Madrid street are one single architectonic body; they correspond each to the other as two necessary ideas. The street without him would be like a face without a nose. He is its caryatid and at the same time its parasite: he gives it consistency and lives from it" (II, 49). They are instantaneous impressions of a stranger in a sometimes hostile, sometimes fascinating world.

Reyes' creative writing during his first year in Spain includes not only *Cartones de Madrid* but also the most famous and one of the most lyrical and evocative of his works, *Visión de Anáhuac*. It was written soon after *Cartones* and forms a perfect emotional counterbalance to it. The one records his first contact with a new environment; the other, his nostalgia for what he has left behind.

---

[16] Henríquez Ureña, *Obra crítica*, pp. 212–213.

He re-creates with a masterful combination of descriptive objectivity and emotional intensity the scene spread out before the astonished eyes of the Spanish conqueror on his arrival at the seat of the Aztec Empire, Tenochtitlán, "that orb of sonority and brilliance." The vision, as Reyes imagined it, was exactly this—one of reverberating sounds and brilliant flashes of color, where all the senses come into play, but where, above all, that of sight captured the resplendent glory of the vanished civilization. His physical description of the plateau achieved its poetic synthesis in that phrase which has itself become part of the legend of Mexico: "Traveler: you have come to the most transparent region of the air" (II, 12).

Octavio Paz, the lucid and profound poet-essayist whose universality and dedication to literature rival Reyes' own, called *Visión de Anáhuac* "a great fresco in prose."[17] And, as the title indicates, it is primarily a pictorial impression. Decorative elements are heightened because of the stylistic treatment that gives them autonomy:

> The people adorn themselves with brilliance, because they are in the sight of a great emperor. The cotton tunics come and go, red, gold, embroidered, black and white, with feather appliqué or painted figures. The brown faces have a smiling serenity, all showing a will to please. Trembling in the ear and nose are heavy rings, and around the neck, eight-strand necklaces, colored stones, bells, and golden pendants. Atop the hair, black and straight, the feathers sway to the rhythm of the step. The muscular legs display metallic anklets and silver-leaf gaiters with leather trim—yellow and white deerskin. The sound of the flexible sandals is heard. . . . A variegated flywhisk flutters in their hands, or a staff writhes in the form of a snake with teeth and eyes of mother-of-pearl, its head of tooled leather and feather knobs. Skins, stones, and metals, feathers and cotton, mingle their tints in an incessant irridescence and—communicating to them their quality and refinement—they transform the men into delicate toys. (II, 18–19)

[17] Quoted in Reyes, "Historia documental de mis libros," *Universidad de México* 9, no. 8 (1955): 10.

An enormous quantity of objects, all colorful and shining, sparkle and reverberate in the atmosphere so as to surround and envelop the reader, capturing him in their luminous threads. A lost world has been sensuously re-created.

The purpose of Reyes' essay is not historical; his is a fundamentally aesthetic evocation of Mexican history. The past lives in the beauty of the legend it encloses, and, because of the fascination of legend, the Mexican has peopled his imaginative landscape with historical fancies: "He thinks he hears, in the open country, the sorrowful weeping of the twins whom the white-garmented goddess carries on her back" (II, 34). For Reyes, then, the pre-Columbian fragment of Mexico's "national soul," which he is seeking to define, is reduced to an aesthetic nostalgia, a love for beauty.

Torrijos

When Reyes spoke of his years in Madrid he liked to divide them according to his three residences, in the streets of Torrijos, General Pardiñas, and Serrano. Each change marked a bettering of his circumstances, and each one was closer to the center of the city. The Torrijos apartment saw the times of worst poverty, as Reyes recalled in a letter to José Vasconcelos: "I . . . have had to write for so long next to the fire, my hands aching, with eternal droplets of water from the rafters falling on my head, and having to deprive myself of the last drop of alcohol that would have comforted me, without any food during entire weeks but potatoes and more potatoes" (April 23, 1920). In his published writings there is little that refers to moments of depression and hardship, for Reyes said he always wrote under the stimulus of "constructive sentiments." But one can cite this passage, the last section of his "Fuga de Navidad" (Christmas Fugue), 1923:

> That man has gone out in the morning, wrapped in a light overcoat which the wind of Castile bathes and penetrates. His elbows are worn, his shoes ragged. Since it is Christmas, beggars approach to ask alms, and he asks their pardon and continues walking. Hunched over from the cold, beneath the gust that ruffles his clothes and would like to rip them away, he looks in his pocket

for his handkerchief, still warm from the household iron. He possesses nothing, and he had a big house with gardens and fountains, and salons with stags' heads. Will they have forgotten him already in his country? Sometimes he quickens his pace, and sometimes he stops for no reason. He has spent his last pennies on toys for his son. No one is exempt; we do not know where we tread. Perchance a slight shift in the daylight leaves us lost, astray. That man has forgotten where he is. And he remains, suddenly forsaken, bewildered with hope and memory, replete with Christmas within, trembling in the gusts of snow, and shipwrecked in the middle of the street. Oh, friends! Who was that man? (II, 137)

None other than Reyes himself.

And yet he has also referred to these years as a time of happy poverty. In the same building lived two fellow *ateneístas,* the painter Jesús Acevedo and Martín Luis Guzmán. Reminiscing in a letter to Guzmán, Reyes recalled the homemade amusements that poverty forced them to invent:

> What different times were those! Do you remember, Martín? . . . On Sundays, those Catalan masons who lived in the "room" next door came to visit us. And, in the afternoon, lacking a better show, you, poor Jesús Acevedo, and I would depict pictures from the Prado: the best, without doubt, that of the Conde-Duque de Olivares painted by Velásquez. Jesús was the horse, and he made ferocious eyes and tried to foam at the mouth. . . . I was the Conde-Duque, and I did not need to puff out my face or pad my stomach. And you, oh Martín . . . you were the landscape in the background! Those admirable and fantastic Madrid backgrounds of cold and delicate atmosphere that one finds in Velásquez! (March 15, 1922)

The philological and erudite research that was to inspire a great part of Reyes' writing in Madrid was begun in that early period, with a 1914 edition of two plays by the sixteenth-century Mexican dramatist Juan Ruiz de Alarcón. He found the necessary research materials in the Center for Historical Studies, one of the organs of an educational council set up to carry out Giner de los Ríos' ideas

of cultural regeneration. It was presided over by Ramón Menéndez Pidal, the leading figure of Hispanic scholarship, who, upon
meeting Reyes, asked him to become a member of the Philology
Section. The Center, divided into several departments, was a work-
shop devoted to Menéndez Pidal's school of historical criticism,
which was based on precise philological analysis, detailed historical investigation, and a thorough knowledge of the sources. The
insistence on clarity, on effort, on discipline, on the elimination of
traditional rhetoric and the revision of historic and literary com-
monplaces—a true renovation of methods of literary criticism—
was due to Menéndez Pidal and his followers.

Reyes was closely associated with the Center and its president
for five years and submitted himself to its discipline with a humility surprising in a creative writer—but not in one such as don
Alfonso, who early learned the value of careful intellectual train-
ing in all fields of literary endeavor, whether scholarly or imaginative. He devoted himself primarily to sixteenth- and seventeenth-
century Spanish literature and to bibliographical tasks. A letter to
Guzmán gives a good description of his work at the Center:

> These days my edition of the Arcipreste de Hita's *Libro de buen
> amor* [Book of good love] has come out. . . . I have already de-
> livered an anthology of Quevedo; and, to La Lectura, I will de-
> liver this afternoon two comedies of Ruiz de Alarcón; on my desk,
> for Calleja, I have in preparation an anthology of the same Ruiz
> de Alarcón, which I will take care of in two weeks. Then, a
> Góngora, etc.: thus I supplement my earnings. None of this is
> "my" work, but we will see if with these efforts I achieve a
> month of leisure to write, in the autumn, another book. (August
> 2, 1917)

He continues, in a rather melancholy humor: "Some day, I will
fall back fatigued to my native land: when no one loves me there
anymore and everyone considers himself happy to have liquidated
accounts with my disposition, my headache, and my complicated
and poignant style."

The relationship with Menéndez Pidal and the Center was a
focal point of Reyes' life in Madrid. The experience of following a

rigorously scientific method of scholarship not only gave him a point of departure for the further development of his own critical method, but supplied as well the solid foundation that underlay his purely creative writings. It also marked the beginning of his friendship with the leading Hispanists of the future, most of whom lived and taught in the Americas after the Spanish Civil War.

During those first years Reyes also began his association with one of the most influential cultural centers of the period, the Residencia de Estudiantes (Student Residence), another spiritual heir to Giner de los Ríos' humanistic educational ideals. The Residencia, founded in 1910, was an autonomous institution whose ambitious goal was the formation of "competent, serious, and liberal Spanish leaders."[18] For this it did not depend on formal instruction for the university students living there, but rather on an ambient intellectual stimulation from visiting and resident scientists, artists, and scholars, and from various cultural programs and activities.

Reyes called himself an honorary companion of the Residencia, and it was the sometime home and frequent gathering place of most of his friends. Juan Ramón Jiménez lived there for a time, as did young poets and artists such as Federico García Lorca and Salvador Dalí. Many gave lectures there, and well-known foreign visitors rarely passed through Madrid without speaking at this famous institution, which the British Hispanist J. B. Trend enthusiastically called the Spanish Oxford and Cambridge. Henri Bergson and Paul Valéry, Maeterlinck and Einstein, H. G. Wells, Chesterton and Belloc, Marie Curie and Paul Claudel, John Maynard Keynes and Count Keyserling—men and women from many countries and of many specialties spoke in its lecture hall. The Residencia also published a magazine, *Residencia,* and a collection of books under the direction of Juan Ramón Jiménez.

During the year that Reyes arrived in Madrid the Residencia moved to a new location atop "Poplar Hill," as it was called after the grounds surrounding its red brick pavilions were landscaped

[18] Alberto Jiménez-Fraud, "The 'Residencia de Estudiantes,' " trans. Robert Williams, *Texas Quarterly* 4, no. 1 (1961): 48.

under the direction of Jiménez, the first resident. The enthusiasm which a whole generation—no, several generations—felt for its ideals and its hopes for a better Spain has perhaps never been more simply expressed than in Juan Ramón's description of the trees in the partially planted gardens:

> There they are, still lying on the ground, their roots protected in baskets of their native soil, giving off an aroma of life and hope. Three thousand of them have been delivered, and each of us will plant his own. Those that are already planted present a cheerful sight, healthy and vigorous, so tender and so strong at the same time, with their firm young foliage fluttering in the breeze. With the nourishing moisture at their base they are beginning to sprout new roots, and their tops are reaching to support the sky. As yet they cast too little shade even for Parsifal, the janitor Cándido's white dog, and the sound of their rustling leaves is so faint as to suggest seedlings in the nursery far away on the other side of Madrid. But what a joy already, this anticipation of greenery, of gold, of slender grace, of light, of birds—on this hill, barren yesterday, this bit of the planet that now belongs to us, where in planting for changing seasons to come, spring, summer, winter, and autumn, with their yearly return of memories, we are setting out the garden of *our* vitality too, *our* ardor, *our* firmness, and *our* glowing vision![19]

General Pardiñas

Reyes moved to the Pardiñas apartment in late 1915 after almost losing his life from a severe attack of typhoid fever. "When I get out of bed, a shadow of my former self," he wrote to Gómez de la Serna, "I find that 'they' have abandoned me. Guzmán has set out for New York, where he is going to open a bookstore and get rich; Acevedo—victim of his eyes—has gone to live in a barrio full of local color. . . . On finding myself alone I—fortunately always a snob—have moved to General Pardiñas Street, #32, 1st floor right, elevator, heat, hot water boiler, bath, gas and electricity" (May 18, 1916). The house faced the small plaza of Salamanca

---

[19] Juan Ramón Jiménez, quoted in ibid., p. 50.

and the tennis courts where in 1920 the Cuban writer, José María
Chacón y Calvo, Reyes, and others founded the Moratín Tennis
Club. In the distance one could see the silhouette of the Guada-
rrama mountains. Unfortunately the chilly horrors of the winter
months belied Reyes' optimistic enumeration of its amenities.
Chacón y Calvo, a fellow resident, baptized Pardiñas as "the house
of ice," claiming that its foundation was an enormous iceberg from
which the cold slowly rose to frost the entire house and everything
in it.[20]

The cold made Henríquez Ureña long for the comparative
warmth of a Minnesota winter, but don Alfonso worked on imperturbably, wrapped in a cocoon of blankets, "with all the resigna-
tion of a paralytic." His mornings were generally spent in the un-
heated manuscript room of the National Library, his chest and
back padded with newspapers, and with little Japanese hand heat-
ers in his pockets; his afternoons, in the Center. His nights he
devoted to his own tasks: the ever-increasing journalistic contributions which were, from 1916 to 1920, his principal means of support, scholarly studies, and editions of the classics. In every free
moment he visited the cafés and strolled along the streets of Madrid, an eager observer of and participant in the life of the capital.
Sundays he would sometimes go to a soccer game, the theater, or a
friend's house, or go on an excursion, but this was an infrequent
indulgence.

It was not easy to find the time for creative writing, what he
called the "background of my labor, the constant and disinterested
work, that which is as normal as breathing, that which I write
only for myself."[21] As he wrote Henríquez Ureña in 1916: "I am
somewhat melancholy. . . . I remember tonight all the verses I
have not written and look with horror at the philological note
cards. I am a little, a little—up in the stars: I do not know if I
explain myself. It depends a little on the shape of the clouds
(which I do not see). And I would willingly make a trip in the

[20] José María Chacón y Calvo, *Ensayos sentimentales*, p. 153.
[21] Reyes, "Historia documental de mis libros," *Universidad de México* 9, no.
9 (1955): 12.

air. I shall not write more, because it would make you furious. If I had a sack of gold and a very big castle, at this moment I would write the best of my life."

He did, however, find time to write one book in 1916, the first of his books to receive any widespread critical attention. It was *El suicida* (The Suicide), a loosely woven collection of essays whose unifying theme might be described as ideas leading toward the formation of a philosophy of life. The underlying motive of the book, which winds like Ariadne's thread through the labyrinth, is the humanist's belief that man's destiny is a search for the truth. Reyes' point of departure is the mystery that surrounds the suicidal impulse. It leads him to an exploration of the two basic attitudes toward life, acceptance and rebellion. His probing into the matter of spiritual rebellion, or criticism, involves him in a discussion of the search for liberty, of the search for renewal and change, and, finally, of the problem of artistic creation itself. It is one of the most interesting books of the Madrid period, since it presents an immediate reflection of his philosophic preoccupations.

In *El suicida* Reyes used a continuous interior monologue. It is a purposely amorphous book, revealing the creative, poetic, and reflective spirit of the writer. Reyes comments that its form reflects the modern world, for "the book as a faithful and immediate image of the multiple states of the soul is something absolutely distinct from the book understood in the classical manner" (III, 294). This "somnambulist's monologue," these "lyric nightmares," as he called them, that poured forth from the recesses of his being in a "wave of unrest," are the ideal form to encompass his irrepressible flow of ideas. As always, Reyes' creative technique was based on the exploration of multiple facets of any given theme. As Henríquez Ureña said: "His intelligence is dialectic: he likes to turn ideas inside out to see if in the weaving there is deceit."[22] And the reader, too, is thus able to participate in the creative process.

During the next three or four years his more personal creative writing included *Huelga* (Strike), a collection of miniature essays

---

[22] Henríquez Ureña, *Obra crítica*, p. 298.

in which he recorded his impressions of the general strike of 1917, and *Horas de Burgos* (Burgos hours), describing his visit to that city, where anecdotal essays alternate with stylized pictures of objective reality. His very popular modern prose version of the *Poema del Cid* appeared in 1919. The many essays he wrote during these years were later collected in various books, the most extensive being his series of *Simpatías y diferencias*, 1921–1926, which he described as "a background, like the habitual level of my literary conversations. Because I always want to communicate and exchange ideas with others, and since I do not have the chance to discuss everything, I write down what keeps on accumulating" (IV, 450).

Serrano

Reyes' uncertainty about his future was resolved in 1920 when he reentered the Mexican Diplomatic Corps (he had been, briefly, in 1913, Second Secretary of the Paris Legation) and soon became chief of the Madrid Legation. The "house of ice" was abandoned, as he wrote his friend Guzmán:

> Now I live in Serrano, that large street parallel to the Castellana, and a step away from the Legation, where I descend like a meteor at any hour of the day or night. In my salon I have put the presentable books—by the binding, I mean, because the century is materialistic and does not pay any attention to the rest. Alongside, I have a dining room crafted by a genius of carpentery, whom I gave some English models, severe and elegant. In another part, a refuge full of enchantment, is hidden the "Cité des Livres": the romantic mound, the delicious chaos, with a round table and large easy chairs. And then, all the rest. The bedrooms overlook a garden. (March 15, 1922)

In these comfortable surroundings he was to spend his last three years in Madrid, years of combined diplomatic and literary activity.

Diplomatic affairs necessarily took up the major part of Reyes' time in these later years, for he joined the Mexican Legation at a very difficult moment. Spain had refused to recognize the current

Mexican government, and relations with Mexico had been broken off. Soon after his appointment as chargé d'affaires, Reyes was able to resolve successfully the diplomatic impasse by making good use of the many friendships he had acquired in his years of residence in Spain. As one can see, however, from his diplomatic memoirs, it was a turbulent period. Spain was in a constant state of political unrest that led in September, 1923, to the military dictatorship of Primo de Rivera.

During this period Reyes had been thinking of returning to Mexico and had given serious consideration to an offer from Vasconcelos to name him Subsecretary of Public Instruction. Loath to leave the atmosphere of intellectual freedom that characterized the Spain of the 1920's, he finally wrote him: "It would grieve me to leave my little job for a dream: and the next day receive a kick from one of those materialistic monsters whom the turbulences of our life have made rise to the surface of public affairs in Mexico. I would like to know up to what point there is freedom to develop one's own plans" (May 25, 1921). And he decided not to accept.

Yet the nostalgia for Mexico was never far from his thoughts. In 1923 he wrote two very dissimilar works, both of which attest to a persistent preoccupation with Mexico. The first is a short story, perhaps his best. A friend's letter awakened memories, he was unable to escape the phantoms from his past, and he sat down to write "El testimonio de Juan Peña," an autobiographical tale in which he sought to capture the flavor of a youthful experience. The story is a simple one. When still a law student he was asked to go out into the country and give counsel to an Indian who, it was claimed, had been unjustly deprived of her land. He and two friends, his "secretaries," undertook the trip, full of a youthful spirit of adventure. The whole tale has a vague air of idealistic fantasy, not because Reyes saw it with a nostalgic eye, but rather because he was able to re-create with such skill the mental and emotional world of those three young men. Imbued with the skepticism of the Centennial Generation, they found themselves in a situation in which "at two steps from the capital, . . . its vague literature, . . . its decadent Europeanism, they suddenly met with a little town of brown, barefoot men."[23] So unreal was this to them that at times they felt as if they were taking part in a farce.

At the same time, however, they were gradually overcome with a sense of responsibility. And herein lies Reyes' narrative talent. The suspense in his story is of the most delicate fabrication. It has nothing to do with plot structure, but lies entirely in the gradual changes in the protagonists' point of view. This, combined with the plasticity of his imagery, which is reminiscent of that of *Visión de Anáhuac*, makes for a masterful tale. Critics have praised Reyes' skill in narration and questioned, therefore, the relative scarcity of the short story in his work. It is a question that remains unanswered.

The other partially autobiographical work of that year is the dramatic poem *Ifigenia cruel*, 1924, fundamental for the understanding of his life and his art, and considered by many to be his greatest poetic work. His interpretation of the classical story in stark, bare verses gives us an Iphigenia who has lost her memory and who, upon recovering it at the sight of her brother, refuses to return with him to Greece. She proclaims her freedom from the laws of destiny and finds the redemption of her accursed blood in the affirmation of her own will. The chorus tells Iphigenia: "You have opened a pause in the destinies, from whence/leaps the fountain of your liberty" (X, 349). Reyes said of his poem that it was "mythology of the present and the easing of a personal suffering."[24] Iphigenia's proud refusal to become again a part of the bitter world of quarrel and bloodshed from which she came, her denial of cherished memories in order to begin life anew, are an example to modern man. In this way it does become contemporary mythology.

And how easy it is to hear Reyes speaking through the voice of the memoryless Iphigenia who wandered lost in a world of which she could not become a part:

[23] Reyes, *Quince presencias*, p. 60.
[24] Reyes, "Historia documental de mis libros," *Universidad de México* 9, no. 8 (1955): 10.

And I walk distrustful of myself,
spying on the sound of my footsteps
to see if I can guess where I am going.

(X, 317)

Her doubts for the future, her loneliness, are Reyes' own. He wrote: " 'Ifigenia' . . . conceals a personal experience. Using the scant gift that was conceded to us, in the measure of our strength, we tried to free ourselves of the anguish that such an experience left with us, projecting it upon the artistic sky, discharging it in a colloquy of shadows" (X, 354). The Iphigenia who prefers her liberty to a return to Greece is the Reyes who left the strife of Mexico and vengeful thoughts behind him in search of his own freedom.

Shortly after the publication of *Ifigenia cruel*, symbolic, perhaps, of a measure of freedom from the weight of the past, Reyes left Madrid to continue his diplomatic career in Paris and several Latin American capitals. Azorín, at the farewell dinner given Reyes by his friends, summed up most succinctly his position in Madrid: "While other American diplomats have had the sympathy of the brilliant intellectual elements, consecrated by the power of the state, official, Alfonso Reyes has received the homage of the select, independent literature, not sanctioned by the state."[25] This was not usual. "The Latin American," said Henríquez Ureña, "often does not know how to orient himself in the Spanish intellectual world, because he either disdains it or admires it without discernment, and as soon as he arrives in Madrid he throws himself in the arms of the fabricator of facile sonnets or erotic novels."[26] Reyes, however, had become an integral part of the authentic intellectual life of Madrid. This is best illustrated by the lifelong friendships and correspondence he maintained with the leading figures of Spanish literature and thought—Unamuno, Valle-Inclán, Ortega y Gasset, Juan Ramón Jiménez, Gómez de la Serna.

[25] Azorín, "Azorín habla de la personalidad literaria de Alfonso Reyes," in *Páginas sobre Alfonso Reyes*, I, 58.
[26] Henríquez Ureña, *Obra crítica*, p. 213.

He practiced that cult of friendship which seems to be in itself a typical form of Hispanic life. His friends were a necessary part of himself, an indispensable complement to his own personality. He relied upon a voluminous correspondence to keep alive these friendships and to remain close to the literary worlds of which he had been a part. His letters were, as Henríquez Ureña has written, "a wonderful medley of personal experience, description, fancy, thought, and opinion—a whole criticism of life and a complete self-revelation."[27] Those that stem from his Spanish experiences and thus concern a period vital to his literary development serve as a basis for the following chapters. They are not only relevant to his personal and literary biography, but also give a unique glimpse into the inner world of a select and rarified intellectual elite. By putting this world in its human perspective, they become a fascinating commentary on the men who dreamt of creating a new Spain.

[27] Henríquez Ureña, quoted in "Digesto sobre Alfonso Reyes," P.E.N. Club de México, Volante no. 14 (31 May 1924): 11.

Miguel de Unamuno

(1864 – 1936)

FOR MIGUEL DE UNAMUNO, philosophizing was a vital attitude, it was life itself. He was well aware that ever since man had become the object of his own meditation, not as an abstraction but as a being of flesh and blood, metaphysical thinking had become an impossibility. In this negation of traditional metaphysics, he was a precursor. He wrote in 1913: "Philosophy is a human product of each philosopher, and each philosopher is a man of flesh and blood, who addresses other men of flesh and blood like himself. And do what he may, he philosophizes not with reason alone, but with his will, with his feelings, with his flesh and his blood, with all his soul and with all his body. The man philosophizes."[1]

By the strangest of paths, Unamuno has come to coincide with

[1] Miguel de Unamuno, *Del sentimiento trágico de la vida*, pp. 29–30.

the anthropologists and sociologists, with the defenders of the "human sciences," who for the last few decades have been taking note of the disappearance of man as an abstract being. In view of the direction taken by the new sciences, the attitude of the traditional philosophers toward Unamuno is a paradoxical one. They look down upon him for having seen what they did not see, a little like the blind who reproach those who are seeing the light.

Unamuno was, then, the opposite of the philosopher who constructs a metaphysical system. His belief in the totality of man led him rather to the contradiction of all systems, or, one might say, to a system based on the principle of contradiction. "Blessed those who have never felt in contradiction with themselves!" he wrote. "Blessed? No! For blessedness has no place in the kingdom of limbo. Nor does he live a life, a true human life—perhaps more than human—he who does not carry within himself a whole nation in perpetual civil war."[2]

Statements such as this abound in his writings. Yet he lamented, in a letter to Reyes, the very condition he praised above: "I am becoming incapable of a smile and each day I feel more solitary. Only mournful laughter, a painful *ricanement*, calms my nerves. I continue on in search of a soul, my own, which escapes me, and I have no glimpse of the paths of my emancipation. And it is just as well while my conscience continues being a battlefield of civil war" (June 2, 1917).[3] Paradoxical? Of course. Not all is aggressiveness, struggle, and anguish in Unamuno. There is also the contemplative Unamuno who longs for the peace that comes from the immersion and dissolving of the self in "intrahistory," that everflowing silent stream of everyday life where eternity and tradition repose.[4] When he wrote those few revealing lines to Reyes,

[2] Unamuno, *Obras completas*, X, 479. In this chapter, subsequent citations of Unamuno's *Obras completas* will be inserted parenthetically in the text with the abbreviation OC, followed by volume and page numbers.

[3] The Unamuno-Reyes correspondence, kept in the Reyes archives, has been published in Spanish by Manuel García Blanco in *América y Unamuno*, pp. 120–166.

[4] This side of Unamuno's personality was studied exhaustively by Carlos Blanco Aguinaga in his *El Unamuno contemplativo*.

Unamuno was immersed in political activity, his peace destroyed by the demands of public life, and he was very much in need of that refuge which he was sometimes able to find in an inner region of his soul.

There seems no doubt that Unamuno incarnated, better than anyone else of his time, the conflicting spirit of Spain. His works, such as *La vida de Don Quijote y Sancho* (*The Life of Don Quijote and Sancho*), 1905, *Del sentimiento trágico de la vida* (*The Tragic Sense of Life*), 1913, and *La agonía del cristianismo* (*The Agony of Christianity*), 1925, not only express his own personality but also present Spanish philosophy, religion, and poetry.[5] It is not just that he unconsciously came to symbolize the spirit of his people; he fully believed that he, in a very real sense of the word, *was* Spain. "The Spanish mountain ranges hurt him as if they were his own spinal cord,"[6] commented one critic. And there can be no doubt at all of the fact that the Spain he analyzed, exhorted, described, and suffered with was the Spain of Miguel de Unamuno. He had, in fact, created it in his own image. Whether the true Spain completely corresponded to that image was another matter. He saw the Spain of peaks and abysses. He scorned the in-between, the mediocrities, the common sense. There are several levels of truth in his phrase: "I judge my Spain by myself." It is like a game of reflecting mirrors where it is impossible to tell which is the original image and which the reflection. But the voice of his country he was. His influence on the national conscience was unequalled by anyone of his own or succeeding generations.[7]

Unamuno's "pulpit" was the University of Salamanca, of which he was twice rector, and where he taught Greek language and literature and Spanish philology for forty-three years. From there he lectured to several generations of his countrymen. Or, perhaps, one could better say, preached to them. There was much of the preacher in Unamuno, and he has often been compared to a

[5] Federico de Onís, "Introducción," *La Torre* 9, no. 35–36 (1961): 19.

[6] Max Aub, "Retrato de Unamuno, para uso de principiantes," *Ínsula* 19, no. 216–217 (1965): 4.

[7] Ricardo Gullón, *Última lección de Unamuno*, p. 16.

Protestant clergyman. Aware of this, he cultivated that image. At a time when a generalized anticlericalism was the popular attitude in intellectual Spain, he dressed purposely to resemble a pastor—always in black, with his waistcoat buttoned to the neck, so that no tie was needed, and all one saw was the round white circle of the collar. Once it was adopted, he never abandoned this way of dress. It was true to his religious nature and to his "evangelical" zeal.

His tool was the essay. He, like Reyes, wrote in a conversational style, addressing himself personally to the reader, who is forced to feel himself alluded to directly. But Reyes insinuates himself subtly and courteously into the reader's good graces. Not so Unamuno, who used the essay not so much to present ideas, solutions, and possibilities as to attack, awaken, and confuse: "Who has told you," he said, "that I always write so as to clarify ideas? No, sir, no! Many times I write to obfuscate, that is to say, to show you that that idea which you and others like you think is clear, is in you and in them and in me obscure, very obscure. I, like my friend Kierkegaard, have come to the world more to cause difficulties than to resolve them" (OC XI, 278–279).

In every literary genre Unamuno expressed himself with equal intensity. Nowhere in his work can one escape from the force and fascination of his personality. Unamuno's novels and plays are passionately subjective, concentrated, intense, so as to better reveal the naked soul. He explains that in his novels he eliminates any geographical, chronological, or descriptive passages. What is left is a gallery of magnificent, tormented, unforgettable characters—human beings of flesh and blood—passionately and obsessively coming to grips with the basic philosophic problems of their existence—and Unamuno's—and ours. In each one of these fictional characters we recognize some facet of Unamuno, for here he could give life to possibilities he had had to discard in his own limited physical existence. And, at the same time, Unamuno was challenging death. By creating a multiple character in his novels that was himself and that would live again and in different ways

in the reader's imagination, he saw a way to achieve immortality.[8]
It is against the fear of a final void or nothingness and the consequent disappearance of his own individuality that Unamuno
unceasingly fought.

Unamuno the philosopher cannot be separated from Unamuno
the essayist, novelist, dramatist, or poet. In the essay it is more
the outer Unamuno who is on display, the public figure, the cru-
sader, the polemicist; in the novel, in the drama, and, most of all,
in the poetry, he achieves a more profound treatment of his inner-
most struggles, of his existential anguish. And there remains yet
another field of writing, in which one renowned critic feels that
Unamuno has gone still further toward revealing self-expression
—the epistolary genre. Of Unamuno's voluminous correspondence,
Guillermo de Torre wrote: "Definitely, Unamuno's letters could
very well remain, not so much as his masterpieces, but rather as
the most authentic versions of his essential 'I,' multiform and
unified at the same time. For the same reason, this correspondence,
in spite of the accidental motives upon which it rests, does not
lose freshness and validity with the passing of the years, but
rather gains in it. Since—as T. E. Lawrence said, thinking perhaps of his own letters—'sincerity is the only thing that improves
with time.' "[9]

Much of Unamuno's letter writing was directed toward Spanish
America. His fascination with the New World had begun in his
childhood, and he had even thought of emigrating. His continuing
interest was expressed in several planned and unrealized trips, in
his friendships with Spanish American writers, in his writings in
Spanish American magazines and newspapers from 1899 until the
year before his death, and in his many essays and articles, the
first in 1894, on Spanish American themes and books.[10] Several

---

[8] These ideas are developed by Gullón in his *Autobiografías de Unamuno*,
pp. 256–257.

[9] Guillermo de Torre, "Unamuno, escritor de cartas," *Insula* 19, no. 216–
217 (1964): 9.

[10] García Blanco, *América y Unamuno*, p. 8.

volumes of his complete works are composed entirely of articles published in America.

Unamuno enjoyed, because of this, a great prestige in Spanish America, and it was only natural that any fledgling writer from that part of the world would be anxious for his approval. Alfonso Reyes, in 1913, was one of these young and unknown writers, and the first letter in the correspondence between Reyes and Unamuno, dated May 28, 1913, sought just such a recognition for Reyes' first book, *Cuestiones estéticas*:

> The book that I send you was written some time ago, and in the least stable period of life: during adolescence. This accounts for its complexity. Excuse me for this, leaf through it if you have time, and give me your sincere and honest opinion, as is your custom. *I know how to listen.*
>
> Consider me, from this moment, your most solicitous friend, ready to serve you. I live at the center of all the literary relations in Mexico. See how you can make use of me.

It would have been interesting if Unamuno had taken this opportunity to inform himself of the reformist fervor of the group of *ateneístas* in Mexico, but he did not answer Reyes' appeal.

Over a year passed, and toward the end of August, 1914, Reyes arrived with his family in San Sebastián, in the north of Spain. He was resting there, in his brother's home, before beginning the conquest of Madrid, when, suddenly, on the last day of August, the news spread throughout Spain that the government had removed Unamuno from the rectorship of the University of Salamanca. When a third-class railway coach brought Reyes to the Spanish capital a month later, the *madrileños* were still talking about it. Unamuno's removal had even taken the Battle of the Marne out the headlines for a few days, such a furor did it cause in Spain.

Unamuno had been rector of the university since 1900. His dismissal without warning and with no explanation had a decided effect on the future direction of his life. The method of his dismissal rankled more than the act itself, and he never forgave the government officials for dealing with him in such a manner. For several years he chose not to participate in any administrative university activity, limiting himself to the teaching of his two classes.

His friends came immediately to his defense. He was defended in the press, in the Congress, and in the Senate.[11] José Ortega y Gasset, who, though a younger man, was beginning to share Unamuno's eminence as a spokesman for intellectual Spain, cleverly capitalized on the fact that his disagreements with Unamuno were notorious to show that, in this case, something much more important than personal grievances was at stake: "An honorable man," he wrote in a Madrid paper, "cannot see without being fired with indignation that in his presence a fellow man is being crushed, one who leads a clean and perfect life, diligent and ascetic, lacking the defensive power that money gives and without the offensive power that the acts of a deputy give. If beyond these qualities the offended man possesses that of being Unamuno . . . abandoning him would be equivalent to revealing a perversion of the instincts."[12]

In the Senate, the representative of the university openly attacked the government saying, courageously, to the Minister in question: "I am sure that your excellency will not give him back his position, but Unamuno, beheaded in law by your excellency, figures in fact with some few others at the head of the Spanish intellectual world."[13] And Unamuno also defended himself, as could be expected, in a famous speech given in the Athenaeum, a gathering place and forum for the intellectuals of Madrid, ironically entitled "Lo que debe ser un rector en España" (What a rector in Spain should be). It is quite likely that Reyes heard this speech, for he had begun frequenting the Athenaeum only a few days after his arrival in Madrid.

Unamuno's participation in Spanish public life increased markedly after his dismissal. His fighting spirit was aroused and the

[11] Emilio Salcedo, *Vida de Don Miguel*, pp. 189–193.

[12] Quoted in García Blanco, "Don Miguel y la Universidad," *Cuadernos de la Cátedra de Miguel de Unamuno* 13 (1963): 22.

[13] Speech of Luis Maldonado on October 3, 1914, quoted in Salcedo, *Vida de Don Miguel*, p. 192.

period between 1914 and his exile in 1923, years which coincided almost exactly with Reyes' stay in Spain, form a clearly defined epoch of his life, characterized by political activity. As Reyes was to write later: "Can one live in Spain without the temptation of politics? And above all if one lives with pen in hand? . . . And I would like to write a book (except that I lack the time and the mood) about the characteristic manner in which their alternate political participation and abstinence has distorted the writers of Spain (remember Unamuno, Ortega y Gasset, Maeztú)" (IV, 402–403).

Unamuno undertook two main campaigns during these years: first, during the war, against the German sympathizers in Spain, and then against the king and the dictatorship. And there were many minor skirmishes in between, all in the name of liberty and against the forces of tradition. Ricardo Gullón, author of a definitive study on Unamuno, writes:

> Unamuno was correct in calling himself the representative of the liberal conscience, disdained when not combatted—and, if possible, crushed—not so much by the king as by the forces of a reaction hating both the intelligentsia and the people. . . .
> . . . On the Spanish scene, Don Quijote-Unamuno charges forth to combat giants and dragons, and, on doing so, he dramatizes, because of his inherent spiritual disposition, both circumstance and dialogue. In the gray and drowsy Spain of the years 14–23 . . . the voice of Unamuno tirelessly beat at the Spanish soul, preparing the spirits for combat.[14]

By 1917, the year of the first general strike in Spain, which was followed by harsh repressive measures, he was in the thick of the battle. He hated to leave his beloved Salamanca for Madrid, yet he gave two speeches there, in January, on academic autonomy and on the European war and Spanish neutrality. In May he spoke again in favor of the Allied cause, at a large Leftist meeting in the Madrid bullring. Later on, he even made a trip to the Italian front with other Spanish intellectuals.

[14] Gullón, "La novela personal de don Miguel de Unamuno," *La Torre* 9, no. 35–36 (1961): 95.

It was at the time of all this activity that Reyes again attempted to communicate with Unamuno. How had Reyes meanwhile been adapting himself to the Spanish scene? The first year he had written of Madrid: "Why are there crude spirits and hoarse voices? Why the tasteless joke and the impudent burst of laughter? Why is there a surreptitious, muffled, unequivocal current of hatred toward beauty?" (II, 63). Other impressions had succeeded these, but he had surely not put them too far behind him to be able to appreciate the article Unamuno published in February, 1917, entitled "El frío de la Villa-Corte" (The coldness of the capital), in which he said, in reference to the unhappiness of many Latin Americans in Madrid: "I can see very well why a well-tempered, profound, and delicate soul, hungry for humanity, should feel sad and isolated in that cold inn full of smiles and pleasant words and where all the doors are always open" (OC VIII, 551). Perhaps the sympathy he showed here for the spiritual problems of the American in Madrid played its part in encouraging don Alfonso to write him again.

His letter was written on May 22, 1917, almost four years to a day after the earlier Mexican letter, and it had the same ostensible purpose: to present Unamuno with one of his books. It begins by making mention of the earlier communication:

> I sent you from Mexico, some years ago, a certain book of mine —*Cuestiones estéticas*—written in the fervor of adolescence, for which I received no acknowledgment. Now I send you *El suicida, Libro de ensayos*. Also a certain erudite pamphlet which you can ignore. The hazards of my country have thrown me upon European shores, and I now live in Madrid. The skepticism of the capital would like to convince me that don Miguel de Unamuno "no longer reads," but I neither believe it nor place your approval in such low esteem as not to desire it.
>
> Who knows? Why shouldn't this badly printed book interest you? For all we know, the one who is most worthy of us and understands us better may live on the other side of the ocean.
>
> In any case, I am sending what I have: receive it as a token of my severe and conscious admiration.

Unamuno as usual belied the critics and denigrators who had obviously counseled Reyes not to bother writing to him, by replying a few days later, soon after having returned to Salamanca from addressing that large political rally in the bullring. As Reyes wrote years later: "He sent me a very expressive letter, which is very far from being a mere courtesy and which was the origin of our friendship."[15] The letter reads:

> I have just seen in my register, in fact, my dear sir, that I received and catalogued in my library, some years ago, your *Cuestiones estéticas*, but I confess that I did not read them. You were then completely unknown to me and I lacked, as I lack now, the time to read those I know and those who are recommended to me by someone reliable in taste and criteria. But *El suicida* I have read, and profitably. I read it with interest from the moment I began, because when poor Felipe Trigo killed himself—the cult of Life, thus, with a capital letter, carries one to death—I thought of writing about it. I see that we have much reading in common and similar likes. I have marked some passages of your essays with hopes of commenting upon them sometime. When? I do not know. I like the genre and I like the way you treat it. Perhaps there is too much literature. Something more of active mysticism would be better.
>
> I have also read your translation of Chesterton's *Orthodoxy*. I did not know it and I like it very little. There is too much ingenuity and his paradoxes are cold, without passion. It does not palpitate.
>
> I do not know upon what they can have based themselves to tell you that I no longer read. I read, yes, but what I seek out and not what comes to seek me out. And this they call, no doubt, not reading. *Ars longa, vita brevis*, and I would have no time left to converse with the great ones, with the eternal ones, if I started to listen to all those who, because I do not have time to hear them, now accuse me of being deaf. I read better than ever if not more than ever. (June 2, 1917)

Unamuno speaks with convincing honesty when he excuses himself for not having read Reyes' earlier book. In 1903 he had

---

[15] Alfonso Reyes, "Mis relaciones con Unamuno," *Cuadernos de la Cátedra de Miguel de Unamuno* 6 (1955): 6.

written an essay on this very matter, saying that he was completely overwhelmed with all the Latin American books that he received, and that no one appreciated his criticism anyway: "And if it is terrible to tell them the truth, it is not less so to remain silent. I receive a book with an expressive dedication, and usually a letter with it, a letter in which I am asked to give 'frankly and sincerely' . . . my opinion on it. And woe is me as far as the demanding writer is concerned if I use sincerity and frankness with him" (OC VIII, 201). This almost echoes Reyes' letter, and Unamuno would have had no way of knowing that this young writer *was* capable of listening, as he had said.

Unamuno had in fact done for Latin America what he always refused to do for Spain—exercise literary criticism. As Torre points out, this is all the more significant a concession, considering his mistrust of "literature" as such, in the sense of its being a purely aesthetic phenomenon.[16] There were several powerful reasons for Unamuno's interest in the literature of the New World. It was first aroused not so much by what was peculiarly American in that literature but by what he saw in it that was purely Spanish. He said of the first work he analyzed, the Argentinian gaucho poem *Martín Fierro*: "[It] is, of all that I know that is Spanish American, the most profoundly Spanish."[17] He wanted to free the Spaniard from narrowness and provincialism, by opening his eyes to the true universal Spanish tradition that he had hopes of seeing mature in Spanish America. "One has to leave behind this geographic and nominal Spain," he said, "this sad patrimony of profiteers, go outside in search of the Spain that could have been and that ought to have been. And who knows if from there they might not return it to us . . ." (OC VI, 904).

Spanish America was, then, for Unamuno the Other Spain, and he had very decided ideas about how its literature should develop, and especially about the direction in which it should not go. He repeated in many ways and at many times the idea expressed in

[16] Torre, "Unamuno crítico de la literatura hispanoamericana," *La Torre* 9, no. 35–36 (1961): 541.
[17] Unamuno, quoted in García Blanco, *América y Unamuno*, p. 348.

this phrase: "Infinity and eternity we have to look for in the heart of our corner and our hour, our country and our epoch."[18] In other words, the universality of Spanish American literature and, therefore, its greatness must be based on authentic Americanism. Reyes did not fit into Unamuno's idea of the ideal American author, in whose work he always wished to find a certain descriptive Americanism. But Reyes was concerned with the same problem of the relation between the universal and the particular in literature as was Unamuno. Although Unamuno at the turn of the century worried primarily about the dangers inherent for the Spanish American in his excessive imitation of foreign literatures, Reyes in later years suffered from the excessive nationalism of a Mexico just becoming aware of its own uniqueness. Looking then at the problem from a different angle, he declared: "The only way to be profitably national is to be generously universal" (VIII, 439).

By the time of the publication of *El suicida*, Unamuno had by and large abandoned literary criticism; therefore it is not surprising that he did not write about it. His interest in Latin America had not declined, but his articles on America now dealt with other themes. That Reyes' book found favor with him is, however, undeniable and, moreover, easily explicable.

Unamuno was not a very good literary critic, in the accepted sense of the term.[19] He was not capable of that voluntary "proteanism" which Reyes puts forth in *El suicida* as a necessary attribute of the critical function. A book only interested him and met with his approval when he was able to place it within his own ideological framework, even if he had to force things a bit to do so. As we can see from his letter, he was unable to appreciate Chesterton's English temperament. Reyes might have commented then and there on this weakness in Unamuno's critical method, but he does so rather on another occasion, in relation to Pascal: "Doesn't Unamuno say that Pascal never convinced himself? 'Convinced,

18 Unamuno, *Ensayos*, II, 1167.
19 Torre makes this point in "Unamuno crítico de la literatura hispanoamericana," p. 549.

never'—he writes—'persuaded, perhaps. For this reason he preached to himself.' But this is the portrait of Unamuno and not of Pascal!" (VIII, 243–244).

Thus when Unamuno says that he read *El suicida* with interest, it is natural for him to add that he and Reyes have similar tastes. Felipe Trigo, the popular novelist whose suicide served as the starting point of Reyes' book, was known to both of them. And, in truth, much of what Reyes says in his book responds to Unamuno's way of looking at life. The active mysticism that Unamuno recommends to Reyes in his letter is the quality that Reyes praises in his essay, and it comes very close to describing Unamuno's own attitude toward life. It is, Reyes says, heterodoxical mysticism, the mysticism of the rebel, of the critic, the desire of the creature to better the conception of the creator. Is this not a portrait of Unamuno, the prototype of the heterodoxical thinker, who in his fictional creations strives to place himself in an analogous position with God? All the spiritual energy that Reyes sees concentrated in his concept (he compared it to the idea of knight errantry) is found in Unamuno. It is no wonder that he felt so much at home in Reyes' book.

Soon after this cordial exchange of letters, Unamuno and Reyes met personally, perhaps in the Residencia, where Unamuno used to stay when he visited Madrid. Both Unamuno and Reyes were writing extensively for the Spanish press at this time. The so-called Generation of 1898 had exerted a strong influence on the life of its countrymen through conscientious and dedicated journalism, and as the century progressed the press took on even more importance in political and cultural life. Almost all the important newspapers had sections devoted to the arts. Both Unamuno and Reyes were assiduous contributors to *España*, a weekly magazine with a basically political orientation. This was Unamuno's main forum in his pro-Allied campaign during the war. It was Reyes' outlet for, among other things, his movie criticism. Unamuno may very well have decided to read *El suicida* because he knew of Reyes from his articles in *España*.

Among the many articles that attest to their active participation in Spanish journalism, one finds that their interests several times led Unamuno and Reyes to dwell on similar themes. One such shared concern was a passion for the Spanish language. For both Unamuno and Reyes it was the receptacle and the guardian of Spanish tradition and Spanish spirit, the symbol, for Unamuno, of the unity of the Spanish world, and, for Reyes, of its common Latin heritage. They jointly defended it against the misinformation of such self-appointed experts as the French writer Remy de Gourmont, who asserted that the Spanish of a certain Latin American writer, a Francophile, was a neo-Spanish "more agile than the rough classical Castilian. . . . The sentence," Gourmont continued, "constructed in the French fashion, follows a more logical line, more in conformity with the natural course of thought. . . ." Reyes, after quoting the above, asked, with equanimity, as was his wont: "This matter of neo-Spanish, where does it lead us?" He concluded by saying: "Let us not invent languages among ourselves. We must use the only international language among the Spanish American republics, the only one in which we can all more or less understand ourselves" (IV, 196). Unamuno's approach was much more direct and scathing: "M. Gourmont, who calls himself a philologist and passes for such among the more or less mercurial literati who have not studied philology, would be hard pressed to define and discover that neo-Spanish language he has invented." He concludes: "He would do well, then, . . . to remain within the natural movement of his own thought and not to start writing haphazardly about that which he obviously knows very little and very badly" (OC VIII, 239, 241). Reyes' Mexican courtesy and Unamuno's Spanish brusqueness led them to a similar conclusion.

Many such parallels can be found in the writings of Reyes and Unamuno. They share an unflagging interest in the promotion of cultural relations between Spain and the New World. On this topic they were the two most effective and intelligently articulate figures in Spain. As Unamuno said: "I think that I can affirm without its being taken as petulance that I for my part, alone and solitary, unconnected, without statutes and program, have done for the spiritual union between the Spanish-speaking countries as much as any other person can have done" (OC VIII, 467).

Both writers started from the premise, or rather from the knowledge, that the problem was a grave one "The mutual ignorance between the old and the new Spains was in those days incredible,"[20] Reyes wrote. The tenacity with which Unamuno pursued the subject is good evidence of the little change in the attitude of the Spaniard over the years. He wrote in 1905: "And among the many lies that fly about and spread here, one of the biggest is that of Spanish American fraternity" (OC VIII, 360–361). In 1908 he commented in a letter to an Argentinian writer: "The ignorance about American matters is very great in Spain and especially in that empty and indecorous Madrid which is the last place that foreigners who try to study us should visit."[21] And in 1919, at about the same time that Reyes was concerning himself with the subject, he wrote: "All the rhetoric about the intellectual and moral union of Iberoamerica is here pure hypocrisy. . . . Here there is an artful and indifferent resistance to that which could come to us from the countries beyond the ocean that talk and think in Spanish" (OC VI, 919). Obviously Unamuno considered it an active ignorance, a purposeful rejection, on the part of the Spanish peninsular culture, a resentment disguised by false protestations of love.

Reyes' reputation as an unofficial cultural ambassador linking the two continents was built on the solid foundation of these years in Spain when he undertook his educational campaigns side by side with Unamuno. His basic philosophy could perhaps best be expressed by these phrases from one of his newspaper articles: "Hispanoamericanism is not a question of the 'ties of the blood': it is also one of the ties of reason. There is no good insisting on the ties of the blood. What is lacking is the campaign of reason" (IV, 572). Reyes' appraisal is more optimistic than Unamuno's, for he believed that honesty and good faith would suffice to change the

---

[20] Reyes, "Treno para José Ortega y Gasset," *Cuadernos Americanos* 85, no. 1 (1956): 65.

[21] Quoted in García Blanco, *América y Unamuno*, p. 275.

situation. Unamuno, perhaps because he had lived with it longer, was not so sanguine. And his pessimism about the Spanish political situation tinged his viewpoint: "No, the kingdom of Spain cannot serve as a link between the Iberoamerican republics and Europe," he wrote, "and a dynastic regime that is sustained by lies, that vegetates only by means of falsehoods, this kind of regime cannot aspire to this function. There is no worse slavery than that of lies. And Spain has to free itself from the kingdom of the lie. Deceitfulness is the enemy of civility."[22] This illustrates in passing why official Spain did not look with too much favor upon Unamuno.

A central point in the correspondence between Reyes and Unamuno was the letters that followed upon Reyes' visit to Salamanca in April, 1920. He went in the company of another Mexican writer, Artemio de Valle-Arizpe, who was his partner on a historical commission set up by the Mexican government to search for documents in Spain and Italy. This was the first official connection Reyes had had with the Mexican government since 1914, and the trip to Salamanca was made as part of the investigation. Two of Unamuno's books in Reyes' library were signed by their author on that occasion. Unamuno was living in the house on Bordadores Street that he had occupied ever since leaving the rectorate in 1914, and he received Reyes and his friend in his study, a sunny room piled high with books and sparsely furnished with a plain table and two leather chairs. But let Reyes describe the afternoon: "He talks to us of the latest books; but he is stifling, he feels cramped in the closed room, and then he takes us on a walk in the outskirts, on the shores of the Tormes. He recites his verses. He flashes, he thunders and throws lightning bolts, talking of the evils and the hopes of his country. He remembers America and shudders." Reyes felt, that afternoon, the full force and power of Unamuno's personality: "It seems, at times, that he applies his ear to our heart, like a doctor. It is useless to dissimulate. We are

22 Unamuno, "El Unamuno censurado," *La Torre* 9, no. 35–36: 25.

before a man. A man: angel and demon, saintly rebellion and saintly humility, a civil war in his conscience; aggressiveness and, at the same time, a thirst for harmony, and, above all, a tragic feeling of life" (IV, 390).

Reyes continued on from Salamanca by car with his three traveling companions—two other Latin American writers had joined them—on a trip through Extremadura, carrying letters of introduction from Unamuno. He kept in touch with Unamuno by postcard. On his return to Madrid their correspondence concerns the publication of the works of the Mexican poet Amado Nervo, who had died the previous year. A Spanish publishing house had put Reyes in charge of the preparation of the complete works of Nervo, and he edited twenty-nine volumes between 1920 and 1928. It is only natural that he should think of two essays that Unamuno had written on Nervo as a possible prologue to one of the volumes. He must have asked and received Unamuno's consent while he was in Salamanca, for he sent him the proofs of the two articles immediately on his return to Madrid.

The publisher of Nervo's books then sent Unamuno the Nervo volumes that had already appeared, and Unamuno wrote to Reyes:

> I have received, my dear friend, the eight volumes of Nervo's works and I have already read—reread mostly—half of them, taking notes, which will be useful for me.
>
> I did not know his Juana de Asbaje (it seems to me, I do not know why, that it should be Asuaje) and scarcely she herself. It has been for me a discovery. I want to gloss these lines:
>
> > If it is to live so little,
> > What purpose to know so much?
>
> She meant to say:
>
> > If it is to know so little,
> > What purpose to live so long?
> >   (July 7, 1920)

Both Unamuno and Reyes had been friends and admirers of Nervo. Nervo had been living in Madrid for quite a few years when Reyes arrived in 1914, and had been one of the first to help his young compatriot by introducing him to some of the Spanish writers. It is interesting to think that these two writers, Nervo and Reyes, of quite different temperaments, should be the two Mexicans whom Unamuno was to know the best, and from whom, one must assume, he was to form much of his idea of Mexico. Nervo was a gentle and quiet man whom Reyes said was progressing toward mutism. He had evolved toward a personal mysticism, an inward-looking faith, quite different from the active mysticism espoused by Reyes.

Unamuno's friendship for Nervo seems to have sprung, as with Reyes, from an affinity of interest. "There, in that room of meditation of the poet," he wrote, "we talked of these things, of these matters of the other world, which preoccupy Nervo, as they do me" (OC VIII, 442–443). Nervo's mysticism was also very different from Unamuno's. It was a mysticism very much of the turn of the century, impregnated with a diffuse eroticism that made his poetry popular with a certain type of reader, particularly a feminine one. Unamuno, curiously enough, seemed oblivious to this aspect of his poetry and was very attracted by what he did choose to see, the purely religious elements.[23] Because of this, he overcame his usual dislike of what he considered to be the superficial qualities of "modernista" poetry.

Unamuno's comments on Nervo's study of Juana de Asbaje, or Sor Juana Inés de la Cruz, the most fascinating and brilliant figure of Mexican baroque literature, are most interesting. The intellectual curiosity and the inner struggles of America's first feminist could not help but interest Unamuno. The next month he published an essay, "Sor Juana Inés, hija de Eva" (Sor Juana Inés, daughter of Eve), in which he repeated his interpretation of her verses. "The question that Unamuno sets forth," Reyes wrote, "is very different and is, truly, more tragic" (XII, 150). In fact, the themes of both the verses and the gloss are very much Unamuno's own. In his last poem, written a few days before his

---

[23] Torre, "Unamuno crítico de la literatura hispanoamericana," p. 543.

death, Unamuno's point of departure seems to be a thought similar to Sor Juana's own, rather than to his reinterpretation of it:

> To live the dream, is this not to kill life?
> Why put in it such effort
> to learn that which in the end is forgotten,
> scrutinizing the implacable brow—
> desert sky—of the eternal Master?
>
> (OC XV, 818–819)

Another topic that entered naturally into the conversations between Unamuno and Nervo was Mexico itself and, especially, Tepic. This was Nervo's birthplace and the city where Unamuno's father had lived and worked. It was through his father that Mexico first gained a place in Unamuno's imagination. Unamuno wrote several times about the presence of Mexico in his childhood recollections and attributed to Mexico two factors important in the formation of his character.

He believed, first of all, that the "indianos," the Spaniards like his father who returned home after living in the New World, had a definite liberalizing effect on Spanish public life, and that his own civil conscience was formed under this influence (OC X, 427–428). A second, more intangible factor was what might be called the poetic aura of Mexico: "Mexican traditions illuminated my young imagination,"[24] he recalled. As a boy he devoured his father's books on ancient Mexican civilizations. "I even thought about adopting the ancient Mexican calendar, because ours . . . is so well known! . . . And what I thought *seriously* of was getting books to learn Aztec. At twelve years old!" (OC X, 147). He remembered being fascinated as a child by a scene of the execution of Maximilian in a traveling wax museum. "And today," he wrote, "when I read things about Mexico, and, above all, about its antiquity, the perfumed mist of my first youth envelopes me, and from the printed words escape, like a chord of distant harmonies, the sounds of daydreams of my twelve years, in that blessed age in which history and legend were one" (OC X, 147).

[24] Quoted in García Blanco, *América y Unamuno*, p. 9.

Even at the age of seventy-one the glow of Mexico had not died. In 1935 he wrote that "we still keep in my house a lovely sarape, which was used as a table cover, and whose bright colors are as symbols of the bright colors—flower-like—that adorn the web of those childhood memories of mine of the paternal Mexican tradition."[25] Unamuno's frequent mention of Mexico was a source of pride for Reyes, who wrote in his "Recuerdos de Unamuno" (Memories of Unamuno): "Many times he told me, and I think he put it in writing, that, if he had been younger, he also would have wanted to move to Mexico" (XII, 151).

Amid the nostalgic and imaginative evocation of Mexico in his essays there is a rather dissonant note to which he returns again and again: his irritation at the spelling of Mexico with an x when, according to Spanish phonetic spelling, it should be a j. "The question," he writes sarcastically, "is to give a certain exotic and strange air to the word in order to thus express a certain eagerness for distinction and independence. . . . One has to distinguish oneself even if it be only by means of an x (OC VI, 822). Reyes defended the opposite view, and considered the x a symbol of the essence of Mexicanism. But the philologist in Unamuno refused to see it poetically.

After his visit to Unamuno in Salamanca, that is, after 1920, Reyes saw Unamuno more frequently. He wrote: "I always ran into him in one place or another, each time he appeared in Madrid. He came several times to my Sunday get-togethers."[26] But Unamuno's visits were, luckily, not so frequent as to make unnecessary their communication by letter, for it is here one discovers the first references to another subject that was to interest them both. After receiving Reyes' recently published book *El plano oblicuo* (The oblique plane), 1920, Unamuno wrote him: "Meanwhile, on seeing on the cover of the book a monogram of A.R., it has occurred to me to offer you that which I enclose, ex-

[25] Quoted in ibid., pp. 9–10.
[26] Reyes, "Mis relaciones con Unamuno," p. 6.

plaining first its architectonic construction. 'Cocotology' prepared me for these tasks" (January 21, 1920). "Cocotology" is the Unamunian word for the science of making paper animals. He was an expert in making paper birds, and the café tables of his afternoon *tertulias* were strewn with them.

In that letter he sent Reyes, as he said, a suggested new monogram, preceded by the "architectural" drawing explaining it, along with two monograms of M.U. and one, for King Alfonso, of A. XIII. Neither of them ever mention the fact that one of the M.U. monograms lies with its jaws open toward that of the king, where the three III's form an effective barrier against any communication between them.[27] This is a silent commentary on a very real situation that was to have wide repercussions.

It was the monogram that aroused Reyes' interest in what is a very little studied facet of Unamuno's work: his drawing. Their letters show how this interest developed. Reyes writes:

> My dear Maestro: Maroto recently opened an exhibition in Madrid (which I missed because of ill health) in which some portraits done by you of your wife and yourself were announced. How could I obtain photographic reproductions of them? Where are they? Can I still see them in Madrid? You know that I have your head of Nervo, and I would like to continue increasing my documentation on "Unamuno, the sketcher." (Jan. 29, 1922)

And Unamuno replied:

> I cannot guess, my dear friend, what portrait of my wife done by me is the one announced by Maroto. It must be one of my youngest daughter—which, by the way, turned out very well—that he asked me for and I gave to him. And if you ask him in my name —showing him this letter if you wish—for a photographic reproduction, he will not refuse you. Because my situation has changed since I was elected vice-rector—the position of rector remains vacant and I shall probably occupy it—I can move about freely

---

[27] Ernesto Mejía Sánchez, "Más sobre Unamuno y Reyes," *Boletín de la Biblioteca Nacional* 15, no. 3–4 (1964): 11.

and I am thinking of going there to Madrid. I shall bring the
drawings I have, I shall give you some of them, and of the others
you can make reproductions if you wish. (January 31, 1922)

The documentation of "Unamuno the sketcher" became an
article, published under that title in 1923. Reyes wrote:

> There in his leisure moments, there within his domestic self as
> the head of the household, he distracts himself with his little
> paper birds (some other day we will talk of this philosophic art
> and of its essential precepts: Never use glue or scissors, etc.), or
> he entertains himself with his sketches. Unamuno, as an artist, is
> little known. Many years ago, The *Revista Moderna*, of Mexico,
> published the portrait of Amado Nervo as seen by Unamuno. It
> is a rapid sketch, drawn in a moment of conversation, where per-
> haps the best is the hand. His sketches sometimes attempt to fix
> the features of a face; at other times, to reproduce the stonework
> in churches and cathedrals, human and animal gestures, the
> ecstatic calm of the Castilian fields. (IV, 390)

Unamuno gave Reyes nine drawings, which he included in his
book *Grata compañía* (Pleasant company), published in 1948.

In the two succeeding letters there is a continuation of the discussion of the drawings, as well as a new proposal of Unamuno's.
He tells Reyes:

> The State has given our poor Faculty of Letters the sum of
> 2,500 pesetas for lectures, and my companions there think that
> they should be given by Frenchmen, Portuguese, or Latin Ameri-
> cans. And since we cannot bring these latter over here, we must
> have recourse to those resident here. Would you want to come?
> Would Icaza come? Do you know of any other—Mexican, Cuban,
> Colombian, Chilean, Argentinian, etc., etc.—who would do a good
> job and about whom you would, confidentially, of course, give
> me information? Because then I would write him. Do me, then,
> this favor.
> We would pay him the trip, the stay . . . and each lecture. . . .
> Bagaría asked me for some drawings and I told him that I no
> longer had them since I had lent them to you. If he asks you for
> them, let him choose. Except for the one of my little niece drink-

ing chocolate, because I want to keep that for the interested party. (March 15, 1922)

Reyes' answer tells Unamuno of Bagaría's visit and suggests several possible lecturers. The letter concludes:

On my part, I have the chapter of a book in preparation, of which I published (I refer to the chapter) a fragment in Costa Rica: Visión de Anáhuac. It is about the first visual impression that the conquistador had of Mexico. Does this seem opportune to you? It would go well with what Icaza would read, since I know he has on hand something about culture in the Viceroyalty of New Spain. If this is not a good idea, tell me, since there are other things. And I am truly grateful. My trip and my stay would be at my expense, and the lecture will be very well paid by the pleasure and the honor of the invitation. (March 22, 1922)

Unamuno's idea of acquainting the Spanish students in Salamanca with the Latin American writers was an excellent one. Unfortunately, in spite of his good intentions, and Reyes' enthusiasm and pleasure, these particular lectures never took place.

Unamuno was at this time in the midst of a whirlwind of political activity that was about to culminate in a visit to the king. Events over several years had been leading to this. In 1920 Unamuno had written an article that caused him to be tried for "insults to the king of Spain" and then sentenced to sixteen years in prison, though he was pardoned before he had to serve. At the end of 1920 he also lost an election for national deputy, which distressed him only in that a victory would have made it possible for him to make a trip to Argentina without requesting permission from the government, something he refused to do.[28] None of this seemed to interrupt his work or seriously bother him. What did embitter him was the situation in Spain.

After his sentencing he received messages of support from all over Latin America and in answer to one of them he asked that the Latin Americans "come to the rescue in any way they can of this poor people, exploited, oppressed, and debased by the hypocritical

28 Salcedo, *Vida de Don Miguel*, p. 230.

Hapsburg despotism."[29] This was written in June, 1921, the month before the catastrophe in Morocco when the Spanish army in Africa lost thousands of men, apparently due to following the king's advice rather than that of the government and the minister of war. From this moment onward, Unamuno did not desist in his attacks until he saw the king expelled from Spain.

Reyes received a confidential visit from Unamuno in his legation office one day in early April, 1922, a visit that was to make Reyes the possessor of secret information about one of the most important political crises in Unamuno's career—his visit to the king. Reyes never spoke of it until a 1954 newspaper article angered him by stating that Unamuno had had no affection for him. To deny this accusation he told part of the story, and revealed it completely in a 1956 letter to Unamuno's faithful disciple García Blanco.[30] The whole episode of Unamuno's visit to the king can be traced through don Alfonso's words.

On the seventh of April he wrote a letter to Artemio de Valle-Arizpe, a copy of which he kept in his files:

> Unamuno has had an hour-and-a-half interview with the king. In the morning he had been here in the legation, as a matter of fact, he asked for you. That same afternoon (I had heard about something since that morning, but I did not believe that it was so near to taking place) Romanones took him to the king. The press and the literary coteries, and the political centers, are all commentary and surprise. It has been made known that some years ago the king met Unamuno in some train station, and he told him: "Since then (that well-known dismissal in Salamanca) I have not seen you again. I would like us to talk." Then Unamuno wrote to the king, asking for an interview; BUT THE LETTER DID NOT GET TO ITS DESTINATION. And, since then, Unamuno has become more and more bitter toward the king, until reaching the point of the attack which he recently made upon him in the Athenaeum, and which hurt the king very much.

[29] Unamuno, "El Unamuno censurado," p. 50.

[30] The letter to García Blanco (January 12, 1956) was published by Ernesto Mejía Sánchez, "Más sobre Unamuno y Reyes," pp. 15–16. Mejía Sánchez tells the history of this episode in his article.

Romanones guessed what was happening and, with a master stroke, he joined and reconciliated them. We shall see what comes of it. Unamuno had told me in the morning: "These people in the palace are very worried because the king's son is turning out to be an ill-behaved boy, they have not taken care to give him good tutors, and they fear the kind of character he will develop." We'll see, Artemio, don't get frantic. You will know about everything, if you are not here to witness it first.

Madrid was truly in an uproar over the affair. Again we can follow Reyes: "The literary opinion of Madrid in those times—always fierce—considered this a betrayal on Unamuno's part. He wanted to give a lecture in that admirable and extremely liberal house, the Athenaeum of Madrid, and the audience of young writers, amid shouts, kicks, and whistles, did not let him speak. That is how they behaved in those days."[31] The Athenaeum was one of Unamuno's chief forums in Spain, a place where politicians and intellectuals could meet with complete freedom. At the time of the uproar about Unamuno, Reyes pointed out that anti-monarchical lectures were heard there almost daily, while at the same time the Conde de Romanones, a monarchist, was president. One admirer called it "a sort of walled-in Hyde Park."[32] Both Reyes and Unamuno had spoken there, and often met there informally to participate in the lively discussions that were always going on. Unamuno called it "the most famous cultural institution in Spain—more than any of its universities" (OC X, 344). And Reyes said: "It will be impossible to understand Spanish intellectual life in those years without a complete comprehension of what the Madrid Athenaeum was, where on the one hand the expression of thought had no limits and on the other the direct and immediate relation between workers of the spirit was established automatically . . . in a democratic leveling of which I know no similar example" (VIII, 171). Here, then, in the center of Madrid intellectual life, liberal sentiment was so aroused when the symbol

[31] Reyes, "Mis relaciones con Unamuno," pp. 7–8.
[32] José Rubia Barcia, "Unamuno the Man," in Rubia Barcia and M. A. Zeitlin, eds., *Unamuno, Creator and Creation*, p. 5.

of antimonarchism went to see the king that they would not even listen to an explanation. They accused him of giving in so as to be made rector again. And Unamuno found that he had to explain his position not only to his colleagues in the Athenaeum but even to his Latin American readers.

He did not dare, however, refer to the main reason for the king's desire to see him. This, as far as is known, he told only to Reyes. In his letter to García Blanco, Reyes says:

> I think that the moment has come to reveal to you, in the confidence of our love and veneration for the maestro, that don Miguel told me the following: When Romanones took him to the king, the king told him that he wanted to name him tutor of the prince of Asturias and entrust him with his education, since the boy was in bad hands and had already committed some dangerous pranks, like strangling a cat. I think that nothing was decided at the time, but don Miguel at the moment considered it the duty of a good Spaniard not to take the proposition lightly. Perhaps you already know of the matter. I communicate it to you in any event, asking you, this I do request, that, if it is still a secret, you keep it that way.

After the scandal he had already caused, Unamuno knew he could never mention this matter. It does seem possible, however, that he might not have minded the idea of being thus able to guide the path of the monarchy in the right direction, toward the Republic, perhaps. "If it is human to make a mistake," says the critic who published this letter, "it is not less so to delude oneself, and don Miguel was a visionary like a good Quijote."[33]

Reyes was right in believing that this affair would attest to the respect that Unamuno felt for him. He concluded his article of vindication by making this point:

> Remember that I had been for five years a newspaperman and writer in Madrid, and then, for five more, practically, I was the Mexican attaché. Unamuno, after what had happened—although he was very ready to fight and although, as he said, it had frequently been up to him to "fight in the middle of the bullring"

[33] Mejía Sánchez, "Más sobre Unamuno y Reyes," pp. 14–15.

—needed to explain himself and to unbosom himself to someone, and he chose the only one of the literary group who, although very close to him, could, because he was not a Spaniard, consider the acts with more moderation than any other. But would he have taken this step if he had not felt himself my friend, if he did not know me to be his friend, if he did not esteem me on an intellectual and on a moral level? If this is not sympathy . . . No: no one takes the friendship of Unamuno from me.[34]

The political situation worsened after this, both for Spain in general and for Unamuno personally. The last letter from Unamuno in the correspondence is a good measure of his desperation. Reyes wrote him on October 21, 1923, with a request:

Canedo, Moreno Villa, and I are going to begin to publish soon some small *Cuadernos Literarios* [Literary notebooks] with works of contemporaries and our own, as well as very select and untouched classics. We want your advice: but we also want—and as soon as possible—your collaboration. We would like you to participate in the first series of notebooks that we are preparing with a novel, or whatever suits you best. . . . Our object is to go before the public as soon as possible—ourselves and some friends —without submitting to editorial requirements. And we need people like you to authorize us with your participation. We are doing it with very little money, but we are ready to send you by return mail whatever you want to be paid.

Thank you for the attention you give us. Can we have your original in reply?

The plan had been thought out by Reyes, his close friend Enrique Díez-Canedo, the literary critic, and the poet José Moreno Villa one Sunday afternoon in Reyes' apartment. They wanted to make available the books of Hispanic authors to counteract the flooding of the Madrid market with translations, and they wished them to be "a reflection of contemporary life without reducing it to the intellectual circle of one group, of one tendency, or of one country."[35] The books were quite successful. About thirty of these

[34] Reyes, "Mis relaciones con Unamuno," p. 8.
[35] Quoted in García Blanco, *América y Unamuno*, p. 155.

small volumes came out—the first ones yellow in color with green lettering. Both Reyes and Moreno Villa published something in the collection, along with Azorín, Manuel Azaña, Gómez de la Serna, Pío Baroja and many others. The plan was a brave attempt to carry out a program of cultural propaganda among the Spanish public to benefit Spanish authors, complementary to what Ortega was doing on a much larger scale in the *Revista de Occidente* at about the same time. The collection finally had to be abandoned because of the dispersion of its originators.

They were unsuccessful in their attempt to get Unamuno's collaboration. He answered them two days later:

The original in reply? Oh, my good friend, that cannot be! And it cannot be because I do not have it done; because I have nothing unpublished and ready, finished, that fits into those *Cuadernos Literarios*. I would have to do it. When shall I do it? Look, I received your other letters; I thought of doing something for that Mexican newspaper, but the time went by in sleeping and dreaming, in writing polemical articles, in gnawing at my insides on seeing what is going on—and I did not even answer you as was my duty. I have found just one sole refuge within the ideal this year. I have written some romantic rhymes of a supposed poet—something like Stechetti—and I have framed them in a story. It will be called *Teresa*. There are about (don't be frightened) 2,500 lines. And now I am waiting to see if Ricardo Calvo will stage, finally, my *Soledad*. Books—they turn out to be so unproductive for me! My *La tía Tula* [Aunt Tula] and *Andanzas y visiones españolas* [Spanish travels and visions] fell almost in a vacuum and the second edition of *Paz en la guerra* [Peace in war] is scarcely just beginning to be noticed. Which ties me to the terrible task of *having to* (having to!) write ten or twelve articles a month. And now more, because the stupid censorship exercised by those uniformed Boeotians brainwashed by the ordinance means that of every ten they suppress three or four entirely.

I am discouraged on seeing the way this stupid dictatorship and all this regime so like a casino movie is accepted. That Primo de Rivera has no more brains than a frog. He is a prototype of foppish frivolity and vanity. Not ambition, no, but vanity. And the poor dolts who surround him![36] All the Spanish idiocy is aroused. It is painful to read certain papers. I do not know where we will end up. But let us see if I am able to hatch something for the *Cuadernos Literarios*. Some tragic bufoonery will be the result; some bitter representation of this farce that we are suffering. If I can write anything . . .

I have planned only things for the theater, but I have gotten into my head the idea that they be acted before they are printed. I now have done six dramatic works and I have scarcely been able to have the theater public judge them. I turned another two into novels. And I have two more in the works. And now they tell me that Vidal y Planas is going to stage, without my permission, my *Nada menos que todo un hombre* [Nothing less than a complete man]. Perhaps arranged for the stage by him it will get access to the theater, and arranged by me it will not, but I know that I would do it better than he.

For these and many other reasons—and not the least important, to chat with all of you—I should go to Madrid, but while this Boeotian dictatorship lasts I do not plan to ask permission. It is humiliating to receive the slightest favor from the authorities under this shameful regime. (October 23, 1923)

The response came quickly:

Dear and admired don Miguel: Your letter has moved me, has moved us. It is not difficult for me to feel as a Spainiard would. I truly am one!

You have tempted us; we want to see that *Teresa* soon. . . .

We cannot renounce so easily the plan to count on you for one of the first notebooks. It would not matter if you gave us something already published, taken out of another book, or a small collection of articles that you would like to see together in a provisional edition: a collection that could end, for example, with the recently published one on your thirty years of teaching. That is, a brief anthology of your articles published from 1921 to the present.

[36] This sentence and the two previous ones were not published by García Blanco in *América y Unamuno*. They were published by Mejía Sánchez in his article "Más sobre Unamuno y Reyes," p. 17.

> We are still waiting for you. Canedo and Moreno Villa return
> your greetings. I promise myself—this time, yes—your quick af-
> firmative reply. (October 25, 1923)

Unamuno painted a vivid picture of his state of mind, his spirit,
and his work as the fateful year of 1923 drew to a close. He was
overwhelmed with work, his books were not selling, he was still
expecting *Soledad* to be staged (which it was not, in his lifetime),
and he was disturbed about the dramatization of one of his novels
by someone else. Ironically enough, this novel was dramatized by
yet another author, and it became the most successful and most
frequently performed of his works.[37] His only refuge was *Teresa*,
the long romantic poem in which he gave fictional birth to one of
the many "Unamunos" who never achieved an existence of flesh
and blood.

It was the anguished, embattled Unamuno who took up most
of his time that year. Primo de Rivera's military dictatorship
found its most implacable enemy in Unamuno. He expressed himself in many letters, which were often published, in the same vein
as he did to Reyes. He showed no fear or concern for the conse-
quences. In December a letter of his was published in Buenos
Aires, with no signature. In it Unamuno had written: "I thought
that that royal goose who signed the shameful proclamation of the
12th of September, pattern of ignominy for Spain, was only a
blusterer with no more brains than a cricket, a tragicomic movie
actor, but I have seen that he is a sack of abject and vile passions."
He concluded: "I am drowning, I am drowning, I am drowning
in this sewer, and I feel the ache of Spain in the depths of my
heart."[38] This letter was the direct cause of the order for his exile.
He left Salamanca under guard on February 21, 1924.

The government had again acted in a decisive fashion against
its most prominent intellectual opponent. Again Unamuno was
the center of political furor—in truth he had been for several

[37] Delfín Leocadio Garasa, "Los empeños teatrales de Unamuno," *Ínsula* 19,
no. 216–217 (1964): 23.
[38] Quoted by Carlos Esplá in "Vida y nostalgia de Unamuno en el destierro,"
La Torre 9, no. 35–36 (1961): 117–118.

years. But now repercussions were felt even across the Atlantic. The *Literary Digest* of New York, on June 21, 1924, in an article entitled "Why Spain Deports Unamuno," reproduced from the *Mercure de France* the opinions of Jean Cassou:

> The deportation of Miguel Unamuno has shocked the civilized world. Frenchmen are especially indignant. They remember his enthusiasm for France, the part he played during the war, and his violent campaigns against the "troglodytes"—that is to say, against the belated tho powerful element given over to clericalism and pro-Germanism. His case brings to light the existence of two irreconcilable Spains—on the one hand a very active, very live, but very small group of intellectuals; on the other hand the enormous mass of the country, devoid of political conscience, incapable of reacting to the accidents of civil life, and always ready to be led by combinations of the demagogs and politicians or driven by military force.[39]

And the *Digest* itself explained the importance of it all by saying that it was as if President Roosevelt had deported Charles W. Eliot.

Unamuno was sent by the Spanish government to the island of Fuerteventura. From there he was dramatically rescued and taken to Paris, arriving in October. Reyes arrived in Paris a month later and in December of that year was named Minister of Mexico in Paris. Thus began another phase of their relationship, which Reyes has documented with affectionate attention to detail. Unamuno was decidedly unhappy in Paris. Carlos Esplá puts it best when he says: "The inadaptation of Unamuno to Paris was at all moments complete."[40] He was incurably homesick.

Almost every day of his thirteen months in Paris he met with his Spanish friends at La Rotonde, a picturesque Montparnasse café that had been a favorite of Picasso, of Trotsky, of Modigliani, "a café of political émigrés, of artists, of poets, of *rapins*, of models, of bohemians, a cosmopolitan, rebellious, colorful, extravagant

---

[39] "Why Spain Deports Unamuno," *Literary Digest* 81 (21 June 1924): 17.
[40] Esplá, "Vida y nostalgia de Unamuno en el destierro," p. 140.

clientele."[41] There, as in the Athenaeum, he stayed talking with his friends for hours and hours, in dialogues that were typically closer to monologues. Otherwise, he walked through the parks and the boulevards, reading, preparing articles, and thinking of Spain, oblivious to his surroundings. He had few French friends—Jean Cassou, Georges Duhamel, Valéry Larbaud, Paul Valéry—and did not participate in French cultural life. Reyes describes his last impressions of Unamuno:

> I saw him in Paris for the last time. He was in exile, but, natural-
> ly, he was still living with his imagination turned toward
> Salamanca. He would recite his poetry for us without paying
> attention to the traffic: one of his sonnets against the military
> dictatorship of Primo de Rivera almost cost us our lives at an
> intersection of the Grands Boulevards. He would close his eyes
> before the magnificent Av. de l'Observatoire and he would ex-
> claim with a gesture of impatience: "Gredos! Gredos!" He was
> lost in his dream. (XIII, 151)

Reyes and Unamuno were frequently together during Unamu-no's sojourn in Paris (Reyes was to stay until 1927), and Reyes has written several times about an episode that was for him the highest accolade he could have received from his friend. He recalls:

> One day we went together to the home of Jean Cassou. I left early
> so as to walk along the bank of the Seine, enjoying the warm
> evening, in the company of the poet Rilke. Then Guillermo Jimé-
> nez, who has written it somewhere, took from Unamuno's lips the
> greatest and the most moving praise that I could have received
> and desired: "Reyes' intelligence"—said Unamuno—"is a func-
> tion of his goodness." . . . The maestro's words do not make me
> vain, nor, unfortunately, do I have the right to consider them
> just; but they clearly express his judgment of my person, and
> above all the benevolent refraction which affection produced in
> that judgment. If this is not friendship . . .[42]

[41] Ibid., pp. 125–126.
[42] Reyes, "Mis relaciones con Unamuno," p. 7.

From France, Reyes returned to America, and Unamuno to Spain three years later, in 1930, at the downfall of the monarchy. They were never to meet again, but Reyes' books, affectionately inscribed, made their way to Unamuno from 1926 in Paris to 1933 in Río de Janeiro. There was a chance that they might meet in Argentina, in 1936, but Unamuno was forced to refuse the last invitation to that country he wanted so much to visit. He did so in a letter to Díez-Canedo, then Spanish ambassador in Buenos Aires, while Reyes was his country's ambassador in Río: "My health is not what it was, although it does not prevent me from living an ordinary life and working. I feel myself now, finally, getting old, and feel the need to leave my things in order before having to leave this world. But that which above all keeps me here now is the state of public affairs (*res publica*) in this our Spain, over which I see hovering a catastrophe if Providence or Fate or whatever does not remedy it." And he concluded by saying: "It seems that it is God's will that I shall not be able to cross the sea."[43] And so it was. The last word on this topic was by Reyes, who wrote in 1941: "If Unamuno had survived, surely now we would already have him in these lands, where the soul of Spain is expanding" (XI, 148).

There is no doubt that Reyes was proud of his friendship with Unamuno and never relinquished his memory of it. Unamuno's photograph stood on a shelf by his desk, and the doubt cast on that friendship in the newspaper article mentioned earlier brought a prompt and convincing reply. Reyes' explanation for that article shows both the goodness of spirit and the intelligence that Unamuno recognized in him:

It is possible that then [at the time of the interview], and for whatever circumstances of the moment, Unamuno may have found my image a little tarnished in his memory. That has no importance and does not affect the dominant tone of our good and very cordial relations. Misfortune is, at times, a bad counselor, and don Miguel suffered a lot during his last years, as we all know. Thus his old friends, understanding the discomfort of his spirit in the face of the vicissitudes of his country, have

43 García Blanco, *América y Unamuno*, pp. 13–14.

spread a merciful cover over his final inconstancies. The great man, cast first to one side and then to the other by anguish and by the desire to stop the avalanche with his own hands, was left alone, without coreligionists and without Spain. Peace to his remains.[44]

Perhaps only Ortega has expressed with equal eloquence and justice the tragedy of Unamuno's death. He wrote: "Unamuno's voice has sounded forth unceasingly within the limits of Spain for a quarter of a century. On its ceasing forever, I fear that our country may suffer an era of frightful silence."[45]

[44] Reyes, "Mis relaciones con Unamuno," pp. 5–6.
[45] José Ortega y Gasset, *Obras completas*, V, 266.

Ramón del Valle-Inclán

(1866 – 1936)

UNAMUNO LONGED TO TRAVEL TO AMERICA, Juan Ramón Jiménez went to the United States to be married, and José Ortega y Gasset visited Argentina, but of Reyes' Spanish friends only Ramón del Valle-Inclán had been to Mexico. This gave a particular flavor to their relationship, for Mexico had permeated Valle-Inclán's life in an unusual fashion, and had become one of the "aesthetic coordinates" of his work.

Mexico was part of the Valle-Inclán legend, that mass of anecdotal material in the midst of which Valle himself was often completely obscured. "He was an improbable type," wrote Ramón Gómez de la Serna, his most imaginative biographer, "who adorned life like a reckless and delirious vignette."[1] This is an apt image, for the first impact made by Valle-Inclán tended to be a visual one.

[1] Ramón Gómez de la Serna, *Don Ramón María del Valle-Inclán*, p. 10.

One critic states that Valle has been pictorially interpreted more often than any other Spanish subject aside from Don Quijote and Sancho Panza.[2] Walter Starkie, the Irish Hispanist, who visited him with Reyes in 1924, tells us that "he was tall and meager, and his spectacles gave him the air of Quevedo. His brow rose high and ascetical, and his sharp, piercing eyes behind steel-rimmed glasses glanced here and there restlessly while with one hand he stroked his long beard, which flowed down over his chest like the plumage of a bird. He wore a black cloak draped over his left shoulder."[3] And Reyes sketches him thus: "Don Ramón is a rudimentary figure, of easy contour: looking at him incites one to draw him: with two little circles and a few vertical lines his face is done (pince-nez and beard); and with four straight lines and a curve, his right hand (index, middle, ring, little finger and thumb). Face and hand: the rest does not exist, or is only a slight prop for that face and that hand. In fact, the teacher who defines needs no more: the face is the dogma, and the hand is the commentary" (II, 85). Reyes' abstraction and Starkie's pictorial description both show him as a striking figure, "the best walking mask that strolled, all year long, on Alcalá Street,"[4] as Gómez de la Serna phrased it.

His extravagances of dress and aspect, which he developed during his first visit to Mexico, were matched by those of speech and action. Valle, like Unamuno, had a public image that had to be maintained, often at the expense of his inner self. Valle did not live his life, he portrayed himself, and that self absorbed a great deal from his fictional characters. He identified particularly with the Marqués de Bradomín, the decadent Don Juan who was the protagonist of his first four novels, the *Sonatas*. The anecdotes he invented about himself—he was never known to say a true word about his own life—and the exotic atmosphere in which the Marqués moved combined to create the image he desired.

Valle not only created, then, fictitious worlds in literature, but

[2] Gerald Gillespie and Anthony Zahareas, "Valle-Inclán," *Kenyon Review* 29, no. 5 (1967): 610.

[3] Walter Starkie, "A Memoir of Alfonso Reyes," *Texas Quarterly* 2, no. 1 (1959): 70.

[4] Quoted in Guillermo de Torre, *La difícil universalidad española*, p. 117.

also his own fictitious figure. All this, just as with the eccentricities of others of his literary contemporaries—Unamuno's peculiarities of dress, for instance—had a definite significance. They were one sign of the widespread and all-encompassing literary movement which, originating in Latin America toward the end of the nineteenth century, spread to Spain. *Modernismo* was a form of protest against the narrow, stifling culture of the turn-of-the-century bourgeois society, and one of its most characteristic aspects was exoticism. The *modernistas* created for themselves other worlds in which they could breathe more freely and find fulfillment. Thus Valle made himself the protagonist of a heroic world—a sign of rebellion and also, it seems, from comments of his friends, an indication of insecurity and timidity. The picturesque bohemian held center stage.

But actually who was this don Ramón del Valle-Inclán who so intrigued and impressed Reyes? He was, first of all, one of the five leading members of what Azorín had called the Generation of 98. However, unlike Unamuno, whose prestige grew after his death, that of Valle diminished, and it is only recently that he has begun to be de-mythified, that the many masks have been removed, and that the brilliant satirist and stylist has been given his due. In the years immediately following his death, it was Unamuno and Juan Ramón Jiménez, themselves linguistic innovators, who clearly saw that the true importance of Valle was in his creation of a "language."[5] Unamuno wrote that "Valle-Inclán made for himself, using as material the language of his people and of the people with whom he lived, a language . . . of his own, a personal and individual language."[6] Juan Ramón called his language "flame, hammer, seed, and chisel of the unknown, all in disarray, he himself not knowing why or how. A supreme language become man."[7] In this passion for the word lay the source of Valle-Inclán's literary genius.

---

[5] Ibid., pp. 113, 132. Also Ignacio Iglesias, "Valle-Inclán de nuevo," *Mundo Nuevo*, no. 5 (November 1966): 76.

[6] Miguel de Unamuno, *De esto y aquello*, I, 415.

[7] Juan Ramón Jiménez, *La corriente infinita*, p. 101.

Valle's early novels, the *Sonatas*, chronicle the loves in the four seasons of the Marqués de Bradomín's life in a very stylized and impressionistic prose. The settings are exotic—one takes place in Mexico—and his characters exalted. The influence of Barbey d'Aurevilly, Casanova, and D'Annunzio is strong. It is one of the characters in the *Sonata de estío* (Summer sonata), 1903, who gives voice to Valle's artistic credo: "I laugh at all that is human and all that is divine and I believe only in beauty."[8]

Valle continued throughout his life to stylize reality, but his focus and his theme changed radically. Not only is there an abrupt change in his aesthetics but also in his ethics, in his world view. The comment quoted above contrasts sharply with an interview Valle held in 1920 in which he claimed that "we must not cultivate Art now, because it is immoral and miserable to go on playing in these times. The first thing is to bring about social justice."[9] A variety of influences had "broken the barriers" of Valle's aristocratic aestheticism. The change within himself must have been taking place during the First World War when the death blow was dealt to the European "belle époque" and thus to the Marqués de Bradomín, who in a way epitomized this spirit in Spain.[10] At the same time, the Spanish government system, a holdover from the nineteenth century, was creaking through its last years, and social unrest and political and military disasters began to take their toll. On the cultural plane, all the new literary and artistic "isms" of these vanguardist years began to undermine the traditional artistic values.

With these influences impinging upon him, Valle in 1920 published three works: *Divinas palabras* (Divine Words), which Reyes calls a tragicomic parody; *Farsa y licencia de la reina castiza* (Farce and license of the popular queen), a grotesque deformation of the reign of the nineteenth-century Isabel II; and parts of *Luces de Bohemia* (Lights of Bohemia), the "first great work of 'denun-

[8] Quoted in Torre, *La difícil universalidad española*, p. 127.

[9] Ramón del Valle-Inclán, quoted in José Rubia Barcia, "The Esperpento: a New Novelistic Dimension," in *Valle-Inclán Centennial Studies*, p. 77.

[10] Guillermo Díaz-Plaja, *Las estéticas de Valle-Inclán*, p. 246.

ciation' in contemporary Spanish literature,"[11] and, one might add, a precursor of the theater of the absurd. This is a key year in Valle's development, when he initiates that period of literary creation which we today find most important. Hand in hand with the de-mythification of the legendary Valle by the contemporary critic came the realization of the significance and actuality of Valle's unmasking of Spanish traditional and cultural legendry. As Torre points out, "Valle-Inclán's art follows an inverse process in relation to what is customary in so many other cases. He begins by being a traditionalist and he concludes as a revolutionary,"[12] both stylistically and ideologically.

It is in *Luces de Bohemia* that Valle baptizes the new genre on which his fame rests. It is, he says, an "esperpento." One of the characters in *Luces de Bohemia* defines the form thus: "Classic heroes reflected in concave mirrors give the 'esperpento.' The tragic sense of Spanish life can only be rendered with a systematically deformed aesthetic. . . . Spain is a grotesque deformation of European civilization."[13] From that time on, everything Valle wrote had the quality of an "esperpento," for, though he applied it only to his plays, the "esperpento" was more than a genre, it was his vision of the world, and he saw everything in that deforming mirror which dehumanized and mechanized man until he became a grotesque puppet. Valle's models were no longer Botticelli or Rossetti, but Bosch and Breughel, El Greco and Goya.[14] And with his "esperpentos" Valle makes as bitter and cruel an attack on the Spanish monarchy as Unamuno ever did in his essays and public polemics. He had, like Unamuno before him, come face to face with the tragedy of Spain.

Camilo José Cela, one of the most original of contemporary Spanish novelists, has expressed the opinion that Unamuno and Valle, so very disparate, but both so very Spanish, "encompass between them all the possibilities of the Spanish being." This is a

---

[11] Ibid., p. 247.
[12] Torre, *La difícil universalidad española*, p. 124.
[13] Quoted in ibid., p. 154.
[14] Pedro Salinas, "Significación del esperpento o Valle-Inclán, hijo pródigo del 98," *Atenea* 164 (October-December 1966): 108, 115.

daring statement to be made about a people who encompass so many extremes. Cela contrasts the two men: "Valle is a dandy and Unamuno an intellectual. Valle is an aesthete and Unamuno a humanist. Valle a writer and Unamuno a thinker. Valle dreams of being a cardinal and Unamuno of becoming a saint." And he concludes: "Egoists, each one in his glorious manner, anarchic, grandiose, Valle and Unamuno—the former on his luminous stage, the latter in his shaded solitude—represent the front and back of that coin, always ready to be tossed in the air, which is called Spain."[15] Valle, like Unamuno, was an eccentric and a prophet.

Reyes witnessed precisely those years of the definition and establishment of the mature Valle-Inclán, and commented on the process with foresight and sagacity. He was keenly aware of the significance of Valle's literary development, and also very appreciative of the enchantments of the "mythical" Valle-Inclán.

Valle created his legendary figure in the world of the café. "That indefatigable fictionalization of his own life . . . was—in its immediate aesthetic profundity—one of the greatest delights of his conversation," wrote Reyes.[16] He re-created, in several fragmentary impressions, the atmosphere of the café life which he shared with Valle. When Valle was in Madrid, Reyes tells us, no day passed without his going to the café:

> In the mornings, he slept. He lunched about one, and before three (he always went on foot and very quickly) he was already in the Athenaeum, directing the rehearsals of the Theater of the New School . . . playing everyone's role, creating the works all over again with his personal interpretations.
>
> As evening approached, the day began to be bearable for him. Then he would decide to walk the streets, accompanied by some silent friends. . . .

[15] Camilo José Cela, *Cuatro figuras del 98 y otros retratos y ensayos españoles*, pp. 22, 25.
[16] Reyes, "Presentación," in William Fichter, ed., *Publicaciones periodísticas de don Ramón del Valle-Inclán anteriores a 1895*, p. 7.

By seven, he was in the Café Regina, where we always saved the place of honor for him.

I do not know at what hour or where he ate dinner, but he would not return to his house any more, and he would go on in continuous *tertulia* all night. . . .

Conversation stimulated him. It puts him into action intellectually. Dawn surprises him dauntless—like Socrates in "The Banquet"—serenely given over to the delights of conversation. (IV, 277–278)

The Spanish novelist Ramón Pérez de Ayala, in an article written a few months after Valle's death, comments on the brilliance and tragedy of his conversational skills: "Dialogue was his terrain, and a contradiction or a polemic would animate him as a breeze does a live coal. He slipped out of and overcame every adverse argument with a disconcerting witticism: ingenious and sensible at the same time. . . . So it is that Valle-Inclán consumed a great part of his genius, like sterile incense before an empty altar, in the conversations of the café *tertulia*."[17]

This was very true of his later years. He wasted what he might have created in the obsessive necessity to give fuel to his public image. Even Reyes writes as early as 1921: "But when does Valle-Inclán write? In the twenty-fifth hour, undoubtedly. An hour that he has found outside of time, as one who finds a hiding place. He arrives there alone, on tiptoes, 'trembling with desire and fever' " (IV, 278).

It was in the epoch of the Café Regina (don Ramón later moved his *tertulia* to other cafés) that don Alfonso first frequented Valle-Inclán's *tertulia*. The café was the center of Madrid social life, especially of the literary life. This was where things happened and people met. The only writer among Reyes' friends who kept apart from this world was the shy and retiring Azorín, who found it more pleasant to invent for his own personal enjoyment several literary societies complete with engraved stationery and a mysterious membership, but with no real existence. He had the joys of

---

[17] Ramón Pérez de Ayala, "Los muertos del año," *La Prensa* (Buenos Aires), 28 February 1937, section 2.

erudite and literary companionship with none of its problems. There was a Lope Club and a Góngora Club. Reyes considered himself a member of both, and Gómez de la Serna had a delightful time speculating upon how the members spent their time.

Valle, in contrast to Azorín, seemed to have no life at all outside the café. The Regina on Alcalá Street is one of those about which Torre, a young man at the time, writes: "The cafés that are now legend were then fluid anecdote, and on the marbles of their tables, in the mirrors over the red divans, was written vividly all the literary history of Spain."[18] Gómez de la Serna was not overly impressed by the Café Regina, perhaps out of loyalty to his own *tertulia*. The café "never had character," he said, "with its air of a pantheon full of columns,"[19] but it seems likely that the liveliness of the gathering dispelled any such gloom. The most frequent *tertulianos* during these years were the editors of the magazine *España*, men such as Manuel Azaña and Luis Araquistain, who were to take their place in history during the Spanish Republic, the politically-minded intellectuals who were to become the intellectually-minded politicians. Sometimes Antonio Machado, the Mexican scholar Francisco Icaza, Enrique Díez-Canedo, Eugenio d'Ors, Américo Castro, and José Moreno Villa would join them. Valle was in his apogee, and his *tertulia* was a brilliant one. Its fame even reached New York, where, on the occasion of don Ramón's visit there in 1921, a newspaper gave out the information that "any afternoon in Madrid from 6:00 to 8:30, you can find don Ramón at a table in front of the Café Regina."[20]

"That slight black figure with the ivory face, wrapped in his cape, trotting quickly through the open areas of the Salamanca barrio, against the monotonous background of a fence, beneath the rows of acacias and street lamps" (IV, 277)—this was Reyes' view of Valle as he walked by the Pardiñas house, stopping by for Reyes on the way to the Regina. There, settling down to enjoy Valle's anecdotes of the evening, don Alfonso spent many of his pleasant-

---

[18] Torre, *La aventura estética de nuestra edad*, p. 110.
[19] R. Gómez de la Serna, *Retratos contemporáneos*, p. 309.
[20] Reproduced in *La Pluma* 4, no. 32 (1923), facing p. 80.

est hours in Madrid. "Valle-Inclán's improvisations well nigh hypnotized Reyes, who played up to him," wrote Starkie, "encouraging him to embroider his anecdotes. . . . All of the rest of us sat in silence, lulled by the musical tones of the poet. . . . While the master was speaking, Reyes whispered to me: 'He is unique. As his imagination works he discovers, as though by magic, the tones and cadences to express his thoughts, and he seems then to create before us a poetic drama.' "[21]

Mexico had a favored role in Valle's stories. He styled himself as "Colonel General of the Armies of the Tropics" and took pleasure in describing his heroic exploits. "He would talk to me," Reyes recounted, ". . . about that man [a Mexican general] with the face of a lion who drank brandy with gunpowder, and who would go out on horseback when there was a riot in the streets" (VIII, 79). When Valle was away from Madrid, Reyes said, the only consolation left to his companions was the thought of all the tales he would have to tell on his return. Reyes wrote nostalgically: "How many such afternoons! From the terrace of the Regina together, we have seen the afternoons dying, crumbling within the frame of two public clocks. . . . As dusk falls, the two spheres become congested with light, and it is a glory to see the time die beneath the stroke of Longines" (IV, 276).

The Valle-Inclán of the café does, however, occupy too great a space in his biographies. It became too easy to accept the myth, which, although it was one aspect of his creative talent, was not the man himself, but only one perspective, significant in its revelation of his attitude toward life. A more prosaic account would begin by stating that Valle was born and raised in a small Galician town. There, it appears, he first heard about the Americas from the stories of a maid who had worked in Cuba and who familiarized him with its "landscapes of mystery and witchcraft."[22] In 1890 he went to Madrid, and two years later sailed to Mexico (Reyes was three years old at the time), where he stayed for less than a year. When Reyes arrived in Madrid many years later, Valle-Inclán

[21] Starkie, "A Memoir of Alfonso Reyes," p. 70.
[22] Francisco Madrid, *La vida altiva de Valle-Inclán*, p. 44.

was living with his family in Puebla del Caramiñal, in Galicia, but his trips to Madrid were very frequent.

Valle's letters to Reyes all fall within the years 1923 to 1926. During this time Valle suffered a severe setback both in his health and his economic situation. His letters refer to both. The first reads:

> I received your good and moving letter, sick in bed, which I have not gotten out of yet, although I am, it seems, a little better. . . . I have been suffering from this sickness for quite a while, but the pain has never been so bad. I have been in bed for more than a month, bored, sad, and in pain. If I recover, I hope to see you soon in Madrid. We will talk about our Mexico. (November 14, 1923)[23]

Valle had quarreled with his publishers and his next letter refers to that problem:

> With great joy I would send you this *Tirano Banderas*, which I spoke to you about in my previous letter. But after all these years, sick and old, I have fallen into the claws of Renacimiento. I am bound by an absurd and usurious contract. Because of this contract only Renacimiento can publish my works. But Renacimiento does not publish them, and since I owe them money, they will end up in control of all my work of thirty years. Renacimiento's intention of not publishing my works and of making things difficult for me through starvation is obvious. Recently they have put on sale *Sonata de estío*. It has been printed since April 30th, according to the colophon! And they began to print it way back in the summer of 1922! With the other books, four unpublished and ten re-editions, they have done nothing in the whole year.
>
> I am thinking of going to Madrid to see if I can find a way out of this cave, but my illness keeps me in bed. I have been urinating blood constantly for a month. Nevertheless, I shall make an effort and there we shall see each other, God willing. I do not

---

[23] Several of Valle-Inclán's letters to Reyes have been published in Spanish in complete or fragmentary form in: Emma Susana Speratti Piñero, "Valle-Inclán y México," *Historia mexicana* 8, no. 29 (1958): 70–72; Speratti Piñero, *Elaboración artística en Tirano Banderas*, pp. 147–150; Reyes, *Obras completas*, IV, 406.

think that I shall die from this one. Excuse the long lament of
this letter, but this illness has weakened me so much that I find
consolation in complaining like a woman. You are so good that
you will pardon me. (November 16, 1923)

It seems probable that Reyes had asked Valle to publish *Tirano
Banderas* in his collection of *Cuadernos Literarios* and, for different
reasons, had as little success as he had had with Unamuno.

Reyes was upset over Valle's long illness and financial difficulties. He must have felt the injustice of a writer of Valle's caliber
having to subsist on the borderline of poverty, for he informed
President Obregón of Mexico about the situation. Valle's admiration for Obregón, whom he had met in Mexico, might well have
suggested the idea to Reyes. Valle kept a picture of Obregón on
display in his house, and mentioned him very favorably in one of
his letters to Reyes: "The news in the papers is very confused, but
through the chaos I have a presentiment of the triumph of the
Federal Government. General Obregón is called to do great things
in America. His courage, his serene spirit, his knowledge of military tactics, his intuitive strategy, and his lucky star as a predes-
tined man assure him of victory" (December 20, 1923). Don
Ramón's friendship with President Obregón was also well-illus-
trated by anecdotes. The most amusing of them has Obregón, one-
armed like Valle, turning to him at a party and saying: "Don
Ramón, lend me your hand to applaud."

In any event, Reyes' intervention was successful, and the Mexican government aided the ailing Spanish writer, mindful of his
long interest in Mexico. It was this money that enabled Valle,
when he solved his difficulties with Renacimiento a short while
later, to return with his family to live in Madrid. Don Alfonso
alluded to this episode only once, in the introduction to *Las vísperas
de España* (Evocations of Spain), written in Buenos Aires the year
after Valle's death: "When I was living in Paris, in ill-fated times,
for him, I was the intermediary in the Mexican petition for this
invariable and pure friend of our country" (II, 43). Reyes, however, was still in Madrid when Valle wrote him in March and

April, 1924, thanking him for his intervention and acknowledging
the arrival of the money: "How can I tell you how much I appreciate the generous and delicate offer of President Obregón, and
the friendly intervention of yourself in this matter? I accept very
gratefully, although with the intimate sorrow that my friendship
for Mexico has not been able to show itself with all the disinterest
which I could have wished" (March 31, 1924). And on April 14
he wrote again: "If at any time, after I recover my health, I can
serve you or Mexico in some way, I only await your command to
put all my will at your service."

Reyes intervened in Valle's life at a decisive moment. The letters are one illustration of the truth of the statement in a recent
article that "during the years when D'Annunzio was achieving the
heights of his popularity and was becoming a 'national monu-
ment,' Valle-Inclán still lived in a hovel and had to beg advances
from his publishers in order not to die of starvation."[24] Reyes' own
articles on Valle-Inclán do not deal with his personal life but
rather with the public figure and, most significantly, with the
writer.

He came closest to evoking the mystery and fantasy that surrounded don Ramón in a description of a lecture given by Valle in
the Athenaeum, or rather, in his description of Valle as a lecturer.
The portrait is worthy of the subject in its vividness and plasticity.
Hearing Valle speak and watching him perform was not an
ordinary experience, as don Alfonso recalled it:

> His eyes begin to sparkle, his voice becomes warm, and his hand
> of wax, more eloquent even than his words, continuously sketches
> and describes a rhythmic, isochronal, transcendental curve. The
> hand comes and goes. At times, the index finger seems to reach
> out to sustain a corollary that tries to escape. Other times that
> large fish's fin opens out and beats the air, or becomes a plane for
> the projection of his ideas. A metaphysical shuttle, the hand
> comes and goes. The face is fecund like a cipher and the hand
> unravels the infinite connotations of the face.

[24] Manuel Durán, "Actualidad de *Tirano Banderas*," *Mundo Nuevo*, no. 10
(April 1967): 50

Reyes was struck by the supernatural aura which surrounded Valle. "When he talks of death, he does it with personal knowledge, assuming the responsibility of having been dead once." When he raises his hand to his forehead it seems to Reyes "as if he were fitting into place the lid of his head." Although the topic of the lecture had been aesthetic quietism, Valle had aroused his audience to a high emotional pitch:

> After the lecture, we took with us, along with a feeling of charming and delicate courtesy, the taste of something rough, harsh, and even savage. What is it? I will tell you: the empty sleeve!
> . . . Like those alarm clocks that vibrate and jump at the firing of their potent machinery, that fragile human drapery has also vibrated and jumped, jolted by an idea greater than itself. Then, as the right hand opens out like a wing, as the right hand stretches forth like an oar in a storm, the left stump has raised itself up, waving in the wind—with what is now a bloody elegance—an empty sleeve. (II, 85–87)

The loss of his arm, in a café quarrel, served Valle—and others— as an inexhaustible source of anecdotes, but Reyes' visual description is more revealing of the "satanic mystery" that surrounded Valle than any of these. Certainly this vivid portrait with its imagistic ascent into the realms of fantasy can stand among the most evocative of the impact of Valle's personality.

Nor has Reyes' literary criticism lost any of its pertinence with the passage of the years. His fine critical sense sought out in the early 1920's the very facets of Valle's work that have withstood the test of time. In his principal critical article, "La parodia trágica" (The tragic parody), Reyes' main purpose is to discuss the birth of the "esperpento." However, he who has called Valle "this true literary Janus, one of whose faces looks at the *Sonatas* while the other contemplates the 'esperpento,' "[25] begins his essay with a very illuminating commentary on the *Sonatas*. He approaches them from the point of view of character presentation: "Not only

---

[25] Reyes, "Presentación," in Fichter, ed., *Publicaciones periodísticas*, p. 7.

must one conceive the themes panoramically; also the figures, the characters. In order for a hero to appear panoramically before the eyes of the poet he must 'have a past,' like loose women; he must have a history. Only figures weighted down with a past are rich in a future."

Reyes proceeds to apply this theory of the "panoramic" character, which explains so well the particular flavor of Valle's books, to his re-creation of Don Juan:

> The figure of Don Juan springs forth in the most intimate region of Spanish sensibility. Art, in successive treatments, has given this gallant hero a certain tint of general citizenship in the kingdoms of the human soul. Don Juan is a panoramic figure. One can see him from above: he has a past, he is swollen with a future. Until today, Don Juan has been a man who reacts when taxed with two motives of action: love and death, the one as strong as the other. And the poet adopts Don Juan, and it occurs to him that he might react, might give of himself, to a motive of contemplation; to nature, to a landscape, and to the seasons of the year, which are the periodic respiration of a landscape. And here the *Sonatas* are born. The Marqués de Bradomín embodies thus one of the themes that has the strongest national (universal) roots, he gives it a new shading, and he makes it prosper by means of a preoccupation as ancient as the world. the lyricism of spring, summer, fall, and winter, and the ethic of the ages of man.

And without pause Reyes approaches the "esperpento," saying: "And one day it occurs to Valle-Inclán to apply his aesthetic equivocally; to deflect it slightly from the lines of nobility toward the lines of caricature; to no longer make a vital graft within the traditions of a theme or of a character, but rather a mimicry of life, using the appearances of a ridiculous doll" (IV, 101–104).

Reyes also notes the significance of what is perhaps the main interest of contemporary critics, Valle's language. "Even the language in which he writes is now something very much his own. He writes prose 'in Valle-Inclán'—a language made for the use of his soul, through elective affinity and natural selection" (IV, 278). His observations on how Valle wrote have also been born out by

present-day commentary: "This platonic man always knows be-
forehand what he is going to say and to write. He proceeds by
archetype, by large-scale previous ideas; and he lets the conse-
quences roll on toward particular events, with the security and
confidence of one who has completely dominated the disciplines"
(IV, 278). Recently, detailed studies have shown that the flamboyant Valle-Inclán was indeed an indefatigable worker and a
patient and careful artist, like Reyes himself, who strove continu-
ously for artistic perfection. Reyes in later years wrote again of
this quality in Valle: "The fine poet, whose masterly prose re-
volves in that golden zone where poetry begins, already occupies
that special place which corresponds to those who consecrate all
their effort to the love of beauty."[26] A pure and disinterested passion for the literary vocation was a bond between them, just as it
was between Reyes and that other completely dedicated Spanish
writer, Juan Ramón Jiménez.

Another topic that Reyes touched on in relation to Valle's writing was a refutation of a senseless accusation of plagiarism made
by one of Valle's contemporaries, the academician Julián Casares.
Valle had a habit of encrusting passages from other works onto his
own to give them the authentic flavor of another period or place.
In the case in question he had indicated very obviously in the text
what he was doing. Reyes comments that this is perfectly legitimate, as later critics have all done, adding, "more clarity cannot
be demanded of an artist. There is always a feeling of modesty, of
licit modesty, of good aesthetics and good education, in not going
about uncovering the wrong side of the tapestries we are weaving"
(IV, 282). Don Alfonso was himself interested in the various
influences on Valle-Inclán, as Valle's letter shows:

> Since you are curious about knowing literary influences and un-
> raveling their importance in writers, I am going to tell you those
> which I think most strong in the hour of my youth. Our friend
> Canedo, on noticing the influence you mention, that of a Portu-
> guese with whose work I am *totally* unfamiliar, must have made

[26] Ibid., p. 9.

a mistake. It could well be the influence of an unknown third person, both on the Portuguese and on myself. On the other hand, few have seen the influence of Chateaubriand. In the memoirs of the Marqués de Bradomín (Sonata de invierno), the visit which the marqués pays to the king and queen remembers intentionally that which the romantic viscount made to Charles X in exile (Memoirs of beyond the grave). (December 20, 1923)

Valle was less serious in pinpointing an influence on Reyes' writing. The fantasy that pervades the pages of *Plano oblicuo* brought forth this remark as recounted by Reyes: " 'You do not deceive us, Reyes,' said Valle-Inclán, leafing through the book. 'You smoke marihuana, as I do, or you take something.' 'Distilled water,' I told him. All of this does not come in, but rather goes out. I keep it inside, simply, and perhaps for this reason it is worth little."[27] Other critics, too, saw traces of exoticism in these early writings of Reyes. But any exoticism they possessed was, as he said, native to him: it "was the fruit of the Mexican atmosphere of my youth." But, in truth, its multiple origin, as he himself described it, was much the same as that of Valle-Inclán: memories, books, and fantasy.[28]

It is reasonable to suppose that in the midst of these literary discussions, one or the other, either Valle or Reyes, would turn his attention to Mexico. Reyes needed to do no propagandizing here. Valle had a marked affinity for Mexico, a somewhat mysterious attraction; though many have remarked upon it, no one has been able to offer a clear explanation for it. Don Alfonso, as might be expected, was one of the first to comment upon it, and he thus opened the way for what was to be a very fertile field of study— that of Valle's relationship with Mexico.

Valle himself has had quite a bit to say about the reasons for his first journey across the sea in 1892. They varied with his mood. In a newspaper interview in Mexico in 1921 he stated that the

[27] Reyes, "Historia documental de mis libros," *Universidad de México* 9, no. 7 (1957): 11.
[28] Ibid., p. 12.

purpose of his trip had been to avoid having to finish his studies in law school. He added that it was the country "in which I found my own freedom of vocation. I owe, then, to Mexico, indirectly, my literary career. . . . Here I began to follow my own path."[29] With these statements he brushed aside the fact that he had abandoned his law career in 1890 on the death of his father and had published a few short stories and newspaper articles in Madrid before he left for Mexico. But he was undoubtedly moved to simplify his autobiography by the desire to make more clear the literary debt he felt toward his host country. In view of Valle's very slight previous experience as a writer, Reyes seems correct in saying that his first trip to Mexico was "an efficacious dazzlement, which opened his eyes to art. . . . The man that Mexico returned to Spain already contained all the seeds of the poet" (IV, 285).

Valle's most famous statement on his reason for going to Mexico is recounted by don Alfonso as Valle-Inclán told it to him. In this story don Ramón was a young boy in Galicia who whiled away his time in card games, having developed his own method of betting only on those cards which were spelled with an *o*. An old man, hearing this, told him: "Look . . . you should seek out other, broader horizons. Go out in the world, don't rot in this corner.' 'And,' don Ramón would conclude, 'following the cabala of the letters, I resolved to go to Mexico, because Mexico is spelled with *x*.' "[30] This, then, was don Ramón's magic phrase, first formulated in a dramatic moment in the Athenaeum in 1915 and often repeated since then. It is tempting to think that perhaps he had in mind Unamuno's well known disdain for this spelling, for he would have greatly enjoyed irritating him. But even if this is true, it is legitimate to question his meaning further, for he never abandoned this catchword.

Laying aside for a moment the fascination of the *x*, it is not difficult to see why the young Valle-Inclán decided to leave Spain and

---

[29] Interview by Miguel Lanz Duret in *El Universal* (Mexico City), 19 September 1921, reprinted in Fichter, ed., *Publicaciones periodísticas*, p. 40.
[30] Reyes, "Presentación," in Fichter, ed., *Publicaciones periodísticas*, p. 8.

travel to the Americas. He had a romantic temperament, and needed to find other realities from which to fabricate his imaginary world. He was attracted to Mexico precisely because it was different, especially from his native Galicia of mists and legends. The abandoning of his own country was for the *modernista* a symbolic gesture in which was reflected the spiritual barrier between himself and the society in which he lived. The Latin American dreamed of Spain and of Paris. The Spaniard placed his illusions in the New World. New York was the exotic atmosphere for both Federico García Lorca and Juan Ramón Jiménez, just as for Valle it was and always remained Mexico.[31]

Mexico meant for him the sensuality, the delirium, of the tropics. He found there a complementary side of his personality, just as Reyes found his, that of severity and intellectual discipline, in Spain. Valle-Inclán incorporated Mexico into his personal mythology, as an integral part of his character. "Such a friend, so rabidly in love with our country,"[32] wrote Reyes. The attachment had deep roots. He was drawn by spiritual and artistic necessities, and what better way to refer to them than by the image of the mysterious x?

Reyes, from the first, was intrigued by Valle's whimsical phrase: "Oh, x of mine, minuscule in yourself, but immense in the cardinal directions toward which you point: you were a crossroads of destiny," he wrote (IV, 279). Years later, he made this letter the theme of a selection of his writings on Mexico, entitled *La X en la frente* (The x on the forehead), 1952. It became for him a symbol of his own Mexicanism: one writer's fantasy had born fruit in the spirit of another.

No matter what Valle's purpose was in going to Mexico, Reyes felt that Valle came away with a true feeling for the new land. "You, don Ramón," he wrote, "are at all times the best friend of Mexico. You love it for its good qualities, and you understand (and perhaps love a little also) its defects. You love it in its tran-

---

[31] For a complete discussion of this subject see Ricardo Gullón, "Exotismo y modernismo," in his *Direcciones del modernismo*, pp. 84–111.

[32] Reyes, *Marginalia, Segunda serie*, p. 34.

quility and in its turbulence. You love it for the lake and the volcano" (IV, 280). And he continued in another essay: "There are many who love America in its well-being and its smile. Valle-Inclán withstands the test of true understanding of America: that which enamors him in America is that pathetic vitality, that anger, that combativeness, that immense affirmation of sorrow, that rubbing of shoulders with death" (IV, 286). This is in direct contrast to his questioning of Ortega y Gasset's understanding of America after his visit to Argentina: "Could he be equally seduced by the America that weeps and fights?" (IV, 263) Reyes had asked. He obviously felt that the extravagant Valle-Inclán had somehow penetrated deeper into the secrets of America than the philosopher Ortega, a prophetic observation because he wrote these lines before the publication of Valle's great American novel, *Tirano Banderas,* which confirmed the profundity of Valle's American vision.

Valle-Inclán made three trips to America: he visited Mexico in 1892 and in 1921, and in 1910 he accompanied his wife on a theatrical tour of South America. On his arrival in Mexico in the spring of 1892 he immediately began writing for the newspapers, publishing during his stay various articles and short stories, almost all in the Mexico City paper *El Universal.* There is still little known of his activities in Mexico, where he stayed for a little less than a year, returning to Spain in early 1893. His autobiographical account of that period is a fictional one in which he told of his voyage as if he were the Marqués de Bradomín, saying: "I was . . . a soldier in the lands of New Spain."[33]

One episode of his stay, however, is known and documented, and it proves to be very interesting in the light of his future attitude toward the Spanish emigrant in Mexico, or *gachupín,* as he was derogatively called. Three weeks after his arrival in Mexico City an article was published in which the Spanish residents of Mexico were referred to as "the garbage that that Mother [country] throws at us continually and which comes only with the object of enriching itself." At this period in his life Valle felt called upon

---

[33] Quoted in R. Gómez de la Serna, *Retratos contemporáneos,* p. 273.

to vindicate himself and his compatriots. He did this by demanding a duel with the editor of the newspaper in question, but was satisfied in the end by an explanation and apology.[34]

From this initial contact with Mexico there remains the recollection of the episode of the duel and also Valle's first literary use of an American theme, in "Bajo los trópicos" (Under the tropics), which he wrote and published in *El Universal* while in Mexico in 1892. There is a definite development in the role Mexico played in Valle's work, which Reyes was the first to trace, in his essay "Valle-Inclán y América." He begins by pointing out what so many have since studied. "In a hundred places America appears in Valle-Inclan's work: sometimes purposefully; at other times, in a vague, unconscious background, if one can speak of unconsciousness in a writer who always ponders the seven harmonic evocations of every word" (IV, 283).

Valle's first short article on Mexico was later used by him in the creation of the short story "La niña Chole" (1895), which, in turn elaborated upon, became the *Sonata de estío* (1903).[35] Here we can again let don Alfonso speak:

> In the *Sonata de estío*, we find the niña Chole, the sweet and cruel mestiza whom the Marqués de Bradomín discovers amidst the ruins of Tuxpan, wrapped in the little silk rebozo and dressed in the 'huipil' of the ancient priestesses, against a landscape of carved stones, golden sands, palm trees, Indians and mulattoes with machetes, and horses covered with silver. A precious miniature, scarcely disturbed by a certain phrase of the niña Chole about the passage due Charon. . . .
>
> Here the maestro inaugurates his artistic, subtle interpretation of the Mexican atmosphere, choosing the scenes, the words, the types most charged with color; gently courting the facts of reality so that they all become expressive; transporting us to a conventional moment of time, where he can bring together what is most mordant and alive in the characteristics of several epochs. Thus, he applies to American matters the procedure with which he

---

[34] Fichter, *Publicaciones periodísticas*, p. 29.
[35] Fichter traces the origin of *Sonata de estío* in ibid., pp. 23, 39.

treated peninsular themes; he takes advantage of the suggestions of the primitive chroniclers and soldiers who used the pen of memoirs when they could no longer wield the sword of the deed; or some fleeting evocation of the America of Chateaubriand—this true creator of "virgin jungle," where the trees cry out as in Dante; and he always strives for that Parnassian objectivity of the Flaubert of *Salammbô,* across whose starry background are slowly pulled the curtains of a Catholic and Celtic melancholy, tremulous with tears and palpitating with insatiable desires. (IV, 283–284)

Don Alfonso saw then that the *Sonata de estío,* in spite of its Mexican setting, is basically the same as the other three *Sonatas,* in that in none of them does Valle actually look at reality. His purpose is to abandon it, not describe it. There is no sign of anything but an aesthetic preoccupation, none of the social and human interest he was later to exhibit. His interest here is in transferring his hero to a new territory, to another stylized atmosphere. The Marqués de Bradomín does not come to the real America, but to a romantic evocation of a country which the author had seen, but whose image he preferred to base mainly on literary rather than on actual experience.[36]

Mexico does not appear in Valle's work again until 1918 when, in a sonnet, the Indian for the first time takes the central position:

> The colt was nocturnal. The rider was
> of copper—an Indian born in Tlaxcala.[37]

A year later, in a poem from *La pipa de kif* (Pipe of kif), 1919, there is another vision of Mexico, which don Alfonso also comments on in "Valle-Inclán y América": "The herb-seller's store is an aromatic warehouse of American odors, with special predilection for the exotic and—if possible—the grotesque note, corresponding to the aesthetics of the poem. The synthetic power is disconcerting, and that Jalapa, that Campeche, that Tlaxcala

---

36 Speratti Piñero discusses his use of Mexico in *Sonata de estío* in *La elaboración artística,* p. 105, and in "Valle-Inclán y México," p. 62.

37 Quoted in Speratti Piñero, "Valle-Inclán y México," p. 66.

glimpsed through the smoke of marihuana, like beautiful monsters of hallucination and remembrance, are never forgotten. Decidedly, Valle prefers the Mexican America: the most mysterious and the most profound" (IV, 284). Reyes cannot hide his satisfaction at this fact.

In the summer of 1921, Mexico still unforgotten, Valle received an invitation from President Obregón to be guest of honor of the Mexican Republic at the centenary celebration of its independence. It was Reyes, then Mexican chargé d'affaires in Spain, who presented him with the invitation, telegraphing him at Puebla del Caramiñal, fearful that he might refuse. "But don Ramón withstood the test," Reyes wrote. "When he was perhaps most involved with his family and with rural pleasure, rusticating in picturesque Galicia, he heard the loud ringing of adventure. And by return telegram, he decided to leave" (IV, 279).

He arrived in Mexico City in September and remained there several months, during which time "he went to the cafés, gave some talks . . . presided over a literary gathering at the Teatro Principal . . . gave a lecture in the amphitheater of the University's Preparatory School,"[38] traveled throughout the country, and was much feted. He was intensely interested in the changes brought about by the Mexican Revolution. In an interview with a Mexican newspaperman, instead of identifying himself with the Spanish colony as in his previous visit, he alienated it by coming out in favor of Mexican agrarian reform. His interest in Mexico had widened to include social and political as well as aesthetic factors. Speaking of his first trip, he said that in Mexico he had found "silent but significant lessons in art and beauty."[39] Reyes noted that one of his main observations after returning from his second was that the struggle between the Indian and the landowner still persisted. The conclusions Valle drew from this can be seen in the following passage from his letter of December 20, 1923, to Reyes:

[38] Rubia Barcia, *A Biobibliography and Iconography of Valle-Inclán*, p. 18.
[39] Interview by Roberto Barrios in *El Universal* (Mexico City), reprinted in *Repertorio Americano* 3, no. 13 (28 November 1921).

But I note that I am getting away from the spirit that first moved me to write you. You can already guess that it is the Mexican Revolution. If I have to be frank I shall tell you that I was waiting for that attempt of the landowners. Revolution cannot be made half way. The "gachupines" possess seventy per cent of the territorial property. They are the extract of Iberian barbarism. The land in the hands of those foreigners is the most harmful form of possession. A thousand times worse than mortmain. Our Mexico, in order to do away with revolutions, has to nationalize the land, and the landowner.

. . . More than the Mexican Revolution, it is the latent revolution in all Latin America. The revolution for independence, which cannot be reduced to a change of viceroys, but to the cultural triumph of the Indian race, to the plenitude of their rights, and to the expulsion of Jewish and Moorish "gachupines." Better, of course, would be a throat-slitting.

If you think that in this tumult of news a clarion call in *España* would be appropriate, just tell me. I have tired myself and I scarcely have the strength to finish. I am still very weak.

His revolutionary ideals are clearly expressed. Don Alfonso commented that his second trip "only confirmed his attraction to Mexican things, and his understanding of our ideas, our victories, and our misfortunes."[40]

While in Mexico this time, Valle announced that he was going to write a book on the conquest of America entitled *Hernán Cortés*: "In writing *Hernán Cortés*, I will relate Man and Landscape," he explained. "Can you not understand the emotion of these men of iron, beneath this tropical sun, face to face with the snow-topped mountains, the rushing water, the juicy fruits, the brown flesh?"[41] That same epic moment was described by Reyes in *Visión de Aná-huac*: "And it was then that, in an enviable hour of astonishment, having crossed the snow-topped mountains, the men of Cortés ('dust, sweat, and iron') appeared upon that orb of sonority and brilliance—the spacious circle of mountains" (II, 17). This confrontation between the conquistador and the geography of the

---

[40] Reyes, "Presentación," in Fichter, ed., *Publicaciones periodísticas*, pp. 8–9.
[41] Quoted in Guillermo Díaz-Plaja, *Las estéticas de Valle-Inclán*, p. 250.

New World imagined by don Ramón is in fact the underlying theme of Reyes' *Visión*. There is a definite affinity of outlook.

Valle's book never appeared. The contemporary situation in America began to interest him more. On his return from Mexico he wrote a poem entitled "¡Nos vemos!" (We'll meet again!) dedicated to the Mexican Indian, clearly indicative of his new frame of mind. The poem, a precursor of similar ones by other poets, is a call for revolution, and concludes:

> Mexican Indian,
> hand in hand
> I tell you my faith:
> the first
> is to hang the landowner
> and afterward sow the wheat.
> Mexican Indian,
> hand in hand,
> God for a witness.[42]

He expressed the same views in his letter to don Alfonso, and in *Tirano Banderas*, which he was soon to write, the advice given in the poem—"to hang the landowner"—is carried out by one of the characters.

In other words, in *Tirano Banderas* Valle expresses the very opposite view from the one he wished to defend in a duel in his first visit to Mexico. He attacks the *gachupines* whom he had defended in his youth. This apparently complete reversal in his attitude is not a difficult one to explain. In 1892 he was young and impulsive, and felt himself to be included in the attack. In the 1920's his growing social consciousness had caused him to reflect on what he had seen. As has been the experience of Spanish exiles of later years, he found himself in complete disaccord with the type of Spaniard who had left his country solely to better himself economically and who seemd inevitably to ally himself from afar with the most retrogressive elements and tendencies of the mother

---

[42] Valle-Inclán, "¡Nos vemos!" *Repertorio Americano* 4, no. 17 (17 July 1922).

country. His was a common and very understandable reaction. "I work on an American novel of 'gachupinesque' bossism and avarice,"[43] Valle wrote to a friend, making it clear that the term *gachupín* was, when used by him, a generic term applied to a particular class of man, not to a nationality.

In tracing the thread of Mexico in Valle's work until immediately after his second trip to Mexico, Reyes concluded by examining the "esperpentos" in that light. He found his country's presence in the language. "There is a reminiscence, which comes and goes, of Mexican words, of Mexican turns of speech and puns. It is a murmur that wanders in the liminal part of his soul, but the writer lets it be felt with full consciousness of what he is doing. Those of us who are in on the secret, savor it and smile. And we are grateful for this artistic dignification which don Ramón gives to various of the humble mistakes of our people" (IV, 284–285).

Tirano Banderas: Novela de tierra caliente (Tirano Banderas: Novel of the tropics) appeared in 1926, after Reyes' departure from Spain. It verifies the complete change in Valle's attitude toward Mexico and in the use to which he put his Mexican experience since the time of the *Sonata de estío.* Fundamental to an understanding of Valle's intentions in *Tirano Banderas* is part of a letter he wrote to Reyes, the most natural consultant in such matters:

> I am working now on an American novel: "Tirano Banderas," the novel of a tyrant with characteristics of Doctor Francia, of Rosas, of Melgarejo, of López, and of Don Porfirio. The hero a synthesis, and the language a sum of the American idiomatic expressions from all the Spanish-speaking countries, from the mode of the [Mexican] "lépero" to that of the gaucho. The Republic of Santa Trinidad de Tierra Firme is an imaginary country, like those European courts which Abel Hermant depicts in some book. I lack facts for this book of mine, and you could give me some, dear Reyes. Opposite the tyrant I present and trace the figure of an apostle, with more of Savonarola than of Don Fran-

[43] Quoted in Cipriano Rivas Cherif, "La comedia bárbara de Valle-Inclán," *España* 10, no. 409 (1924): 8.

cisco Madero, even when he has something of this illuminated saint. Where can I see a life of "The Blessèd Don Pancho"? I trace a great cataclism like the earthquake of Valparaíso, and a social revolution of the Indians. For this latter I need some information about Teresa Utrera [*sic*], the saint of the Ranchito de Cavora. My memory no longer serves me and I would like to refresh it. Is there something written about this saint?

It can be shown, then, that from its inception Valle's intent was to present a synthesis—a very personal and somewhat arbitrary one—of Latin America as a whole. His search for documentation reveals that this was not to be a haphazard understanding. There is no doubt, however, that Mexico was primarily in his mind when he wrote it.[44] It was, after all, the country that he knew by far the best.

Death permeates *Tirano Banderas*. Curiously enough, the fascination with death belongs equally to the Galicia of Valle-Inclán's birth and to the Mexico he grew to love. Valle assimilated to perfection—as if they were his own—the popular Mexican traditions of the Day of the Dead, probably because of his Galician heritage. His tragic farce could not have had a more effective background than this macabre festival, in which the tyrant becomes, himself, one of the dolls of death, "a skull with black glasses." Here, indeed, the picturesque Mexico no longer serves merely a decorative function but becomes an integral part of the "esperpento," lending itself to the distorted and parodic effect that is essential to both theme and technique. The result is "a stylized world of cubist fragmentation, animalization, and mechanization."[45]

Tirano Banderas is a tragic commentary on the long procession of anarchy and tyranny that has plagued the Hispanic world. What Valle discerned as he confronted Spanish American reality with the prophetic insight of the poet was that its social and political evils were not due solely to tyranny but also to the particular

---

[44] This point has been admirably studied by Speratti Piñero in *La elaboración artística*, pp. 147–150.

[45] Gullón, "Técnicas de Valle-Inclán," *Papeles de Sons Armadans* 127 (October 1966): 66.

endemic conditions that permitted the tyranny to exist. The tendency toward anarchy that let power fall into the hands of the violent, the corrupt, and the irresponsible was the theme of his novel and his diagnosis of the evils besetting both Spain and the nations she had founded in the New World. It was not that he discovered the key to the Spanish problem in the Americas, but that, like Unamuno, he saw that the problems of Spain were not Spanish but Hispanic ones. The anguish he felt for the Spanish situation was made more acute by his recognition of its intensification in Spanish America. He chose the "esperpento" as the form most adequate for the expression of his social analysis, because only by distortion of the reality could he catch the attention of those who did not wish to see it as it was.

The myth, in the hands of an artist such as don Ramón, far from being an evasion of reality, confronts us with it as the artist sees it, deformed, perhaps, but all the more powerful in its impact. The exotic Mexico of the *Sonata*, when completely integrated into the writer's world view, is no longer exotic. This is the significance of the evolution of Valle's exoticism from the *Sonata* to the "esperpento." "Reality slipped into the invented landscape, and the residue of the vision seeped into reality; the symbiosis emerged artistically perfect."[46] Valle-Inclán, a moralist in some ways very much like Quevedo, arrived at a humanity and a profundity very far from the seeming unconcern with the problems of Spain he exhibited in his youth.

The later years, the epoch of the first "esperpento," were those don Alfonso shared with him in Madrid. Valle died in 1936, but Reyes kept the memory of their friendship alive. In 1952 he wrote the introduction to William Fichter's study of Valle's early period in Mexico, a task that must have given rise to many pleasant recollections. And, a few months before his death, the memory of don Ramón, still enveloped in a slight aura of fantasy, again sparked Reyes' imagination. With a mixture of tenderness and subtle humor he evoked an unusual and at the same time appro-

---

[46] Gullón, *Direcciones del modernismo*, p. 111.

priate image of "the one-armed man of Madrid." This passage, accompanied by a photograph, is found in the private bulletin which don Alfonso compiled for his own pleasure and that of his friends. It is entitled "The 'Tzantza' of Valle-Inclán" and reads:

> During my summer trips through the Cantabrian towns, I bought from a popular Basque artist two rag dolls, caricatures of Unamuno and of Valle-Inclán. The first has been lost. The second ... is there seated on his books, with its legs crossed in an attitude that was habitual with him. I sleep in my library, which is rat- and mouse-proof. During the night, nevertheless, I usually hear little suspicious noises, little footsteps and running feet. I have accustomed myself to think that Valle-Inclán trots and prances along my shelves, that the doll is a true "tzantza," like those that the peasants make of imprudent Europeans and that sometimes come to life.[47]

Valle-Inclán could not have asked for a more "esperpentesque" fate.

[47] Reyes, "La 'tzantza' de Valle-Inclán," "Biblioteca Alfonsina" no. 6–7 (June–July 1959): 1–2.

José Ortega y Gasset

(1883 – 1955)

AT THE OUTBREAK OF WORLD WAR I at least two generations of writers were competing equally for the attention of the Spanish public. Their coexistence seems so complete that it is easy to forget the differences in their ages and their orientations. About twenty years separated writers of Unamuno's and Valle-Inclán's generation, whose group cohesiveness—if one can speak of that in reference to such individualists—stemmed from the disaster of 1898, and those like José Ortega y Gasset, Juan Ramón Jiménez, and Ramón Gómez de la Serna, contemporaries of Reyes, whose mutual experience as they came to maturity was the repercussion in Spain of the First World War.[1] The relationship between Unamuno and

---

[1] Ángel del Río, *Historia de la literatura española*, II, 305.

Ortega y Gasset has the paradoxical quality that characterizes this interplay between the old and the new.

Ortega met Unamuno while still a student, and by 1904, when he was twenty-one, they were corresponding. In that year Unamuno published two of the younger man's letters, letters which the critic Ángel del Río considered to be the first signs of the definition of the new generation.[2] There is no doubt that Ortega entered the world of thought and literature under Unamuno's influence, but even in the early years it was as much a counter-irritant as a positive stimulus.

The two men were to follow diverging and often opposing paths, each seeking to guide his countrymen along his chosen route. The Spaniard had to be awakened and revitalized. The horizon of his interests must be broadened. But how? Unamuno believed that he must first delve deep within himself to discover his authentic, his eternal, being, and from that base build outward toward the formulation of a new national conscience. Special care must be taken, he thought, not to contaminate this with superficial modernities alien to its nature. Ortega energetically and sometimes bitterly combatted Unamuno's personalistic and "eternalizing" approach. He was not searching for the eternal Spaniard, for Unamuno's man "of flesh and blood," but for the modern man inseparable from the atmosphere in which he lived. "I am myself and my circumstance" was his famous phrase. The Spaniard must be made aware of "the theme of our times," as the title of one of Ortega's books reads. Life here and now is important, not the search for eternity. Spain must be Europeanized. It must open its doors wide to culture, modernize its intellectual life. And above all, it must have intellectual discipline.[3]

Ortega's approach had the attraction of clarity, of offering a more immediate and perhaps more logical hope for the future, of being more in tune with the times. Ortega and those who appeared on the Spanish scene with him were more European-minded than

---

[2] Ibid., p. 304.
[3] See discussion in Guillermo de Torre, *La aventura estética de nuestra edad*, pp. 252–253, 263.

their predecessors, less individualistic and anarchic, more interested in values and concepts than in man and his emotions. But Unamuno's inescapable and unforgettable voice held the fascination of the irrational and had an unmistakable ring of authenticity. Ortega himself, in a Goyesque sketch, slightly tinted with Ortegan disdain, a model of his metaphorical style, portrays the aura that surrounded Unamuno's commanding figure: "And although I am not in agreement with his method," he said, "I am the first to admire the strange attraction of his figure, that extreme silhouette of a mystic energumen who thrusts himself upon the sinister and sterile background of peninsular vulgarity, hammering the Celtiberian heads with the oaken trunk of his 'I.' "[4]

He might not approve of Unamuno, but he could not escape him. And the Spaniard of the interwar period had the enviable opportunity of being able to witness a veritable pageant of ideas as staged by two towering figures of contemporary thought. The "frightful silence" that Ortega presaged at Unamuno's death was still in the future in those dynamic years.

Ortega, unlike Unamuno, did not cultivate several literary genres. His chosen field was the essay, and he rarely strayed from it. His mastery of it was such that it is difficult to say whether he should be considered primarily as a writer or as a philosopher. Though he often indicated a decided preference for the latter distinction, Ortega admitted in later years that he might have to be considered a "centaur of both"—art and philosophy.[5] He did resemble Unamuno in that his interests were exceedingly broad. His essays cover a wide range of subjects, and nothing was too insignificant to merit a questioning glance. "Intellectual love" was the phrase he chose to describe his vital approach to life and to ideas. Many of his essays are included in the eight volumes of *El espectador* (The spectator), a personal journal which he published periodically from 1916 to 1934. His books include interpretations of Spanish reality such as *Meditaciones del Quijote*, 1914,

---

[4] A 1908 article quoted in Eduardo Ortega y Gasset, *Monodiálogos de Unamuno*, p. 32.

[5] Torre, *La aventura estética de nuestra edad*, pp. 264–265.

and *España invertebrada*, 1921, or presentations of general philosophical and social problems as in *El tema de nuestro tiempo* (*The
Modern Theme*), 1923, and *La rebelión de las masas* (*The Revolt of the Masses*), 1930, or of artistic problems as in *La deshumanización del arte*, 1925.

It is not surprising, perhaps, that of all his Spanish friendships,
the two which Reyes was forced to defend in later life were those
with Unamuno and Ortega, the most polemical figures. In Ortega's
case, as in Unamuno's, the attack came in a newspaper article.

It was in 1947 that Ortega gave an interview to a Mexican
reporter in which the following exchange took place:

> "Do you have friends in Mexico?" we asked.
> "I had," he answered, "like Alfonso Reyes."
> "Well, what has Alfonso Reyes done to you, maestro?"
> "Nothing concrete or personal. But he has done so many foolish
> things . . ."
> "Like what, maestro?"
> A gesture of displeasure and disdain is embellished with these
> words:
> "Insignificant small-town gestures."
> Don José Ortega y Gasset could not remember any other of the
> friends he affirmed he had in Mexico.

Quite a difference from Azorín, who, when interviewed at the age
of eighty by a Mexican journalist, began by inquiring after Reyes'
health.

Ortega's uncalled-for attack upon Reyes, which raised a furor in
Mexico among the exiled Spanish intellectuals, was the culmina-
tion of a relationship that had shown, over the years, an unusual
blend of intimacy and withdrawal, intellectual rapport and dis-
cord, respect and disapproval.

Reyes' arrival in Madrid coincided with the beginning of
Ortega's rise to eminence in Spain. That year saw the publication
of Ortega's first book, *Meditaciones del Quijote*, in which he presents what was to become his answer to Unamuno's philosophical
irrationalism, and also the delivery of his famous lecture "Vieja y

nueva política" (Old and new politics), which marked his appearance on the Spanish political scene. During the next ten years, the length of Reyes' stay in Madrid, and also the years of what the philosopher José Gaos has described as the second stage of Ortega's development, Ortega was to gather in his hands those organs which were to give him an incredible amount of intellectual authority and power—the most influential newspapers and magazines of the time: in earlier years *El Imparcial*, then *El Sol*, *España*, and *Revista de Occidente*, as well as an interest in the Calpe publishing house. Friendship with such a man was of great help to Reyes in his first years in Madrid, when he earned his living principally through journalism. "In the new firmament of Spain," he wrote, "the Spain of after 1898, . . . José Ortega y Gasset, although still very young, was a radiant star, around whom circled a whole group of planets. He brought me to his *tertulia* and to his domains, he gave me the seal of approval. . . . He recruited me for the magazines and newspapers in which he participated in some way, he launched me in his enterprises."[6]

It is in journalistic activities that the main link between Ortega and Reyes is to be found. "The noble friendship of José Ortega y Gasset helped me from the first instant, associating me first with the weekly *España*, then with *El Imparcial*, and finally with *El Sol*" (II, 42), said Reyes, thus establishing the sequence of his association with the Ortegan periodicals. *España* was founded by Ortega in 1915. It became the political voice of those intellectuals who later were to found the Second Spanish Republic, and its contributors also included many of the leading literary figures of the period. But within the year Ortega had given up the editorship of the magazine, a fact which Reyes interpreted as proof that "the literary preoccupation . . . [had triumphed] in him over the political preoccupations." This pleased Reyes. He said of Ortega that "philosophy—aided by a certain temperamental inclination—leads him to the unrest of politics; literature, more disinterested, if possible, emancipates him from everything but God" (IV, 259).

[6] Alfonso Reyes, "Treno para José Ortega y Gasset," *Cuadernos Americanos* 85, no. 1 (1956): 65.

Ortega did not share Reyes' view, and, in the long run, the "politician" triumphed over the "pure man" Reyes hoped to save and finally despaired of saving.

Reyes' first contributions to *España* were movie reviews written in collaboration with Martín Luis Guzmán. (Ortega told him: "The secret of perfection is in taking on tasks somewhat inferior to our capacities.")[7] Except for a few earlier articles in *España* itself, Reyes believed that he and Guzmán were the first to write movie criticism in Spanish, and, in fact, he remembered only one other man in the field, a newspaperman in Minneapolis with whom he used to correspond. They treated the new art with seriousness and paternal affection, though sometimes even Reyes' supply of good will would prove insufficient. Thus his epitaph for "Fósforo," their joint pseudonym, reads: "Here lies one who despaired of seeing a new art reveal itself" (IV, 200). The movie criticism lasted only a few months, but Reyes continued contributing articles to *España* throughout his years in Spain.

In 1916 Ortega asked Reyes for an article on Chesterton's *Orthodoxy*, which Reyes had just translated:

> For "The Mondays of El Imparcial" I need an article of yours of one column on "Orthodoxy," the translation of which I received and I thank you for. If possible—I think, moreover, that, as we'll discuss later, it's important for you—it should be done by Friday night. One column: simplicity and amenity.
> We'll talk later. (n.d.)

Reyes' article appeared as planned in the cultural section of *El Imparcial*, the liberal newspaper owned by the Gasset family and directed by Ortega's father and later by his brother Eduardo. Reyes was in charge of the movie section here too, but a quarrel between the two branches of the Gasset family caused the dismissal of some of the staff, Reyes among them, and he was left without a newspaper connection.

Again Ortega intervened. On the first of December of 1917, he

---

[7] Quoted in Reyes, "Historia documental de mis libros," *Universidad de México* 9, no. 9 (1955): 12.

founded *El Sol*, which, until its demise at the time of the Spanish
Civil War, was Spain's great intellectual newspaper. Its Thursday
page of history and geography was Reyes' responsibility. José
Gaos, a disciple of Ortega's who later emigrated to Mexico, recalled
the importance that Ortega's periodicals had for the members of his
generation who were then university students: "We read *El Sol*
daily from top to bottom, or just about, and among its great
weekly pages, a cultural bible for us, that of history and geography." They began, he continued, to read *España* and then the
Revista de Occidente, and there, too, they found Reyes, "so involved, and in such an effective way, in the most relevant undertakings of Spanish intelligence of those years, that I suspect that
many of my companions and I myself took Alfonso Reyes to be
one of the still younger but already best reputed Spanish maestros
of the recent generations."[8] They had no idea he was a Mexican.
Reyes' articles in *El Sol* went far beyond the normal limits of
history and geography (don Alfonso interpreted the terms as
meaning anything that happened within time and space) and are
now collected in several volumes of his *Complete Works*.

Spanish journalism had reached a high point of literary com-
petency in the early decades of this century. Ortega had been
born into a newspaper family. He had published his first article
at the age of nineteen and had very high aspirations for his
journalistic contributions. He "tried to introduce through the
medium of newspapers not only ideological issues or cultural information but also a certain amount of academic, if highly polished,
philosophical clarification."[9] He wanted above all to communicate:
"Whoever wants to create something," he wrote, "has to succeed
in being an aristocrat of the marketplace. For this reason, docile to
circumstance, I have seen to it that my work springs forth in the
intellectual marketplace, which is the newspaper."[10] Reyes had a
similar motive for his journalistic endeavors: the desire to create
an increased cultural awareness in the reading public.

8 José Gaos in "Testimonios inéditos . . .," *La Gaceta* 6, no. 65 (1960): 4.
9 José Ferrater Mora, *Ortega y Gasset. An Outline of His Philosophy*, p. 15.
10 Quoted in Torre, *La aventura estética*, p. 318.

The essay lent itself perfectly to the exigencies of newspaper writing. James W. Robb, the leading authority on Reyes' essays, feels that "Ortega is perhaps the Spanish essayist with whom Reyes had the closest affinity: not only for the Ortegan perspectivism and other conceptual or philosophical leanings shared by Reyes . . . but for the illumination of the essayistic style with artistic vision, the concept with the vitalistic poetic metaphor. Ortega is more strongly philosophical, Reyes, more intimately personal and concerned more centrally with the literary phenomenon."[11] It is true that both authors' form of presentation is primarily an imagistic one. Their very thinking processes are by nature metaphoric. Ortega first presents one of his basic philosophic theories on the relations between man and surrounding reality by describing his own walk through the woods surrounding the Escorial. Reyes carries us through the labyrinth of his philosophic digressions in *El suicida* by having us follow the thread of Ariadne. In Reyes, newspaper chronicles or literary criticism, and, in Ortega, philosophical arguments have been transformed into subjective, lyrical works in which facts or ideas cannot be separated from the imagery that has molded them.

Ortega's greatest journalistic venture was the *Revista de Occidente*, founded with the aim of incorporating Spain into a spiritual and intellectual unity with the rest of Europe. The magazine and its publishing house brought European and particularly German culture to the Spanish reader with its translations of, for example, Johan Huizinga's *The Waning of the Middle Ages* and Edmund Husserl's *Logical Inquiries*. A new generation of Spanish writers was given incentive and direction; standards of self-exaction and severe self-discipline were instilled in them, and only those who met these criteria were invited to contribute to the magazine or have their books published by the *Revista*. Thus Ortega, with the *Revista* and its publishing house as his instrument, became the undisputed leader of the young writers. His magazine stands as a

---

[11] James W. Robb, *Patterns of Image and Structure in the Essays of Alfonso Reyes*, p. 17.

great achievement of a brilliant epoch in the literary history of modern Spain.

Though the first issue appeared in July, 1923, not long before Reyes departed from Spain, he was able to offer his assistance in the initial days of the magazine—Ortega wrote to thank him for it—and he did publish a few articles in it. There is one article, to which he contributed and which he inspired, that illustrates very well the spirit of the times. It is entitled "El silencio por Mallarmé" (The silence for Mallarmé). An anonymous invitation had been sent to a dozen writers asking them to participate in a ceremony commemorating the twenty-fifth anniversary of Mallarmé's death with five minutes of silence. "Without speeches. A ceremony—so to speak—without ceremony. What would have pleased Mallarmé," the invitation read. It was to take place in the Madrid Botanical Gardens at eleven o'clock on the morning of October 14, 1923. The invitation closed with this simple sentence: "You will find there your friends."[12] No one knew, at first, who the initiator was. Eugenio d'Ors was suspected and he commented delightedly: "What happiness! The hour has come. I have assured you that we would not have civilization until our anonymous deeds could be attributed indistinctly to any one of us."[13] Ortega, however, "noticed immediately," wrote Reyes, "with that sagacity of his, that that initiative had a certain foreign flavor, and, in this case, Latin American. And in that way he discovered that the one responsible for it all was the Mexican" (VIII, 442).

The *Revista de Occidente* conducted a survey to discover what everyone had thought during the five minutes of silence, a unique psychological document. Ortega took several pages to describe the progress of his ideas in only two minutes. Reyes emphasized the harmony that existed among the group of writers of which he was a part, and described his thoughts: "a sensation of general contentment, a sense of fraternity with my companions, and the vague surprise that such a candid homage could be carried out, without

[12] Reyes, *Mallarmé entre nosotros*, p. 9.
[13] Quoted in ibid., p. 13.

irony and without duplicity, in the midst of this skepticism. Something like gratitude."[14]

Juan Ramón Jiménez, confined to his house with a cold, was obviously intrigued with the ceremony, for he wrote Reyes three letters about it. The first suggests capriciously that he was really there also, but that no one saw him. In the second he recreates poetically his five minutes of silence:

> I who, kept in by a cold, as you knew, remained at home working, was perfecting that morning this poem, written in 1913: "After the sudden splendor . . ." According to my calculations, in the five minutes of the "silence for Mallarmé" I must have been—with the image of the quiet museum of vegetal black marbles, which you were mysteriously complicating, of our carbonaceous, dirty, noisily neighbored, very sad Botanical Garden —seeing myself among the bars of golden light of the octosyllabic lines in the second half of my poem.
>
> I am sure of having pleased the honorable, hard-working, retiring poet of the Don de Poeme.[15]

The third letter written about ten days later, is different in tone:

> This dawn, while sleeping, I have formulated the following infantile definition of Mallarmé:
> "A very exact, cultured, and worthy gentleman of bad taste, who writes—while smoking—on Sundays, on little Japanese slips of paper, the enigmatic alphabet of pure poetry."
> —Points emphasized by the awakened man: "Of bad taste": portieres with tassels, expensive paper for rough drafts, rubber chairs, entwined initials, rhythmic syntax, fashion sheets, smoky hybridism, and the gold of inventions and philosophies of the epoch, badly digested, with perfect eternal liquidations. "Sundays": pure poetry is fiesta, glory, leisure, exception. "Alphabet": cipher, compendium, treasure, norm, secret, synthesis, center, origin.

[14] Reyes in "El silencio por Mallarmé," *Revista de Occidente* 2, no. 5 (1923): 242.

[15] Juan Ramón Jiménez, *Cuadernos de Juan Ramón Jiménez*, ed. Francisco Garfias, pp. 220–221.

A new adornment, dear Alfonso Reyes, devotee of the pertinent maestro, for your little Mallarmé drawer?[16]

This letter is something of an afterthought, a wish perhaps to disassociate himself from any seemingly indiscriminate worship of Mallarmé, and at the same time a yielding to the impulse to make a little fun of that "candid homage" of which Reyes was so proud. Thus his ironical and somewhat unkind mention of the "little Mallarmé drawer." Juan Ramón's character was not such as to be carried away by enthusiasms, as Reyes could be, or Eugenio d'Ors, who wrote don Alfonso the Friday before the ceremony: "Having entered your Order and with a vow of obedience, I am ready to preserve not only silence for ten minutes but even chastity."[17] Nor did Reyes' devotion to Mallarmé diminish with the years. In 1938 he published a small book, *Mallarmé entre nosotros* (Mallarmé among us), and in 1958 he included in the *Biblioteca Alfonsina*, the private newspaper he sent to friends, a floor plan of Mallarmé's Paris apartment.

The *Revista de Occidente* was the last of the journalistic links between Reyes and Ortega, links that were the focal point of their relationship during his years in Madrid. Their correspondence shows other aspects of their association as it continued, rather erratically, through the years.

In Paris, not long after leaving Spain, Reyes received a letter from Ortega that seems to foreshadow his ambiguous attitude of later years, for, while adopting an admonitory and professorial tone, he showed a sincere respect for Reyes' judgment. The letter, dated January 11, 1926, is as follows:

Dear Alfonso: No, not at all—I have never thought even for a moment of attributing to you the paternity of that phrase. You can be sure that in no case, whatever the circumstances may be, shall I commit the error of not knowing you. The only point of complaint that was in my letter—I spoke of "faulty information

---

[16] Quoted in Reyes, *Mallarmé entre nosotros*, pp. 31–32.
[17] Unpublished letter dated "today Friday" [October 12, 1923].

and judgment" or something similar—has in no case anything to do with any lack of loyalty: it alludes rather to what I consider a faulty intellectual attitude in respect to persons and things, rather generalized among young or almost young writers and especially you Americans—and I am referring to the best. A certain irremediable narcissism makes them avoid that minimum of docility toward the structure of the theme or person without which the judgment is inevitably false. Not because what is said about the thing or person lacks, perhaps, exactness, but because only the unessential, the anecdotal, is said, that which it amuses the writer to say, so that unavoidably there results an error in perspective and a capricious sketch. You will remember that when you had the kindness to write something about me after my trip to Argentina, I made bold to offer some observations to you. Some years have passed and I still think today that they were just. I still think that one would have to say many, many adverse and favorable things about me before gaining the right to mention, for example, the sirens of Buenos Aires. I tell you all this with no other purpose than that of tranquilizing you, making you see *de facto* the continuity of my affection and intimacy. In regard to the painful experiences through which you are passing, believe me that you do not need to waste half a word to make me understand it. You know very well what I think deep down of the Americans. Your situation is too lucid and pure for it not to irritate the general run of scoundrels. I know perfectly well that with morals faring so poorly in our peninsula, they are much worse in those countries. But you must not for a moment let yourself incline toward grief. A wise mixture of energy and irony should make you invulnerable.

Now I would like to ask you that you be a little more specific —I do not need to tell you that you can count on my absolute reserve—about your judgment on my possible trip [to Argentina]. It concerns the following: a Chair has been created by the Spaniards over there in combination with the University. It seems that they first took a poll in the newspapers about who should be the first to hold it and the result, fairly unanimous, it seems, has been to call me. The Board of Trustees that administers and governs this institution is presided over by the Secretary of Education. Would it be possible to do something meaningful? What concrete dangers do you envisage? I would appreciate some words on the matter.

Whatever the phrase was that had upset Ortega, it evidently had some importance. Reyes scribbled a note on the margin of Ortega's letter attributing it to "the imbecile and maligner ————." And he evidently wrote explaining the matter to Enrique Díez-Canedo, who responded on the thirtieth of January: "Your letter about the Ortega affair made me furious. It is about as absurd and unjust as one could imagine. It is not easy, I think you know, to get him to the level of simple conversation about a matter that he considers of a serious nature. I, who have a certain intimacy with him, have deduced that this susceptibility of a virtuoso, I dare not call it feminine, is skin deep; and I think that he has and preserves a great esteem for you." The whole matter seems to have originated in Mexico, and Ortega took it with his usual seriousness. As the letter progresses we can see that he had little sympathy for what he considered the "frivolities" of others, though certainly he was guilty of a few himself.

Reyes was obviously accustomed to Ortega's susceptibility, and to the paternal tone he assumed when dealing with Americans, for there is a single, heartfelt "ay!" written in the margin opposite that comment of Ortega's on the "irremediable narcissism" that afflicts the American writers. In fact, in a short essay entitled "Carta a un joven argentino" (Letter to a young Argentine) Ortega had written two years before: "I suspect that [the new generation in Argentina] completely lacks internal discipline—without which, strength disintegrates and volatilizes. . . . To approach matters, curiosity does not suffice; mental rigor is needed to master them." And he added, as in his letter to Reyes, "the American . . . tends toward narcissism."[18]

In his letter, however, Ortega was not speaking in general terms as a reflection of his policy of advocating more "thoughtfulness" in the Spanish-speaking world. He referred specifically to an article

18 José Ortega y Gasset, *El espectador*, p. 492.

Reyes had written in 1917. It had displeased him at the time, and he chose not to forget it.

The incident stemmed from Ortega's first visit to Argentina in 1916. His lectures at the University of Buenos Aires and other cultural centers were an overwhelming success: "He not only delights, he causes wonder in his audiences, who, for the first time, hear philosophy spoken of in a diaphanous and beautiful language."[19] He arrived home with nothing but enthusiasm for Argentina, "that country, that offspring of Spain . . . today more discerning, more curious, more capable of emotion than the mother country," and bitterness toward Spain, where "the good things that happen in the world find . . . only a pallid reflection."[20]

Reyes saw at once what other critics were to comment upon later. "It is the old story of Ulysses," he said. "We cannot be happy on returning to Ithaca—even though the faithful Penelope of the homeland is awaiting us—if we have heard in other seas the captivating song of the sirens" (IV, 262). And to make matters worse, as far as Ortega's pride was concerned, he added that he was afraid the sirens were false ones. Ortega knew only Argentina. "Can the America that weeps and fights also seduce him?" (IV, 263). Was it not possible that a bitter disillusionment would follow? Reyes' comments were more prophetic than he would have wished.

Reyes recognized that this voyage represented for Ortega "a profound and fecund crisis" (IV, 261). In 1917 he somewhat doubted the outcome. He feared that Ortega's bitterness against Spain augured ill for the triumph of Ortega the writer over Ortega the politician. But in 1922 he wrote a parable in which he finds a salutory lesson in the trajectory Ortega had followed. It goes thus:

> Educated in severe ideals, the young maestro began life seeing to it that the aftertaste of the newspaper office *tertulia* did not cling to him, for in his first years as a writer it could have contaminated him.
>
> Later, at the time when a man chooses the two or three fundamental directions of his conduct, the influence of a German city,

[19] Torre, *Las metamórfosis de Proteo*, p. 54.
[20] J. Ortega y Gasset, *El espectador*, pp. 183, 187.

the studious life, Cohen's philosophical discipline were modeling his soul.

The zeal for regenerating Spain set it afire, and, having returned to his country, he became the guide of the young; he pointed out political remedies and artistic orientations; he unsettled the new spirits; he was the Disturber, much more than the Spectator, as he likes to call himself now.

A trip to our dazzling America, at that opportune time when the voice of the Devil of Midday begins to be heard, completed the generous widening of the horizons of this soul which, abandoning the almost ascetic sternness of another hour (Reader: I also was a child without smiles, and I reveal to you, with profound emotion, this process toward happiness), opened itself to a more vast and full comprehension of life, in which even frivolity and games now have a place.

And thus, from the path taken by this traveler—in so few years —comes a great lesson on living the opportune life, giving our desires what is theirs by vital right. (IV, 264–265)

Reyes' opinion of the change wrought on Ortega by his first trip to America coincides very well with what Torre wrote years later: "That trip is equivalent to his first excursion into the wordly world. . . . Before, he was a man of his study and his books; he will continue being so substantially, but he also begins to enjoy turning himself at times into a man of salons and polite dinner table conversation."[21]

Ortega, then, like Unamuno and Valle-Inclán, felt close to America. He even told Reyes that he would like to be called Ortega, the American, and he decreed: "My biography could not be written . . . without dedicating some central chapters to Argentina. That is to say that I owe, no more and no less, a portion of my life—situation, emotions, profound experiences, thoughts—to that country. Just that way, absolutely."[22]

The influence, as is natural, was a reciprocal one. His message had a far-reaching effect on Spanish American thought, for one of the obvious conclusions to be drawn from his view of reality as

[21] Torre, *Las metamórfosis*, p. 54.
[22] Quoted in ibid., p. 52.

the interaction between the individual and his circumstance was
that the Spanish American could formulate a philosophy as valid
or more valid for himself than any created by European thinkers.
Ortega's ideas were decisive stimuli to the self-study and self-
analysis that were characteristic of the Latin American intellectual
scene in the thirties and forties. Ortega's publishing efforts were
also responsible for the introduction of much contemporary European thought into Latin America. And finally, as Torre says:
"Thanks to the magnetic force and the persuasive art of his
powerful personality, many American spirits came to catch on to
the fact that Spain—intellectually—existed."[23] This was also one
of the principal aims of Reyes' journalism while he was in Spain.
As a Spaniard, however, Ortega tended to take a superior stance
when viewing the American, to see him as a "promising primitive,"[24] an attitude that was reflected, I think, in his letter to Reyes.

The next item in the correspondence, a telegram, belongs to
the period of Ortega's second visit to Argentina, from August,
1928, until January, 1929. Again he gave several series of lectures,
some of them an anticipation of *La rebelión de las masas*. Again he
was received with enthusiasm. He renewed his friendship with
Reyes, then Mexican ambassador to Argentina, but signs of a
certain strangeness in his attitude toward Reyes began to be apparent. Reyes' telegram to him on shipboard shows that Ortega
left without bothering to say good-bye. "Truly grieved, I discover
in newspapers your for me unexpected departure. Secluded for
days at home I was told nothing and you were cruel in not telling
me. I shall always remember with emotion our new encounter, so
pleasing to my heart and spirit. Be happy and remember me"
(January 5, 1929). Reyes even tried to see that his greetings
reached Ortega in Montevideo by cabling the Mexican Legation
there to meet the ship, but the telegram arrived too late. He never
received an answer to his shipboard message.

Ortega later refused to assist Reyes in getting his books published

23 Ibid., p. 51.
24 Martin S. Stabb, *In Quest of Identity*, p. 80.

by the Calpe publishing house, or at least so Reyes stated in a letter to Amado Alonso on December 11, 1932:

> I see that they publish many others, and I was saddened forever by the clear and frank ill will of José Ortega y Gasset, who let me be courteously refused by Calpe; thus, just as it sounds. This man has always been very strange in his manner with me. He left Buenos Aires without letting me know a word or saying good-bye to me. My brotherly feeling toward him had gone so far (DO NOT TELL THIS TO ANYONE) as to lend him a little room that I had there for certain types of interviews, because he did not know where to receive a certain lady. . . . Later he shamelessly stole from me a joke about the Kantian hour of Buenos Aires (when, as the afternoon falls, they sell the Critic and the Reason in the streets), something that I told him and I told him that I was going to write it . . . and that he admired very much. I went to him afterwards in order to publish some books and he did not help me, on the contrary, he let me know that my books were not good sellers, something which I have never doubted anyway.

Yet in spite of the resentment he reveals here, Reyes felt a certain intellectual affinity with Ortega. He wrote him a long letter in 1930 in which he provided him with a detailed account of the Argentinian literary scene, telling him: "The least that I owed you was this long history. I owe it to the respect and admiration that you inspire in me, now and always. I owe it to the affection that I have for you. I owe it to your friendship and, many times, to the support that you have given me in various orders and in various moments of my life." The letter is a bitterly humorous appreciation of the pitfalls of life in the literary world of Buenos Aires, and could easily serve as a supplement to the interpretation of the Argentinian psychology and way of life which Ortega published in the seventh volume of *El espectador*, upon his return from that country. It had just arrived in Argentina when Reyes wrote, and undoubtedly inspired him to give vent to his pent-up frustrations. Reyes writes:

> That state of mind in which you knew me in Buenos Aires kept

me for a long time in a state of somnambulism, and even with little desire to take advantage of the very cordial welcome that the Buenos Aires literary world had given me since my arrival. —One day, without looking for it, I found myself surrounded and frequented by some of the young men whom I consider most scrupulous and exacting in literary matters. Sincerely, I never could share your points of view on nationalism and Americanism, but in this exaggeration (I am the first to lament that it does not excite my enthusiasm) I have always seen the seed of a future harvest for American thought. So much the worse for my personal happiness, if I am more demanding and more skeptical than my contemporaries of the continent. You share with me that feeling of true adoration for youth. You will understand that the visits of these boys began to do me a great deal of good. One day they spoke to me about founding a magazine. And I, who see this city full of magazines, and who have certain experience in how badly they turn out, said to them: when you publish the two or three little things that you have at home and that you haven't decided to entrust to the magazines that already exist, you will no longer know what to do with your new magazine. The best would be for you to found a small and neat collection of notebooks. It did not fail to surprise me pleasantly (since I still did not know the dangers of this system of anticipating my wishes) that, in two or three days, the boys presented themselves at the house, already bringing me a publisher for the "Notebooks of the Plata,"—"the collection—they added—that you are going to direct." . . . My first reaction was of great optimism. I started to think again about my literary work, somewhat abandoned. It occurred to me that perhaps I could rid myself forever of the bothersome task of looking for publishers and booksellers. I dreamed of uniting my dispersed and badly published books (so dispersed and badly published that not even I can find copies when I look, nor do I think that you, spontaneously, would realize that I have about fifteen published volumes, between true books and pamphlets that aspire to be books). From that moment date my communications with you to ask for your intervention with Calpe. My project was premature or it was not understood from afar; practically, I had to abandon it. But let us return to the Argentinian boys, who,— meanwhile—always with the method of anticipating reality, had already hastened to announce the "Notebooks of the Plata" with a disconcerting profusion, inventing titles and creating an editorial program to a great extent fantastic. Afterwards I have seen—a typical Argentine phenomenon and a complete facade—that in this literary atmosphere the announcement of a book is equivalent to its appearance, and it is discussed and killed before it comes out. . . . My desire to feel myself associated finally with the world in which I was living was so great, and did me so much good, that I suffered many, many annoyances just to be able to go forward with a task whose results have been rather meagre, since barely four little books have been published. . . . Several times I met our Nosotros friends, and I never understood the remonstrances they made, asking me why "I had gone over to the other side"; I thought it was a way to remind me that I have not given them any of my contributions for a long time. I have taken so long to understand the characteristics of this little literary world, where everyone is in groups and the politics of the groups are more important to them than true work! I was making an effort to shut the eyes of my Mexican perspicacity; I did not want to see. Pedro Henríquez had thrown up to me so much my bad impressions of the first moments that I wanted at all cost to convince myself that everything was sweetness and light. —The other day, Bernárdez and Marechal arranged to found a magazine . . . which would come out every three months, with the seasons, and which would have an anthologic character. . . . The same things happened that I had been noting from the first. Before the magazine came out, the two boys went from group to group saying that they were going to do this and that, and to exclude these and the others. I do not know how far they got in their extremes, but I infer it from the other extremes that I later had the misfortune to witness. . . . I was disconcerted: I thought I was dealing with a group of people who understood one another, and it turns out that they were capable of almost quarreling over a small literary discussion, and over the conditions of a magazine that still did not exist! Always the same strange phenomenon! Always considering as a sufficient literary act the announcement alone! Always substituting for reality a symbolic anticipation of it! (Does this not corroborate your admirable appreciations of the Argentine character and the never fulfilled promise of the pampa?) —The atmosphere con-

tinued charging itself with fictitious enthusiasm on the one hand.
On the other, the "furtive signs" kept surprising me. I published
in Libra a whimsical piece called "Las jitanjáforas," which differs
not at all from my habitual humor, and which in times more con-
scious of literary cheer would have been taken for what it is: a
literary game. Would you believe that I didn't lack for someone
who told me that I had scandalized many people? And even another who came out with that of *going to the other side*? "I see
now that you have gone over to the young people. You do well,
because they are the future." I have not even defended myself. I
do not defend myself for breathing, nor do I ask excuses for the
circulation of my blood, I do not give explanations for my internal
secretions. At a banquet, Méndez Calzada says to me suddenly, in
relation to a story of Quiroga's that I liked: "How can you applaud such things, you who are a partisan of dehumanized art?"
I do not know when I may have made this profession of faith, nor
do I see how one can conclude this from my poor books, where
there is a little of everything, letting me live in them, as is my
wont—without previous doctrine. Later, it is Evar Méndez himself: "Doctor, how can you praise this or that of the group of
Claridad, you who are a surrealist?" And I, who can't get over my
astonishment. And I tell you these superfluities because they all
have a meaning and they come to this: the necessity that there is
to classify things as soon as possible and to judge them together,
so as not to understand each one separately; all, a saving of effort.
But the effect is an insupportable mental stupidity. —The boys,
always cordial with me—although full of inconsistencies among
themselves, which already had me intranquil and upset . . . —decided one day that the moment had arrived to resuscitate their old
combat magazine: "Martín Fierro." I felt a danger coming—now
my instinct was very alert—and I hastened to counsel them: "The
times have changed. You have already won all along the line.
Now advanced art is exhibited in Amigos del Arte, which is, let
us say, an official house. Attacking the bourgeois is senseless. The
bourgeois of this society already accept all the audacities of the
new literature. You have no reason to continue fighting an enemy
that no longer exists. Instead, undisciplined and haughty elements
have detached themselves from you, such as for example all those

free and easy pens of the newspaper *Crítica*, all those impertinent young men who think that it is enough to be ignorant to
be deserving. Those are your true enemies: your false brothers.
And you should now in 'Martín Fierro' do a job of purification.
Cleanse your own house."—I do not know how they understood
it, nor if they felt like stopping to think about it. . . . They showed
me the announcement (the announcement!—that was what mat-
tered and not the deed itself!) of the proximate appearance of
"M.F.," an announcement already published by them—always
getting ahead of themselves and along the way forcing my hand,
just about then I understood them!—in which my name, without
their having consulted me, appeared mixed up with theirs in a
form that would be enough to accredit me as an old rake.

But why make it a long story? I understood that we were very
far apart, and that I was being the plaything of an environment
whose reefs I did not know. . . . I found myself, friend José, in
the same situation in which, in Mexico, the Mexican legalist and
pettifogging politician don Manuel Iglesias found himself, when
he discovered himself to be the true and only President of the
Republic by means of I do not know what Byzantine constitu-
tionalisms, in moments in which the armed opinions were fighting
for Porfirio Díaz or for Lerdo de Tejada. Don Manuel Iglesias
would arrive in a town, with his servant, and no sooner had he
rested a little when he had to flee. "We are going right now, for
the Lerdo people are coming!" "Let's go, for here come Díaz'
men!" And the servant would ask him: "Tell me, Sir, and when
are ours coming?" Everybody was "the others," and none were
"mine."

Conclusion: I am saying good-by to all groups and factions. . . .
I'll tell you more: these bad impressions confirm me in my desire
to separate myself. This letter is absolutely confidential. (January
10, 1930)

The corroboration of Ortega's ideas is overwhelming. Don Alfonso was being subjected to myriad irritations and miscomprehensions by the "man on the defensive," Ortega's phrase to
describe the Argentinian, and the title of one of the two essays on
Argentina he wrote at that time. By trying to be friendly to every-

one, Reyes only succeeded in offending everyone and in being accused by all sides of having "gone over to the others." How Reyes must have delighted in Ortega's comment that tact was of no value in Argentina because "in Buenos Aires every movement that one makes wounds someone, violates some secret personality, offends some intimate phantom."[25] He had experienced this constantly. The principal example which Reyes gave in his letter as characteristic of the temperament of the Argentinian writer was that the mere announcement of a coming book or magazine was equivalent to its publication, saying in effect what Ortega had written in his other essay: "The pampa . . . promises." Ortega had commented that the Argentinian lived for an illusory future rather than within reality: "Perhaps the essential element in Argentine life is this, to be a promise. It has the gift of peopling our spirit with promises. . . . Almost no one is where he is, but rather in front of himself . . . and from *there* he governs and executes his life *here*, the real, present, and effective one. . . . Everyone lives *from his illusions* as if they were already reality."[26] And Ortega continued, echoing what he had written Reyes in 1926: "The typical Argentine has no other vocation than that of being already what he imagines himself to be. He lives, thus, given over . . . to an image. And one can only live an image by contemplating it. And, in fact, the Argentine is always looking at himself reflected in his own imagination. He is exceedingly narcissistic."[27]

Reyes' years in Argentina (1927 to 1930) coincided with a period of intellectual ferment. Vanguardist movements had discovered a fertile field. Different literary groups sprang up. In 1924 the famous magazine *Martín Fierro* was founded by the elite of the "new sensibility," the standardbearers of pure literature (such as Reyes' maligned "jitanjáforas"). Excitement was high and loyalties were fierce. *Martín Fierro* went out of existence in 1927, but it was, in general, these young writers, those in favor of pure art, who surrounded Reyes and over whom he exerted a considerable

[25] J. Ortega y Gasset, *El espectador*, p. 959.
[26] Ibid., p. 919.
[27] Ibid., p. 955.

influence—no matter how skeptical he may seem of this in his letter.

His letter brings into perspective those characteristics and beliefs which Reyes had in common with Ortega. His interest in and his desire to be of help to the coming generation, offering them freely his advice and his time, paralleled Ortega's love for the young aspirants to literary fame for whom he did so much in Spain. This communion of interests was what had prompted Reyes to tell Ortega about the problems he had encountered. Reyes had directed his attention toward those young people whom he considered most "scrupulous and exacting in literary matters." The choice of adjectives is significant. Of primary concern to him as well as to Ortega was a writer's sense of vocation and of self-discipline. Thus he spoke to his young friends of tightening their own standards and raising themselves to higher levels when they wished to resuscitate *Martín Fierro*. Perhaps his greatest disillusionment with the literary world of Buenos Aires was his realization that it accepted and fomented mental laziness, a charge that could never be brought against either Reyes or Ortega. What emerges most clearly from the letter are don Alfonso's good will and good intentions and his consequent distaste for the smallness and meanness of the Buenos Aires literary scene. He considered Ortega to be the one most qualified to comprehend the significance of his observations. Written at a moment of disenchantment, the letter was more bitter than was usual with him, but his frankness and sincerity cannot be doubted.

The years passed, the Spanish Civil War broke out, and Reyes offered Ortega his home, receiving in return a very warm reply: "I thank you intensely for your affectionate letter, which brings me your old friendship. Always deep down I counted on it and this certainty is the most proven homage that I can offer you" (April 8, 1937). Then, in 1938, two letters passed between them concerning a mutual friend, Victoria Ocampo, the Argentinian writer, who is founder and editor of the prestigious literary magazine *Sur*. Ortega wrote:

I thank you very much for your letter, although it comes to add to the portion of melancholy that there already may be in my life. With one collar or another, today's dogs are everywhere the same. But one must demonstrate now that one possesses the most inexhaustible source of life that exists: vocation. Withdraw unto yourself, plan some work which is sufficiently broad, in which you can work for years, an undertaking which, while giving you concentration and continuity, will lend soundness to your judgment.

It would interest me very much to receive from you an opinion, one I could receive from no other person so competently, on the situation in the present and in the foreseeable future of our Victoria in Argentina. I do not need to tell you to what degree what you tell me would be in the strictest confidence. Since Victoria's new form of life—what we might call her publicity—began quite a bit after my leaving that country, I am trying to determine with precision the course of her action. Because I do not hide from you that it bothers me a little. Experience has shown me, from what I have seen in others who in that moment of life have begun a similar expansion of their activity, that it is always a dangerous trajectory and in these times much more so. Since I am sure that you have also arrived at that height of serenity which makes us see things clearly, and since, on the other hand, you know very well the present Argentinian scene, your information and judgments would have for me an exceptional interest.

You have me here at your disposition wandering about Europe. (February 6, 1938)

Reyes replied:

Your letter is for me very comforting. In fact, I am proposing to follow your advice exactly: to concentrate for several years on some undertaking in conformity with my vocation. Soon I will tell you concretely the direction my life will take.

Our Victoria, as you know, does not have a political mind. Notwithstanding, in Argentina the pressures of the moment are so urgent, and the conservative leanings have made themselves so disagreeable, that she did not wish to keep silent in the face of an occurrence so manifest as that of Spain and she made or wished to make a mere general manifestation of democratic spirit. Although she is maintaining herself firm in this line of classical liberalism,

I do not think she is disposed to go beyond it. Since today no one is satisfied with theoretical or doctrinaire positions, and action and intervention are demanded of everyone, she has to suffer miscomprehensions from both sides. Superior people respect her and understand her, but who said that today superior people hold sway in the world? (February 26, 1938)

Victoria Ocampo is a remarkable woman. Mildred Adams, writing in the *New York Times*, compared her work in Latin America with Harriet Monroe's in Chicago and Sylvia Beach's in Paris. When Ortega arrived in Argentina in 1928, she was just beginning to shape her life of dedication to literature. They became fast friends. She recounts in the Adams interview how he baptized her magazine: "You know how the review got its name? I must have told you. Ortega y Gasset, who had started his own magazine seven years earlier, had been in Buenos Aires and gone back to Spain. I called him on the telephone, and told him what we proposed to do. Did it sound like nonsense? Ortega shouted 'No!' You had to shout over the transatlantic telephone in those days. We talked about a name, and I suggested a few, but he didn't like any of them. 'Make it *Sur*!' he shouted, '*Sur*!' "[28]

The first issue of *Sur* appeared in early 1931, with a contribution from Reyes, and dedicated to Waldo Frank. And Ortega kept in touch from afar. Julián Marías, Ortega's disciple and the foremost authority on his work, has described how Ortega always watched anxiously over any person or thing that concerned him to see if he or it were going to live up to its promise; and, Marías said, he would, "carefully scrutinize the disquieting gestures, the bad symptoms, trembling in case the unstable fabric of those hopes might sink."[29] This is exactly what he is doing in his letter to Reyes, and it seems obvious that he was referring to Victoria Ocampo's public stand in favor of the Spanish Republic. She had clearly expressed her liberal sentiments in *Sur* in the August, 1937, issue. She was starting then on the path which was to lead her

[28] Quoted in Mildred Adams, "First Lady," *New York Times Book Review* 2 October 1966, p. 40.
[29] Julián Marías, *Ortega*, I, 164.

later to oppose Perón, and to be jailed by him, but her expression of solidarity with the Republic was undoubtedly looked upon askance by Ortega. His doubts may be seen as but a prelude to his ambiguous political attitude in the future and to his inexplicable attack upon don Alfonso. The great difference in their political viewpoint must have alienated him completely from Reyes.

The advice Ortega gave Reyes at the beginning of his letter is something he repeated to the Argentinians in his third visit there in 1939: "Withdraw within yourself," he said, "and don't let yourself be carried away by the current."[30] Ortega seemed to be following his own advice by alternately withdrawing into disturbing silences and writing strangely reticent commentaries. This did not gain him new friends in Argentina, and he sorely felt the change in attitude. Torre writes: "It does not satisfy nor convince when one who has worked . . . all his life on the 'questions of the time' takes now, with the excuse of being 'apolitical,' an evasive attitude. Some more, some less, all reproach him for not situating himself 'at the height of the circumstances,' . . . for forsaking his responsibility." The ambiguities in his writings of these years, Torre adds, "are perhaps but an indirect consequence of a disillusionment: the balance from a state of mind engendered by that reciprocal deception."[31] The sirens of Buenos Aires had let him down and he them.

Then, in 1940, Ortega broke almost two years of total silence before the Hispanic world—he contributed to that era of "frightful silence" he had prophesied on Unamuno's death—only to censure in print those foreign intellectuals who had expressed sorrow over the Spanish situation. In like fashion, suddenly and with no apparent reason, the interview quoted earlier in the chapter appeared. Ortega's comment on Reyes' "insignificant small-town gestures" seems at first an echo of the old Ortegan idea of universality. In 1917 he had dreamed of an epoch when all the Hispanic world would be one, saying, "But, for that, it is necessary that the Spanish writers—and on their part the Americans—free themselves from

---

[30] Quoted in Torre, *Las metamórfosis*, p. 57.
[31] Ibid., pp. 57–58.

the provincial small-town gesture."[32] But certainly he cannot be accusing Reyes of provincialism, he who was in his own country so much attacked for the very opposite. What Ortega is censuring, as will be clearly seen from Reyes' reply, is the fact that Reyes had aided the exiled Spanish intellectuals and had founded the Colegio de México in order to give them a place to work and write.

It is typical of his writing of the postwar period that he does not say so directly. Was he afraid to express himself? Ortega did not, like Unamuno, remain forever faithful to the same basic principles. Was he not experiencing difficulty during these years in conciliating his old and new political views? "To what else, if not, can one attribute the fact that his attacks, before so clear, seem directed against shadows?"[33] asks Torre. This hypothesis applies very well to his attack on Reyes.

The Spanish exiles felt themselves called upon to defend don Alfonso, and a series of articles appeared in the Mexican newspaper *El Nacional* under the collective title "The Truth about Ortega y Gasset," and with such subtitles as "The Necktie: Backbone of Ortega" and "A Case of Professional Deformation." All point to the deplorable gap between the man and the great writer, and lament that Ortega was not able to sustain the role of moral and intellectual leadership that by all rights should have been his.

The most significant of these articles was that written as an "Open Letter to Alfonso Reyes" by José Gaos, Ortega's former disciple, who had remained faithful to Ortega's own principles. He judged Ortega's comment in the following manner:

> If they do not refer to minutiae, unworthy in any case of being justified, but rather to matters in which your attitude and activity in relation to the Spanish intellectuals in particular and to our countries in general has been expressed, does it mean, then, that Ortega condemns this attitude and this activity of yours, when you are interpreting and acting upon not only the official policy of Mexico but even that of the Mexicans who, having received the Spanish refugees with distrust, at the least, have come to rectify

---

[32] J. Ortega y Gasset, *El espectador.* p. 185.
[33] Torre, *La aventura estética*, p. 262.

their opinion with regard to the majority of them, when not the absolute totality? Can it be that Ortega shares the fury and, where this does not apply, the resentment of the Franco government?

It was, he added, ironic that those who had so many times defended Ortega's silences should now find that one of the few times he expressed himself it was in this vein. And he concluded by lamenting the loss of that faith in Ortega which both he and Reyes had clung to so long and so tenaciously:

> In anti-Franco Spain . . . Ortega has lost his intellectual and above all moral authority almost completely. "Almost," because there still remained some of us who made an effort not to let ourselves be contaminated. What a deep and sincere grief to find ourselves pushed toward the loss of a respect that we had thought necessary. Well, I know in fact that we share no sentiment more fully with you, dear Reyes, along with many others at this moment, than that of confirming one more time with growing discouragement that the terrible nihilism of our days is leaving nothing and, what is worse, no one in whom to put one's faith, hope, and affection, without which life is a gift of ridicule.[34]

Reyes could not resign himself to such a loss. He wrote immediately to Ortega, calling attention to the unjustness of his attack:

> José:
>
> . . . My only crime consists in having found a roof for those companions whom you yourself educated and embarked on the adventure, since I have occupied myself only with those who belonged to our family, not with the professionals of public emotion who have satiated themselves with throwing it up to me. Didn't you know that? I am sure that you are ill informed in my respect, and that otherwise you would be the first to approve of me. Look well toward the horizons, over the fences of the "small town."
>
> If perhaps I believed in certain Spanish hopes, you well know that I learned them from you. That violent men have twisted them is neither your fault nor mine.
>
> Since my return, I have been the victim of attacks from both

[34] Gaos, "Carta abierta a Alfonso Reyes," *El Nacional* (Mexico City), 21 September 1947.

extremes. It is our common destiny. I thought that you, from over there, would see this. I have never been more abused in my life, and I kept silent in order to better protect—without causing polemics that would have obscured my action—the settling among us of my brothers of other times; from that time in which I, without a universal cause to back me, with no one who knew me, still too young and incautious, landed over there also, in search of asylum, victim of similar things. I did not want them to suffer what I had suffered, those who one day shared there with me their scanty resources.

In regard to yourself, do not confuse me with that group of people who have taken advantage of the times to attack you without any risk to themselves. I have respected your sorrow in silence, I have not permitted anyone to treat you disrespectfully in my presence, I have luckily found—among your former companions —more than one who shared my state of mind. . . .

Alfonso (September 17, 1947)

The letter, written without the customary polite phrase of salutation, elicited no response from Ortega. Reyes wrote again in the same vein three years later. He began by recalling the earlier incident and questioning the motive for Ortega's silence. He continued.

Time has passed. My wound has healed, and each time I convince myself more, when I reread you, when I remember you, that something superior to the sad contingencies of our times keeps me tied to your affection. Tell me that you reciprocate this or—you being who you are—I will have to despair of all men. I am not necessary to you, but you—I do not have the slightest hesitancy in saying so—are necessary to me as part of the harmonious whole, of the orb of ideas and emotions in which I live.

Let's have a word, José, a word of yours that would raise both of us above all the error, all the misery that surrounds us!

Alfonso (July 31, 1950)

When Reyes wrote this time, he was impelled by that innate love of concord and amity which marks all of his personal relations, rather than by any real need to receive a friendly word from Ortega. There is a note in the margin of his copy of the letter, next to the first paragraph given here, which says succinctly, "I said it out of kindness." There was no answer.

In 1954 we find Reyes at the head of a group of Mexican writers who planned a testimonial for Ortega, when it was thought he might receive the Nobel Prize. He did not, then, hold any rancor toward Ortega. Reyes always preferred to look at the positive side of things and, in this case, to believe in the existence of a spiritual affinity that rose above the problems of the moment. He explained:

> We were not always in agreement, because the life of the spirit is one of churlish independence. . . . But there were always between the two of us hours of perfect cordiality, of complete comprehension, of affectionate intimacy which I doubt he consented to with those who appeared to accompany him most closely; and always, too, there was between us something like that stellar friendship of which Nietzsche speaks and which joins the movements of two stars no matter how much we see them go their separate ways. . . . Even the sparks of bad humor are, then, a pledge of cosmic affinity. A cruel phrase, a complaint, are then worth the same as a greeting.[35]

The only remaining communication in the correspondence file is a note to the editors of the *Revista de Occidente* in which Reyes asks that his best wishes be conveyed to Ortega, who was then, in 1955, on his deathbed.

It is surprising that so few letters could shed so much light on the relationship between Reyes and Ortega. They show that Reyes put his heart into it, as was true with everything he did, and was constant in his proofs of affection. Ortega was satisfied to receive his admiration and respect, but, after the first few years, he became rather cold and distant. There is nothing specific in his letters to show the change from the generosity he exhibited when don Alfonso first arrived in Madrid. In an epistolary relationship, however, the silences count as much if not more than the written word. And, unfortunately, Ortega's silences are not favorable to him. Julián Marías quotes Ortega as having written in 1916 that "when

[35] Reyes, "Treno para José Ortega y Gasset," p. 66.

passion drowns the masses the intellectual must stay quiet, because if he talks he has to lie, and that is what an intellectual never has a right to do."[36] This does not seem an adequate explanation. One cannot help wondering what he felt on receiving don Alfonso's letter in 1947, which for so many reasons he should have answered.

Reyes' "epitaph" for the man he still chose to consider as a friend is perhaps the best answer one could make, for it is clear-sighted in its comments on the weaknesses and strengths of Ortega's character and just in its recognition of his greatness:

> We lose in José Ortega y Gasset a writer who has left a trace of fire in the language and the mind of our century. . . . He was a solemn man . . . with a sensibility so sharp that he would wound himself with his own sharpness, or, rather, that he ended up piercing himself with his sword. . . . In his temperament mundanity and austerity combatted each other pathetically. . . . When the years have gone by, performing their long-term justice upon the inequalities and accidents and other miseries of daily events, this image will be raised to a place among the highest in Spain, of that I do not doubt.[37]

Ortega could not equal Alfonso Reyes' generosity of mind and his spiritual strength, or, perhaps, he simply could not rise to the occasion. But Reyes was right: above and beyond "the miseries of daily events," Ortega's work rises in all its magnitude.

[36] Marías, "La voz de Unamuno y el problema de España," *La Torre* 9, no. 35–36 (1961): 151.
[37] Reyes, "Treno para José Ortega y Gasset," p. 66.

Juan Ramón Jiménez

(1881 – 1958)

THE GENIUS OF THE NICARAGUAN POET Rubén Darío brought *modernismo* to its most brilliant heights. In Spain, at the turn of the century, Darío gathered around him all the young Spanish poets, and among them a young Andalusian who arrived in Madrid on a gloomy April morning in 1900, at the express invitation of Darío himself. He was Juan Ramón Jiménez, who was to become the central figure of Spanish poetry after the initial period of *modernismo*, just as Darío had been during its early stages.

Modernismo was more than just a literary movement: "It is not something to do with a school or a form," Juan Ramón Jiménez said, "but an attitude. It was the rediscovery of the beauty which had been buried in the nineteenth century by the general tone of bourgeois poetry. That is 'modernismo,' a great movement of enthusiasm and liberty for beauty."[1] Juan Ramón's poetry, like *modernismo* itself, surpasses the concept of schools. His first books of verse, most copies of which he later succeeded in destroying, gave "an impression of roses and tears, lilies and acacias, sonatas, sad avenues, moons, women who fade away, dreams and laments."[2] They were written under the postromantic and symbolist influences characteristic of the early *modernismo*. This period of his work culminated in the *Sonetos espirituales* written in 1914 and 1915, Reyes' first years in Madrid. After this, Jiménez felt he could go no further in the direction of "exquisiteness and preciosity."[3] Valle had arrived at a like conclusion at about the same time.

The "second epoch" of his verse begins with *Diario de un poeta recién casado* (Diary of a poet recently married), 1916. His new understanding of poetry came about, as one of his most perceptive critics, Ricardo Gullón, explains, from varied influences, among them the presence in his life of his bride of 1916, Zenobia Camprubí, his trip to the United States, and his consequent contact both with it and with the sea. He evolved toward what he called "naked poetry," and toward a concept of aesthetic perfection which ruthlessly discarded all that was not the very essence of poetry itself.[4] His movement toward simplicity was paralleled by increasing philosophical profundity, culminating in *Animal de fondo* (Creature from below), 1949, in which he achieved his lifelong goal, a vision of ideal beauty or essence, which he had conceived as a universal consciousness of God.[5]

Juan Ramón was a contemplative and solitary poet. He searched for his idea within himself, not in his surroundings, and his verse is based on interrogation, on abstraction, not on outside reality. He has been accused because of this of narcissism, of escapism, and of lack of commitment. But even if one chooses to ignore those essays

---

[1] Quoted in Ricardo Gullón, *Direcciones del modernismo*, p. 33.

[2] Antonio Sánchez-Barbudo, *La segunda época de Juan Ramón Jiménez*, p. 24.

[3] Gullón, Introduction to Juan Ramón Jiménez, *Three Hundred Poems, 1903–1953*, trans. Eloïse Roach, p. *xxiv*.

[4] Gullón, *Estudios sobre Juan Ramón Jiménez*, pp. 85, 132.

[5] Paul R. Olson, *Circle of Paradox: Time and Essence in the Poetry of Juan Ramón Jiménez*, pp. 217, 218, 227.

of his that deal with contemporary and even political questions, the eternal themes of his poetry should certainly be considered not as a negation but as a purification of reality, as essential reality.[6]

Juan Ramón shared with Unamuno and Ortega the concern for the regeneration of Spain. Like them, he felt a sense of mission, a desire to impart to life and to work that austerity and ethical purity which were part of the teaching of Giner de los Ríos. His sense of vocation, his complete dedication to an ideal of perfection, may explain why the far from humble Ortega chose to call him *maestro*. Though his efforts at reform remained within the scope of poetry, they gained in intensity, as Gullón points out, what they lost in extent.[7] For certainly none of the reformers who preceded or followed him were more fervid in their fight against the evils they all recognized: vulgarity of mind and a weak creative impulse. None epitomized refined sensibility and pure creative effort more perfectly than Jiménez.

The proposal of his candidacy for the Nobel Prize, made officially by the University of Maryland in 1956, was based not only on the poetry itself but also on Jiménez' contribution as a teacher of poetic generations. As a poet he marked the beginning of a new period. And he and Ortega were without a doubt the two most instrumental literary figures in the formation and the guiding of the new generation of writers.[8]

Jiménez was one of the first writers whom Reyes met on his arrival in Madrid, but their memory of that meeting differs. Jiménez recalls it as taking place in a streetcar, while Reyes says that it was in a publisher's office where he first saw that "French or rather El Greco beard: the poet Juan Ramón Jiménez, attentive and nervous, with rare medical information, acquired by means of exquisite illnesses."[9] The close association between the Reyes and

---

[6] Gullón discusses this question in *Estudios sobre Juan Ramón Jiménez*, pp. 79–80, and *Direcciones del modernismo*, pp. 42–43.

[7] Gullón, Introduction to Jiménez, *Three Hundred Poems*, pp. *xxv–xxvi*.

[8] Ibid., p. *xxvi*.

[9] Alfonso Reyes, "Historia documental de mis libros," *Universidad de México*, 9, no. 7 (1955): 14.

Jiménez families began sometime later, after Jiménez' marriage in 1916. Jiménez' multiple recollection of don Alfonso's smile admirably synthesizes the many moments they shared: "In his lower-floor apartment in General Pardiñas, in his main-floor apartment in Serrano, in the Mexican Embassy, in my own house," Juan Ramón recalled, "it greeted me, fine, terse, reaching to his eyes."[10]

Reyes' inner smile is easily perceivable to the reader of his "Apuntes sobre Juan Ramón Jiménez" (Notes on Juan Ramón Jiménez). The first of these two short, informal essays is "Juan Ramón y los duendes" (Juan Ramón and the elves) and depicts a poet isolated in a tower, not of the traditional ivory, but of a more mundane cork-like material. "He is a priest of silence," wrote Reyes. "Juan Ramón needs, demands of life the most complete and absolute silence in connection with his work" (IV, 270). And, in fact, Jiménez announced to Reyes in one of his letters: "I again have the carpenter in the house, since I am going to see if, at last, I invent my purification room" (October 25, 1920). His noise phobia had become acute. Reyes recounted that the room, padded with a special soundproofing substance from the United States, gave a very strange effect, because all the normal background sounds were completely absent, with the result that sudden noises became unbearably obvious. Reyes, enjoying his role as legend builder, further embellished his anecdote: "Last autumn the Venezuelan writer and diplomat Pedro Emilio Coll returned from his vacation with a strange nervous ailment: his head was full of noises. And the mischievous magician of Pombo, Ramón Gómez de la Serna, imagined a comic dialogue between Coll and Jiménez in which the latter ended up fleeing from the intracraneal racket of the former" (IV, 271).

A more serious appraisal of the poet accompanies the humorous one. Reyes witnessed the years in which Juan Ramón's poetic ideas were undergoing a decisive change; he was settling into a way of life from which only the Civil War was to uproot him. The affirma-

---

[10] Juan Ramón Jiménez, *Españoles de tres mundos*, p. 180.

tion at this time of his tendency to isolate himself was only part of this process. He was to dedicate himself completely to the continuous creation and recreation, organization and reorganization, of his poetic work. This is the theme of Reyes' second essay. Reyes saw him as "looking for the definitive outline of the constellation of the soul and the terrible place of each star. . . . I cannot conceive of a more heroic task, a higher task, more worthy of engaging the efforts of a man, even when at the same time it imposes a constant sacrifice" (IV, 273–274). The younger man had before him an example of unparalleled artistic dedication, which could not help but be a stimulus and an encouragement. He described Jiménez as a "perfect animal of poetry, [who] flees from his own claws or hoofs and goes directly toward his wings" (IV, 366).

Reyes' essays on Juan Ramón were written for immediate publication in the Madrid newspapers. Juan Ramón's portrait of Reyes is a more polished literary piece, a meditated synthesis of memories, published in 1940. It formed a part, a few years later, of his collection of "lyric caricatures" entitled *Españoles de tres mundos* (Spaniards of three worlds), 1942, and is an extraordinary portrait, very revealing of his affection for Reyes. His physical description of Reyes soon becomes a symbolic one:

> If I remember rightly, Alfonso Reyes had then a little Mexican moustache, smooth and with a drooping curve, which harmonized with the warm roguish eyes and the dimples in his cheeks, source of his smile. This abbreviated and rounded gentleman was at that time still a mischievous child—and it seems to me that he will continue so—and already a distinguished veteran, both in the figure of a young man. Not two distinct faces, one toward the past and the other toward the future, caught at the neck as in a classical figure, but two in one and in a general spherical union, giratory, present, with its axis in the spinal medulla. A being double, triple in instinct, grey matter, desire, and fostering of existence.

Juan Ramón depicts Reyes as a protean personality. The changing facets fuse into one with the rapidity of the face's revolutions, and express the complete integration of don Alfonso's personality in spite of its mutability. He saw him as the confluence of many roads, "all traversed to the utmost, with surrender and with analysis, with profundity and with happiness, with decision and with serenity, without losing anything, not even a comma, in the international and universal transit." Don Alfonso had that rare quality of being able to give himself up completely to his enthusiasm, yet at the same time to conserve his analytical sense. He lived with passion *and* with lucidity. Everything of worth and moral value he made a part of his own store of knowledge and culture—"Alfonso Reyes, saviour of all that is savable," is Jiménez' felicitous phrase.

"From where did he come," asks Jiménez, "thus prepared in that which was foreign to him?" In questioning the source of Reyes' cosmopolitan grasp of cultural values, Jiménez touched upon a quality which Reyes came to believe every Latin American inherently possessed. It was the basis of his faith in the future of Latin America, whose universal outlook he believed to be ideally suited to its supreme mission, that of creating a new cultural synthesis and a new humanism. We are a race of synthesis, he has said, echoing Jiménez' description of him as a synthesizer of Mexico. The answer to Juan Ramón's query, in Reyes' own terms, would be, then, that Reyes was one of those who had profited from the international quality of Latin America's cultural background. Juan Ramón was impressed by this quality that separated don Alfonso from many of his contemporaries.

The last sentences of the portrait relate don Alfonso to those images with which Juan Ramón was wont to describe perfection:

And a graceful castle wherever he may stop, and a tent, just in case, for that which is free roams outside the castle, in the greater open air where the simple and richest truth springs forth. He arrives at the necessary place, sets up his receiver and his transmitter, and is ready to give and receive with enthusiasm. Listen to him laugh and sing now. (He was serious.) He throws to us through the warm or rigid air, depth of valley, mountain or plain, the flowers and fruits from wherever it may be, west, north, east, south, and the rest, in the enchanted season which he makes total.[11]

Juan Ramón saw in Reyes a stability and serenity of temperament which he did not himself possess. Don Alfonso had the solidity of the "graceful castle" and also the freedom of movement of the camping tent. If he was a man of the "open air," he had arrived at that ultimate and pure state "when man can live tranquilly outside and with no more fear of anything or anybody on earth or in space."[12] Thus had Juan Ramón described in another essay of the same period his "aristocrat of the open air." And the "total season" in which Reyes exists is that of the title of one of Jiménez' books of poetry, where the totality is one of tranquillity, completeness, and accomplishment. Juan Ramón's conception of Reyes had not changed during the years of separation, had not been marred by the misunderstandings and resentments that gradually eroded many of his friendships. (Juan Ramón had made a private list of "good men" and "bad men" and Reyes figures on the former, a *very* short list.) His memories of don Alfonso were all pleasurable ones.

Reyes was in all likelihood referring to Jiménez' silhouette when he wrote him on January 4, 1940:

> Seeing myself reflected in your friendship has been for me a singular pleasure. Since you always construct, it helps me to know, if not what I am, what I should always be. I am profoundly grateful for the good your words have done me.
>
> We have never been far apart. If you have an extra moment, tell me about your life. I have struggled since I returned with the harshness of moral and biological adaptation. But these are times of suffering for all. Manuela and Alfonsito (who has already made me a grandfather) both send you their good wishes with mine for 1940.
>
> Always yours, always desirous that you know I am very close to you, always with true devotion and affection.

[11] Ibid., pp. 180–182.
[12] Jiménez, "Aristocracia y democracia," in his *El trabajo gustoso*, p. 71.

This letter was followed by one a few months later in which Reyes wrote Juan Ramón about the silhouette of Rubén Darío that Jiménez had sent him:

> As I always have you before me, it does not surprise me, although it enchants me, that thoughts of me had crossed your mind as you evoked Rubén Darío. I have read nothing on Darío as complete and as noble as the silhouette that you sent me. I have decided to give it to "Letras de México," where they are very anxious to publish it on the first page and with all honor, since they have it on their conscience that, in the absence of the directors, there appeared a poem of yours carelessly placed.
>
> It is as if you lived among us. Your personal friends as well as those who have still not had that good fortune talk constantly about you. We accompany you, believe us, with all our hearts. (April 3, 1940)

Jiménez answered:

> You [are] always so generous and so good to me (and to everyone). A great example for all and for me! . . .
>
> How much we have to thank you for, we Spaniards of all colors . . . and your books! Your conscience and your vigilance reach everything, Alfonso Reyes. (April 28, 1940)

Jiménez' letter is in the same tone as his silhouette of Reyes and also echoes the Darío portrait, in which he had written: "The whim of the unending wave of figurations brings to my imagination a marine Rubén Darío, coming perhaps from the photograph which the good and faithful Alfonso Reyes, always a best friend of Rubén Darío, gave me years ago in Madrid."[13]

What drew them together most closely in their Madrid years was their joint founding of the magazine *Índice* in 1921. Juan Ramón had been much involved in two earlier magazines, *Helios* in 1903–1904 and *Renacimiento* in 1907. In the first three decades of the century new literary magazines seemed to follow one after the other. Few of them managed to achieve more than a short-lived

13 Jiménez, *Españoles de tres mundos*, p. 122.

existence, but in them the literary groups defined themselves—
Helios, one of the most serious magazines, united the *modernistas*
—and the writers had a place to publish what they wrote, and could
try to make themselves known to an often uncomprehending public. *Índice* did not confine itself to one generation of writers. Reyes
said that its collaborators were only the young and the youthful,
yet in it are joined the poets of several generations. Some were
writers already well-known, such as Ortega and Gómez de la
Serna. Others, such as Federico García Lorca and Jorge Guillén,
really began their literary careers in *Índice*.

The format was simple and elegant; its color scheme, yellow
and violet, Juan Ramón's favorite colors. Juan Ramón and Reyes
did not wish to present any literary program. This was not, they
announced in their manifesto in the first number, a magazine of
any particular school:

> Its editors are writers and artists of the most distinct tendencies.
> Spaniards and Spanish Americans, united only by the common
> interest of the exaltation of the spirit and by pleasure in beauti-
> ful things.
>
> In its pages will fit everything that signifies "life," from the
> purest to the newest, from the simplest to the most renowned,
> from the most occult to the most open; and its aspiration is to be
> able to define and single out, in the most complete and perfect
> way possible—with a criterion that is both very ample and very
> narrow—the noblest quality of the Spanish and Spanish American
> genius.

This statement of purpose reflects the aesthetic idealism which
then and in the future guided the lives of both Juan Ramón and
don Alfonso, and indicates the common artistic grounds on which
their friendship was based.

The mere fact of the publication of *Índice* is proof that Juan
Ramón was not living in total isolation, as was said, nor was he
so uninterested in what was going on about him that he did not
wish to modify it—by his own methods, of course. A follower of
Giner de los Ríos' teachings, he thought that the task of reforming
Spanish culture should be undertaken by a minority whose in-

fluences would then penetrate the entire country. The publication of *Indice* was thus an effort to purify the sensibility of this minority, and Reyes' presence, with his common sense and his realistic appreciation of the problems, encouraged Jiménez to carry out his plans. Their aspirations were high, and in like proportion the difficulties arose.

Publishing a magazine was not a simple undertaking, as can be deduced from the letter Jiménez wrote to Reyes on the eighteenth of August, 1921:

> Your letter, with the proofs, arrived on time.
>
> The second issue of "Indice" is dragging along, beating a direct retreat. There is no type for the complete number—24 pages—; we had to send Corpus Barga's material to the civil government for prior censorship, to avoid any problem with the printed copy; and, above all, the slowness and normal disorder, with which you are already familiar, increased now since the "affair" no longer matters to Maroto! The M. business is taken care of. He ceases being editor, and he will only do a drawing now and then. It could not be any other way.
>
> "The General Bookstore Society" has taken charge of 300 copies of "Indice" for their advertising in the provinces and in America. If not, we ran the risk that the magazine would never arrive anywhere. We will talk about all this anon. . . .
>
> Icaza asked me if we could let him have a little of the magazine's white paper. I am going to calculate what we need for the volume of 6 nums. and I will let him have? what he needs. Thus we please him and we facilitate the payment of the draft for this paper, which falls due in September. And afterwards, with more money, we ask the factory for another quantity. I think that we should do it, for I do not know if all the contributors will respond in the "moment of necessity."

These personal and financial difficulties resulted in the different appearance of the fourth issue, the last page of which is an "Explanation to our Friends" in which all the problems of publication are recounted. The tone is disillusioned and bitter: "He who, in present day Spain, has attempted undertakings of such a serious and pure character knows how much one has to struggle to achieve

the results of relative perfection that are normal in other countries."
The ideals of the first issue are repeated with defiance: "Our desire
is 'not to make' a precipitous and facile magazine, with daring
clippings, more or less necessary concessions, and last-minute fill-
ins. *Indice* will continue being 'untimely'—it is idealistic, keep it
well in mind, without any benefits for those who make it—and it
will attempt the maximum ethical and aesthetic perfection possible." But it was not the time for such a magazine to flourish, and
what started out to be a monthly magazine only managed three issues in 1921 and one the following year.

Reyes and Jiménez were, of course, contributors to the magazine. Both published poetry in it as well as prose, and are represented in all four issues, along with Pedro Salinas, Adolfo Salazar,
and Enrique Díez-Canedo. The magazine contained literary studies,
impressionistic and autobiographical essays, short stories, notes on
the contemporary artistic scene, a short drama, poetry, translations,
commentaries, and the wonderful humorous supplements. Responsible for these last were Reyes and his inseparable friend Canedo.

Reyes had a refined, subtle, and erudite humor. Canedo combined a gentle manner and an inquiring mind with an equally
irrepressible sense of the comic. It is not surprising, therefore, that
they enlivened the cultural life of Madrid with their literary jests.
One of the most elaborate of these appeared in the humorous supplement of the first issue of *Indice* and contained three letters pur-
ported to have been exchanged between the poet Góngora and El
Greco, and which, strangely enough, give a preview of the theories
of impressionism and cubism. Not too farfetched an idea, perhaps,
if one considers Aldous Huxley's opinion that El Greco "at eighty
or ninety . . . would have been producing an almost abstract art—
a cubism without cubes."[14] At any rate, the letters were much appreciated in literary circles, except for one very serious scholar who
felt an obligation to combat such "frauds." Reyes' and Canedo's
delight at this response was so intense that they limited themselves

[14] Aldous Huxley, "Meditation on El Greco," *Collected Essays*, p. 147.

to assuring their readers that this gentleman's letter *was* authentic and was safely preserved in their files.

Reyes' erudition never weighed upon him. He had a propensity for the lighter as well as for the more serious side of literature. "He who treats in verse only sublime things," he wrote, "does not live the true life of poetry and letters, but rather wears them falsely, like an adornment for parties."[15] Literature was neither a game nor a livelihood. One lived it.

In 1923 *Índice* was transformed into a collection of small books, and the *Biblioteca de Índice* was born, "A Library of Definition and Concord." Juan Ramón had always been interested in the presentation of a book as well as in its content, and had considerably influenced the aesthetic side of Spanish book publishing. He had been for a while artistic director of one of the publishing houses, which recognized his talent in this field. Therefore, the small volumes of *Índice* are models of their kind, simple and dignified looking, similar to English books of the period. Don Alfonso has mentioned how often he and Juan Ramón had longed to have their own printing press so as to be able to control personally all the aspects of the production of their books. The appearance of Reyes' *Obras completas*, published many years later, is reminiscent of the books in the *Biblioteca de Índice*.

Of the six books that appeared, one was a new edition of Reyes' *Visión de Anáhuac* and another his edition of Góngora's *Fábula de Polifemo y Galatea*. Juan Ramón also wanted to publish Reyes' dramatic poem *Ifigenia cruel* in this collection. Reyes, however, had to refuse the offer because, although in 1923 he was again in the diplomatic service, he still had financial difficulties. He wrote Jiménez on December fifteenth:

> So that you can understand my fear of publishing *Ifigenia* in *Índice*—in spite of how much I have dreamed of it—let me tell you confidentially some things that until this moment I had not decided to tell you:

[15] Reyes, *Cortesía*, pp. 7–8.

I send to you here some papers, clipped in the order in which they should be read, in which you will see that José Vasconcelos, in spite of having ordered from me, by letter, 2,000 copies of *Visión de Anáhuac* (a letter which at the present must be in his hands, since I returned it to him so that he could see his error), at the time of payment alleges reasons of which he could have thought before giving me the order, and he is only buying 300 copies. I have received, then, 500 Mexican pesos, instead of receiving 2,000.

As the end of the year approaches, I have tried in vain to get my companions and the Mexican students here with fellowships to return to me certain advances I gave them on the strength of future salaries. With the fear that the revolution will leave us cut off, they cannot pay me anything. I have, then, to pay for it myself.

With all these financial troubles weighing upon me, it will not surprise you that I tremble before every new expense.

In respect to your extremely kind offer, how can you expect me to accept it? Your kindness so obligates me, and the idea of having my volume beautifully printed in this collection so enthuses me, that for the moment I could not resist it. But the truth is that I am not at peace. I know more than well—let me tell you this with the same frankness with which I am talking to you about my troubles —that you also have to struggle. No: let's leave it and hope that this shower passes, if it is going to pass. I beg you. Give me back the original, which costs me so much effort to request. Put yourself in my situation; you would do—I am sure—exactly the same as I am doing.

Ifigenia was published in 1924, but not in the *Índice* collection.

The letters that passed between Reyes and Jiménez during Reyes' years in Spain are generally little more than notes, but they do show the frequency and the intimacy of the relationship, not only between the two men, but between the two families. "To-night," Reyes writes in one letter, "someone will read aloud to me *The Gardener*: your remembrance will accompany us" (June 4, 1917), referring to a work of Tagore translated by Zenobia Jiménez. He complains of their separation: "I still have not rescued my life; you know that already; and the infinite, infinite tasks that I

oblige myself to do every day have prevented me again and again
from having the pleasure of going to greet you both, but I shall do
it; and I console myself by thinking that, meanwhile, we are never
far apart" (December 3, 1918).[16] Reyes had sent Jiménez *Visión*
and another book and Jiménez responded:

> A million thanks for your letter and for the little book. I have not
> gone to see you because Zenobia has been in bed 24 days, with that
> unbearable dengue, the war of the—peaceful ones. Your "Dance"
> has delighted me; "Visión" is a true jewel; how well you have
> caught the roving foot of the nightmare! Congratulations, hunter
> of spectres! I do not know how you could have read my piece. It
> had an error in each line, fallen words, evaporated lines . . . Oh,
> well, at least it is going to be published in a book! . . . Zenobia
> asks me to invite you to lunch one day with us. Since I know your
> occupations, I would prefer that you fix the day. The only thing
> that I "impose" is "immediacy." And that the child also comes.
> Remembrances from house to house. (December 5, 1918)

Jiménez' fondness for children is well known, and he liked to be
surrounded by them. He mentions Reyes' son often in his letters.

There was a break in the correspondence when Reyes left Madrid. From 1924 to 1936 Juan Ramón found himself more and
more alone. He was critical of the direction being taken by the
poetry of the younger writers—he felt they were moving toward an
empty formalism—and did not hesitate to make his opinions
clear.[17] He kept more and more to himself, except for occasional
rather ill-humored attacks on those of whom he did not approve.
He was writing comparatively little new poetry, spending his time
instead rewriting and rearranging previous work. It was the period
in which he was most withdrawn within himself and, therefore,
not easily awakened from his reverie by letters from afar.

The letters Reyes wrote to him from Paris in 1925–1926 were
never answered, and their correspondence was not renewed until

---

[16] The two letters quoted in this paragraph and the letters of March 4, 1937
and December 7, 1953 cited later in the chapter are not found in the Reyes
library but rather in the Sala Zenobia–Juan Ramón in the library of the University of Puerto Rico.

[17] Sánchez-Barbudo, *La segunda época de Juan Ramón Jiménez*, pp. 111–112.

1937. Juan Ramón had then made his second and definitive trip to America. His way of life and even his character were to suffer significant changes in these new surroundings. His friends found him more open, more sociable. Jiménez himself, in a letter to Canedo in 1943, said that "a profound change took place within me, something similar to what happened when I came in 1916."[18] The literary critic Sánchez-Barbudo commented: "Seemingly he had reacted against himself, against those defects of his, before leaving Spain; and when away from there, free in part from that wall of gossip and plotting which he always felt there, he was in part another man; more alone, perhaps, but less shut off within himself, less hostile, more open to his fellow man."[19]

Reyes received the first "American letter" from his Spanish friends while in Buenos Aires. The Jiménezes were in Havana participating actively in the literary life there, and they wrote to explain their plans for settling in some part of Latin America or Europe. Reyes answered on the fourth of March, 1937:

> It surprises me very much that on thinking of centralizing the matter in Buenos Aires, New York, Havana, and Paris you have not also added the name of Mexico, the only country in the world showing solidarity with Spain. For my part, I had already felt the necessity of collecting the dispersed Spanish intellectuals and to this end I have addressed the President of Mexico, Lázaro Cárdenas, who turned my letter over to the Secretary of Public Education. Although they have not yet given me a definitive answer to my propositions, we already knew through the press that they invited Doctor Marañón, who had the unfortunate idea of declining the Mexican invitation. . . .
>
> We thank you very much for having thought of us, and it would hurt us very much if you had not. We are ready to do all that is necessary.
>
> Until very soon. A warm embrace for my unforgettable and very dear Juan Ramón, whose image comes to my spirit, without exaggeration, every day since the day in which I stopped seeing him. I dream sometimes that life will join us again.

18 Quoted in ibid., p. 115.
19 Ibid., p. 118.

This letter is one of the earliest references to Reyes' activities in aid of his Spanish colleagues, which he justified some ten years later in his letter to Ortega. Juan Ramón never took advantage of the programs set up by Reyes in Mexico City, for he could never conquer his fear of the altitude.

In his reply to Reyes' letter, Juan Ramón made no mention of its more practical aspects, responding rather to his expression of affection:

> The last paragraph of your letter to Zenobia has filled me with happiness and remorse. But the remorse, exterior: in our apartment in Madrid, now Padilla, 38, there "live" many letters to you, packages of my books and notebooks for you, not finished, and even a book of etchings, "El Sol," that you asked me for some twelve years ago at Lista, 8, dedicated to you. You see, then, that the remembrance also lives.
>
> This has always been my life: putting something aside and not finishing it; the restless passage from one thing to another, the ordered accumulation of delay.
>
> But this is not the essence. You know well that in my thoughts and in my conversations with all those who *are*, you are always in front, in your place.
>
> Thank you today for so many things of always, each one of which I have within myself. (March 31, 1937)

Here Juan Ramón is at his best. His friends, and his enemies, have their just place in his mind and there they remain. The remorse for having left unanswered Reyes' letters is in this context unimportant, because the intention and the affection never faltered. The "ordered accumulation of delay" that serves as his excuse was an inseparable part of his work and of his life. In 1953 he said something very similar to Ricardo Gullón: "I have entire boxes full of bits of paper like these and now I shall never be able even to see them. It is a disaster. And all my life has been the same: I have created more than I could re-create."[20]

Their letters reflect the continuous creative activity of both correspondents. Juan Ramón writes a postcard to ask:

[20] Gullón, *Conversaciones con Juan Ramón Jiménez*, p. 83.

Will you permit me to put the letter you wrote us when E. D.-C [Díez-Canedo] died in my "Con la rosa del mundo" [With the rose of the world]?

I am dedicating the book to you. I wanted to dedicate to you one less bad than those I have done up to now. And I think that now I am beginning the less bad.

. . . Since this 1945 I shall send you whatever I publish. . . . Losada will have six new books this year.

And don't you forget me with your books, which, with those of some poets and some things of P. H^e. U. [Henríquez Ureña], are what I keep of Spanish America. (1945)

Reyes sent him two books immediately, and Jiménez, who never did publish "Con la rosa del mundo," commented: "The pace you have maintained for years with your written work astonishes me. I already know you have no time for social things. And I am extremely pleased that you are giving all of yourself. Now I am engrossed in your two latest books, with the delight of always before the 'idea maker' and (ay, idiots of the pen) before the writer" (May 13, 1945).

Reyes, in turn, acknowledged the receipt of *Españoles de tres mundos*:

Naturally I knew and "loved dearly" *Españoles de tres mundos* (where one finds the portrait of me that you drew with a generosity which would need a new name, and which you had sent me already). But it is a joy to possess it thus, sent and dedicated by you. [The dedication reads: "To Alfonso, this third of a book, with much acculmulated (in compensation) affection. Juan Ramón.] Thank you, Juan Ramón. Your friendship, your memory (we are now at a sufficiently advanced level of years, experience, and grief to be able to speak in this way), are one of the best things of my life.

I am ill. Supposedly hepatic upsets, nameless discomforts, and even itches or urticaria. The quantity of evil that one's fellow men make one swallow! But let us not show more than the smile, the best that we may have. How much I would give to have you here, among my books! I do have you here, in your *Españoles*, and I greedily keep you as my companion in this obligatory reclusion of my bad health. Soon I shall send you an ugly didactic thing, one of those with which I earn my living now. (June 1, 1945)

During this period the Jiménezes were living in Washington, D.C. They had spent two very active years in Cuba and a few years in Coral Gables, where Juan Ramón gave several series of lectures at the University of Miami, and then in 1942 had moved to Washington. Juan Ramón worked for a short time on a cultural radio program for Latin America sponsored by the Department of Defense. Meanwhile Mrs. Jiménez was teaching Spanish at the University of Maryland, as part of the Army's wartime instruction program. It was, strangely enough, as her substitute that Juan Ramón began to teach there, and they both soon became permanent members of the faculty. Reyes made several plans to visit them in Washington, and they did meet finally, after twenty-two years. Reyes was on his way home from a Unesco meeting in Paris. Mrs. Reyes recounted how Juan Ramón, not able to wait to see them, called on the phone, but was so overcome with emotion that don Alfonso was barely able to understand him.

The passing of the years had its effect on the correspondence. Matters of health began to play a progressively larger role in the letters. As one might expect, given Juan Ramón's character, it is principally to his state of health to which they refer. However, Juan Ramón became so worried about Reyes' cardiac problems (Reyes suffered a coronary thrombosis in 1947) that he initiated the following exchange of letters:

> *They are taking me* to Argentina and I do not know where else, in July. I hope to return. Not that the trip would not please me in other conditions of health and equilibrium. But . . .
>
> I always hear about you here and I know that you are following your normal life. May that be for many years, Alfonso. . . .
>
> Are there in Mexico any of those "electric chairs" that take upstairs someone who tires a lot or a little? I could send you one. They can be used on all stairs. (June 11, 1948)

Reyes replied on the twenty-fifth of June:

I am enquiring about that electric chair that interests you, but
they tell me that it is from General Electric and that it is much
more easily gotten in the United States. Nevertheless, we will continue looking and I will let you know what I find out. It would be
very good for me: I spent all of 1947 to all intents and purposes in
bed with two cardiac attacks that appeared successively. I didn't
suffer at all, but they assured me that I could die and I went
through a very serious exercise of patience. It now seems that I
am doing well.

And Jiménez:

The chair, my dear Alfonso, was for you.

My question was to find out if the system of electrical installa-
tion in Mexico works with appliances made in and for the United
States. In Argentina they tell me that they cannot use some of
them. Would you tell me if the stairway in your house is straight
and only one flight? . . .

I am also much better from my terrible colitis and my nervous
depression. I have arrived at my accustomed dynamic phase.
(June 28, 1948)

Reyes answered:

Excuse me for not having understood you well. Your offer of the
electric chair fills me with gratitude and confusion: it is the only
electric chair that can please me. But, considering it well, it is
not worth the trouble. The only one that bothers me, and that I
only climb every seven days, is that of the Colegio Nacional,
three floors, with two flights per floor. Impossible to install the
apparatus! I say that I pray an "Our Father" on each step in order
to arrive at the top with breath. But the truth is that I am now
practically well.

I hope that your trip to South America is a very happy one.
Send us postcards, so that we may follow you with our thoughts.
Delighted to hear that you are recovered. (July 2, 1948)

The final note on the matter was written by Jiménez just as he
was leaving for the ship: "I regret the failure, my dear Alfonso; I
was looking forward to doing this, and the chairs are not expensive. It was not an excessive gift" (July 8, 1948).

Juan Ramón's trip to Argentina, despite the misgivings he originally expressed, was an enormous success. As it had for Ortega years before, Buenos Aires gave him a tumultuous welcome, his lectures were filled to overflowing, and everywhere he went he was followed by well-wishers. It lifted his spirits tremendously and pushed into the background for a while the depression that had been menacing his health.

The optimistic phase did not last long, however. By mid-1950 Jiménez was sinking into a depressive state. His need for Spain and the Spanish people was becoming acute. In August he entered the hospital. Reyes wrote to express his sympathy and in September Zenobia answered:

> Many thanks for your letter! What a consolation the remembrance of good friends is! Thanks to God I can tell you that we have now solved the great problem relative to returning home and to the university at the same time because, as the family is so small!! when I go to class J.R. remains alone, with his thoughts, and there is not enough music of the kind he likes "in the air" for him to be able to manage all those hours—18 per week. Everything will work out and the question is to do it properly. We must invent a family. (September 15, 1950)

Professor Graciela Nemes, now a Jiménez scholar, then a student of Juan Ramón's, would stay with him when Zenobia was in class.

But this was not enough. That same autumn, Zenobia took Juan Ramón to Puerto Rico, where he had been invited to give some lectures. She describes the effects of the trip in a retrospective letter written in 1956:

> You know that we came to P.R. at the end of 50, because J.R. was in a depressive state that we could not see any end to, but as soon as he arrived in P.R. he had a great change for the better. . . . J.R. only got to his feet when I told him that the P.R. coast was visible. With great difficulty and some deceit I got J.R. to accept the rector's invitation to stay in the university's guest house. There he went to the table for the 3 meals (in Washington he only got out of bed so that it could be made, and then grumbling) but he continued receiving visits stretched out on the sofa. He

only joined in the general conversation when it was about literature and something was said that he considered contrary to the
truth. Suddenly he got up and was as well as anyone. (January
30, 1956)

So that, after another few months in Maryland, the Jiménezes
left for Puerto Rico permanently in March, 1951. Finding himself
again in contact with a Spanish atmosphere, Juan Ramón completely recovered his mental and spiritual equilibrium and soon
began to write again, after one and one-half years of not writing
a word.

In 1952 the National University of Mexico, celebrating its fourth
centenary, gave honorary degrees to seventeen foreigners, among
them Juan Ramón. It was Reyes who made the arrangements for
the giving of the degree. He wrote Juan Ramón:

> We are in agreement. I will receive your honorary doctoral
> degree from our university in your name, and very honored. But
> it is indispensable that you send me about two pages so that I may
> read them in your name, as is being done by the other absent
> recipients to whom a similar degree will be conferred by delega-
> tion in a ceremony shortly. The rector and the university are in a
> hurry. Please, do not delay your words. They can be very brief
> and simple, since the important thing is your name. I should
> remind you that you are the only Spaniard to whom this title has
> been given. (March 20, 1952)

This is probably the only degree Juan Ramón ever received. He
had never finished a university career. In fact, he felt that his name
alone was quite enough, and he even got tired of that. He substi-
tuted his initials and for a while changed them to K.Q.K. An enemy
of titles and even of names, he wanted to publish a magazine in
which all the contributions would be anonymous, possessing undoubtedly the deep certainty that whatever *he* wrote would always
be recognized. Therefore, it is not unreasonable to assume that part
of his reason for accepting the degree from the University of Mexico was the consideration he had for Reyes. This is confirmed in the
words of acceptance he sent Reyes, entitled "Act of thanks to the

University of Mexico in general and to Alfonso Reyes in particular." It is, in fact, a nostalgic tribute in verse to his friendship with Reyes, whom he calls "My most dear Alfonso, phoenix of widespread wings, always new in the flaming molds."

Reyes, thanking Juan Ramón for "those admirable verses, of unique accent," announced to him in August: "Today, at noon, . . . a brief and solemn ceremony to give the diplomas of Doctor Honoris Causa to the representatives of the absent recipients. . . . Full of happiness and pride, I received your diploma . . . which gave occasion for hearing my name associated with yours. Your poetry for the occasion, since it alluded to me and it was not proper that I myself read it, was very well read by the young universitarian Eduardo Fernández MacGregor." The ceremony was a formal link between Juan Ramón and Mexico.

Meanwhile, Puerto Rico had worked its miracle on Juan Ramón. At Christmas time in 1952 the Reyeses received a card in which Zenobia wished "that 1953 will treat you as well as '52 treated us." And there is a long postscript from Juan Ramón, an optimistic note full of enthusiasm:

After two and a half years of bad illness (a decompensation of my heart block), here I am beginning to begin again! And this is one of the few letters that I will write by hand, a hand unused to everything.

Thank you, my dear, dear Alfonso, for so much of your kindness to me. Those magic books which pour forth from your difficult conscience, at full speed! What a pleasure this edition of your complete poems (although mutilated). Your books, by some strange chance, are here with me (those received since 1926, I mean).

I had occasion to talk with Gabriela Mistral about a Nobel Prize for you. She insists that the prize is only for *creators*. And I told her: Well, is Alfonso Reyes not a creator even in the newspaper article? There are so many things to create in this badly created world! I shall write to you at greater length, when I am stronger. But I do not lack the strength to embrace you both and wish you more time of grace and glory. More, much more!

It is interesting to note that toward the end of his life, after his wife's death, he again reiterated, this time to a newspaperman, his belief that Alfonso Reyes should receive the Nobel Prize.

By the end of 1953 Juan Ramón was giving a course on *modernismo*. It was don Alfonso who was then convalescing and he wrote:

> We are happy to know of your health and your work. May it all be for the good. We are in this semitropical and half rustic city [Cuernavaca], an hour and a half from Mexico City, where I am resting from the altitude, and above all, from the human tumult, each day more insupportable. Unfortunately, one cannot close one's eyes to the present human spectacle.
>
> At the same time, I find myself recovered from my ills, although, naturally, I now carry what the doctors call, with a horrid term, residual scars. I had a new attack some months ago: this time the new precautionary medicine stopped it, but its application is tiring, because it necessitates constant analysis of the blood. Two months later—without any more discomfort than being shut in the house and a certain quiet, which after all is not bad—I have come for another few months "to rest from the treatment." Here I write a little, I read a little, and once a week I take care of the papers I have to concerning the Colegio de México and the Colegio Nacional. I cannot say that I am very happy. I live in relative tranquillity, but I little like everything that is going on outside. (December 7, 1953)

Zenobia continued to be enthusiastic about her husband's health. She wrote Manuela Reyes on March 30, 1954:

> And now let me tell you that J.R. is incredibly active and clear-sighted and does not stop from 6 in the morning until 11 at night except for a half hour of siesta after meals. He is sending contributions right and left, because they are leftovers from his books, and, on realizing that he is now well, many people ask him for them. He hopes to finish 2 or 3 books before the end of the year, to make up for lost time, and he dictates to me three shifts per day. I do not need to tell you what the proof situation is. Some nights ago I counted the contributions just come out, en route, or waiting for rapid mailing and there were 28! You will understand that I try to

curb him a little but I already know that such curbs do not subdue him. The 23rd of next month he is giving the speech for Cervantes' Day at the university. The 29th he is presenting in the Tapia a young girl of 16 who takes communion every morning and is a great dancer. (In Seville they will cross themselves when she arrives.) I tell you this only so that you can see the variety of his interests and activities. One must not forget that he is 72 years old. Now I am the lazy one. I have stopped teaching at the university and I am now only typist and chauffeur.

It is such extraordinary activity that the reader of the correspondence, if he knows Juan Ramón's unstable temperament, can foresee that it cannot last. In his recent book on Juan Ramón's last years, Ricardo Gullón comments that his neurosis seemed to follow an alternating pattern: "excess of concentration in work, without distractions to alleviate the burden, and escape into depression in order to free him from the unsupportable tension. Overcoming the collapse, he would go back to work with the desire to recuperate the lost time and he would push himself until he made inevitable the relapse."[21] This seems to be exactly the process one can follow in Zenobia's letters.

In the autumn of 1954 Juan Ramón's health had begun to worsen again. In various letters during November and December of 1954 and January of 1955, Zenobia recounts the details of the crisis that Juan Ramón was suffering. In the first she indicates the excellent influence that Reyes could exercise on her patient. "What I would give to be nearer to you and have you both near us," she says. And she continues:

J.R. raises his hands in sign of protest, as if wanting to defend himself against them, when he sees me advance with papers in my hand; but when he hears the name "Alfonso Reyes," what he raises is his head, and he exclaims: "Well, naturally, for Alfonso Reyes everything he wants." And when I insist, "Without changing or adding anything?" he says yes a little reticently and I know that he wants to tell me that now he can do nothing. So that, dear

[21] Gullón, *El último Juan Ramón*, p. 93.

Reyes, I am sorry not to be able to offer you more. (November 9, 1954)

She alludes to Juan Ramón's contribution to Reyes' *Libro jubilar* (Jubilee book), a difficult problem at that moment because she was making arrangements to transfer Juan Ramón from one hospital to another. "Lucky you," she tells Reyes, "who found amoebas and can devote yourself to destroying them and not fight with phantoms." She despaired at the impossibility of knowing what treatment to use for Juan Ramón: "I confess . . . my lack of serenity, and this afternoon," she writes, "since 'I shouldn't be with J.R. paying him long visits,' I am going to the beach with a professor of the University of California (who is here writing a book on J.R.) and his family. I do not think I could offer more good will on my part and I think I will soon end up going to the movies and reading detective stories, since I have never been given to whiskey or rum. As you can see, I am in despair" (December 5, 1954).

In the margin of one of her letters Juan Ramón wrote, almost illegibly: "With my last embrace, J. Ramón." Zenobia told Reyes: "Do not get too upset, because even though for him it is true, we all know that it is his present obsession." Reyes' answer shows his concern:

> Your letter of November 9 frightened me very much because of Juan Ramón's marginal words, in spite of the fact that you yourself told me not to let myself get too upset by them. The result is that I did not dare answer you. . . . I see now that it really is something very serious and it grieves Manuela and myself very much not to be able to be of some service to you and not even to accompany you and help you with the care that Juan Ramón requires. The fact that he shuts his eyes to the enchantments of that landscape is for me the most acute symptom, since I know to what extent he lives and breathes for his eyes. (December 9, 1954)

When the situation improved slightly, Zenobia found new reasons for optimism. Juan Ramón was again to begin a slow and never complete convalescence:

> These lines are only to send you the warmest and happiest em-

brace because I can tell you that, since yesterday, our dear Juan Ramón will be saved. . . . Yesterday I saw him with his own hand (although still held up by his nurse) calmly drink two lovely sips of punch and during half an hour talk to me about matters of arrangements which the doctor had recommended as the most opportune for our conversations—both of us equally happy with the profound emotion and with the superficial reaction to dissimulate the true feelings. . . . Finally, dear friends, that "last embrace" almost came true. I am so thankful to God for this change that it seems to me that all life and all the world have changed. (January 2, 1955)

The next month Juan Ramón returned home, and this moment is also depicted by Zenobia with the precise detail that permits us to relive the scene: when she left the hospital one evening, she said, "J.R. came running out after me and got into the car, assuring me, 'I am not going to stay here.' Although we have some hectic moments and the veterans have infected J.R. with some unaccustomed epithets in his exacting vocabulary, from day to day (it has been five) he is reaffirming himself in his usual customs, behavior, interest, etc. and I am the happiest person in the world. . . . May everything prosper as much for you as it does for us" (February 19, 1955).

A few months later Zenobia sent a short essay entitled "¿Fealdad?" (Ugliness?) as Juan Ramón's contribution to Reyes' *Libro jubilar*, even though, as she recounts, Juan Ramón had said: "This is no good for Reyes because it was not written for him!" She continued:

It occurs to me that if he does not get better enough to write what he would like, this could be published with a note to clarify the situation. Nevertheless, I must say that this week he has complained bitterly to me that a poem was circling through his mind all one morning without his being able to make it concrete. For me this was the best of news—after 8 months! The next day I saw, also for the first time in 8 months, how he was making that characteristic unconscious gesture of writing with his index finger, on the table, while he was eating lunch. For him, it would be a terrible displeasure to see the homage to you appear without his signature, and so, without telling him anything, I am sending you everything. (May 17, 1955)

Reyes immediately replied: "I assure you that Juan Ramón's name alone is for me, in every place and in every moment, an emotion, a caress, a superior stimulus. That page is perfect" (May 19, 1955). However, Juan Ramón discovered the transaction and Zenobia wrote back:

> How can I reward you for all you do without even knowing it? A moment ago the mail arrived and I gave it to J.R. without even opening it. As I was closing the car, J.R. already had your letter open and he said to me: "Did you send that to Alfonso Reyes?" He was not at all angry, because he understood my good intentions, but he told me: "That was very little, very modest for a man like him." And afterwards: "I left a recent unpublished poem, would you look for it for me? Then he dictated the first lines and the title and I set out to look for it, although I did not expect to find it at once. I brought two boxes of his latest work and asked him to help by telling me when I was getting near. He asked me for the second box and he settled himself to look for it calmly. When I returned he read me a lovely unpublished poem to me, but he had not found the one that began: "The tranquil light will be alone now" and that was entitled "Sleepless gold in the hollow of him who sleeps." I was quite disconsolate at not having found it but J.R. told me: "Do you know that I have a lot unpublished? I am going to dictate something else to you." And he dictated to me from memory that which follows:

From this broken stone

From this broken stone which the centuries have lapped against,
remembering, forgetting I watch the river pass,
I watch the cloud go by, I watch the nest in flight.
                                         (To Alfonso) (May 24, 1955)

Reyes' *Libro jubilar* (1956) appeared with the two texts from Juan Ramón.

One of the factors in Juan Ramón's recovery was his interest in the Sala Zenobia–Juan Ramón in the university library. The Sala, used by students of Spanish literature and of Juan Ramón's work, is his memorial in Puerto Rico. Zenobia described its initiation to Reyes:

> For three days now I have had the illusion that Juan Ramón would accompany me to the library in the mornings. I do not know if I told you that J.R. had given his private library to the university of P.R., grateful to it in the persons of Jaime Benítez and Federico de Onís. The library gave me provisionally an enchanting room on the ground floor, almost next to the entrance for cars, so that J.R. has to make almost no effort to transfer himself from our little Chevrolet to the room. Since the packers in Maryland sent everything and all mixed up, my job has consisted principally, right now, in separating what is usable for the library from the private papers and in giving the room a familiar aspect thanks to the contributions (from home) of J.R., who was very interested "in absentia." After three weeks the director of the library visited me and was so pleased with my provisional efforts that he gave us the room as a study for J.R. while he lives and as a remembrance of him afterwards. Moreover, he told me to furnish it completely to my taste at the library's expense and, about a month after the efforts had begun, J.R. let himself be convinced, since I told him that I had all the permanent future of his room at a standstill because I did not have his advice for decisions. . . . J.R. left so highly pleased with the modest achievements (you already know that he likes good but simple things) that he assured us it was too good for him. The fact is that in that first visit everything was decided and now for three days he has come every morning. . . . The good part is that without realizing it he is again becoming a part of his literary and university atmosphere (this last an American innovation.) It seems to me that, thanks to not being lost in the North American atmosphere, this setback, in spite of his being older, is going to be shorter than the previous one. . . . Would that we did not have our dear ones so scattered all over the world and some of them what J.R. considers inaccessible because of the altitude or because one has to reach them by plane. (May 6, 1955)

The Sala has the aspect of the Jiménez home in Madrid, thanks to their gifts of paintings and furniture, photographs and memorabilia. Zenobia wrote Reyes after an exhibit there: "The show-cases installed provisionally are on their way to remaining there permanently with the books dedicated with affectionate inscriptions to J.R., starting with Rubén Darío and Rodó and going all the way to a Mexican gentleman of a generation somewhat younger than J.R. whose name is Alfonso Reyes and whose photograph, which we love, is curling because there was no time to put it in a frame and we do not want to take it away even for one day as long as the visits continue" (December 3, 1955).

By the end of the year, in spite of his improvement, Juan Ramón was still far from total recuperation, and Zenobia began to plan a trip to Spain, thinking that, just as when they went to Puerto Rico, he needed a change. Her letters are full of never-to-be-carried-out plans that left Juan Ramón completely indifferent because he expected to die from one day to the next.

Zenobia's last two letters deal principally with her own health, in rapid decline from cancer, and with her worry about what would happen to Juan Ramón if she should die. Always with the courage to talk about herself with serenity, she wrote on the fifteenth of April, 1956:

> Don't think that we have forgotten you, on the contrary. What happens is that after an impossible winter in which I had all kinds of foolish things, from calculi to an attack of amnesia provoked by the notice of the death of my sister-in-law in the paper before knowing it personally, I am finally right in the middle of a new struggle through x-rays. This is the most inopportune thing in the world precisely when I was completing J.R.'s last selected poems from 1918 to the present. Everything has been interrupted. It seems that the thing is being conquered this time too but I have become nothing but an ember and since I can scarcely sit I spend my life in a horizontal position. More than three weeks ago I had to suspend my work in the library, and J.R., without me, nothing! Let us hope that when the 25 sessions of x-rays that remain are over, I have not turned into a spot of grease.

She is speaking about the *Tercera antología poética*, which with the help of Eugenio Florit was published in 1957. Her sickness did not worry her primarily for herself but for the effect that it would have on Juan Ramón and on his work. In August she writes again, informing them of the course of her illness, and saying: "Who could ever have told me that the struggle not to leave him alone would be so difficult?" She says that she has decided on a radical operation and she tells of making a nephew of Juan Ramón her executor "because in this immense solitude how is J.R. going to resist without the help of his family (I do not refer to money)?" There is no letter that shows better her extraordinary valor in the face of suffering.

These are her last lines to the Reyeses. She died in October after her operation and but a few days after they learned that Juan Ramón had received the Nobel Prize. That same year Reyes wrote the following words to be published in the number dedicated to Juan Ramón in the magazine *La Torre* of the University of Puerto Rico:

I love and admire profoundly the great poet Juan Ramón Jimé-nez and have had occasion to manifest it in my books. We have lived together and collaborated a great deal. In my days in Madrid, he occupied for some time an apartment near my house and we saw each other almost daily. Zenobia, his wife and his fairy god-mother, has also been our favorite friend: my wife and I had a true cult for her. In the year 1921, Juan Ramón and I founded together the magazine *Índice*, the first literary home of some young men, now teachers. When, in 1952, the National University of Mexico conferred upon him the degree of Doctor Honoris Causa, I had the honor of being designated by him to receive the insignias in his name, and he sent an "Acción de gracias," in verse, in which he characterized me in terms of generous sympathy, as well as his other Mexican friends. . . . The page that Juan Ramón has written about me in one of his books is one of my most valued treasures. Our friendship has been a crystal; better yet: an un-flawed diamond. He himself can say if I am not one of his closest friends.

No one can dispute him the place he occupies, next to the most exalted, in Spanish poetry and in universal poetry. I would like, now more than ever, to be at his side to accompany him on the rest of his journey. And let it be a long one.[22]

He touched briefly on the highlights of their friendship in this short but moving passage. Their long correspondence terminated with two letters exchanged in September and October of 1957:

My dear Juan Ramón:
I learned through your gracious rector of your happy recovery and I received photos with your new . . . beard, similar to the one I now have. I have just suffered a profound and bloody operation. I am conquering the painful road of recuperation. I can scarcely dictate these lines, in the name of my Manuela and my Alfonsito also, to tell you once again that you always live in our admiration, our mind, our memory, and our affection.

Your brother,
Alfonso Reyes

My dear Alfonso:
Thank you for your good letter and for the visit of Doctor Chávez.
I am not as you imagine and I am very happy that you are as you say. Unfortunately I can scarcely write, even dictating.
I hope that you completely recuperate and that you are very happy.

Your brother,
Juan Ramón

These letters mark the end of a friendship begun in Madrid forty years before. It would not occur to many that there was such a broad base of mutual comprehension between two men of such distinct temperaments, but the correspondence shows that they were united by an identical way of seeing life and living it in literature. Their most significant affinity was perhaps that in each their literary career took the form of an all-encompassing and lifelong mission. They shared that profound joy in work well done. (*El trabajo gustoso* [Pleasurable work] is the title of one of Jiménez' books.)

22 Reyes, "Carta de Alfonso Reyes," *La Torre* 5, no. 19–20 (1957): 17–18.

In social as well as in aesthetic theory they found a common ground. Each made an impassioned plea for the recognition of the universal identity of man. Both felt strongly that the duty of intelligence was to propagate culture, not to monopolize it. There are, of course, traces here in both writers of the influence of Giner de los Ríos. Both believed in the role of the educated minority as a prime motivating force behind social progress. It is natural that Reyes as a diplomat and as one intensely interested in the future of Latin America would have a fully developed and expressed social and political consciousness, but it is not, I think, so often realized that Juan Ramón Jiménez, in spite of the more pronounced aesthetic orientation of his thought, was actively concerned with contemporary world problems—or that his vision of the future corresponded closely to that of Reyes.

Although with distinct goals, both sought perfection, the one in an ideal of pure beauty and truth, the other in the vision of a more just and happy world, united by the spiritual communication between men. They both sought to achieve it through the written word, in a perfect union of idea and form. Each had arrived gradually at the conclusion that their poetics and their metaphysics were one and the same, as can be seen in the title "Estética y ética estética" (Aesthetics and aesthetic ethics) given by Juan Ramón to his collection of aphorisms, and in the sentence by Reyes: "I am faithful to an ideal both aesthetic and ethic, made of goodness and beauty" (IV, 451).

Ramón Gómez de la Serna

(1888–1963)

TYPICAL OF THE INTER-WAR PERIOD in Spain as in the rest of Europe was the proliferation of vanguardist "isms," and, in Spain, the most fecund and original of these was "ramonismo," as it was baptized by its creator and only practitioner, Ramón Gómez de la Serna, or, as he preferred to be called, simply Ramón. What was "ramonismo"? The ever-lucid Ortega y Gasset was the first in Spain to offer a general theory about the vanguardist tendencies, which he described as "the dehumanization of art":

> In order to satisfy the desire for dehumanization it is not, then, necessary to alter the primary forms of things. It is enough to invert the hierarchy and to make an art in which there appear in the foreground, standing forth with a monumental air, the minimal happenings of life.

This is the latent nexus that unites the modes of the new art that appear to be the most distant. . . . The best examples of how by carrying realism to its extremes one surpasses it—by just paying attention, magnifying glass in hand, to the microscopic in life—are Proust, Ramón Gómez de la Serna, Joyce.[1]

This magnifying, then, of the microscopic is the basic tenet of "ramonismo." And its tool is the literary form invented by Gómez de la Serna, the "greguería." He wrote thousands upon thousands of them, either as separate entities, or incorporated into his novels, essays, plays, and biographies. Every critic of Gómez de la Serna's work has proffered his definition of the "greguería." Ramón himself said they were phrases that tried to capture "what beings cry out confusedly from their unconsciousness, what things cry out."[2] The "greguería" can be completely trivial: "There are tomatoes which are boxing gloves ready to punch." "Sunflowers are the pocket mirrors of the sun." Or it can deal with ideas: "The writer wants to write his lie and writes his truth." "We should not be accomplices, even of ourselves." The variety is infinite. They are brief, intuitive, metaphoric phrases, poetic in that they give an original insight into reality. Pedro Salinas points out that this genre invented by Ramón is an example "of that need, which has existed for many years in the modern spirit and modern art, for the existence, side by side, of antithetical human attitudes, of jest and profundity, of capers and sorrow."[3]

For Ramón is a humorist. His humor arises from his disconformity with his surroundings and is expressed in the astounding inventiveness and unconventionality of his viewpoint. "As Ramón sees and defines it, humor is the perception by the intellect of the grim absurdities of life." This is the analysis of Rodolfo Cardona, an expert on Ramón's work, who also points out that this type of humor with its base of irony and paradox came to be an essential ingredient of European surrealist and existentialist writings.[4] It is

---

[1] José Ortega y Gasset, *La deshumanización del arte*, p. 53.
[2] Ramón Gómez de la Serna, *Total de greguerías*, p. *xxiii*.
[3] Quoted in R. Gómez de la Serna, *Automoribundia*, p. 787.
[4] Rodolfo Cardona, *Ramón. A study of Ramón Gómez de la Serna and His Works*, pp. 69, 92.

deeply rooted in the Spanish tradition of Quevedo and Goya as well. Ramón's humor, then, relates to the irrationalist trends of modern European art in general, and is at the same time intensely Spanish.

Ramón creates the image of a world without logic, without form. His works are themselves formless; they have no meaningful structure. Ramón writes: "How difficult it is to work so that everything may result a little undone! But that is how we impart the secret of living."[5] This decomposition of reality into its most minute parts prompted Valéry Larbaud to say that if there were a protective society for things, Ramón would be its first member.[6] He endowed "things" with life and personality, and it is his acute awareness of them that lies at the source of his creative talent. Cardona claims that he was the first writer to create successfully a world in which the inanimate object almost completely displaces persons and ideas.[7]

During these years, those following the First World War, it seemed as if Spain were at last going to become a part of the European cultural stream, and that the efforts of enlightened intellectuals in the eighteenth and nineteenth centuries would finally bear fruit in the twentieth, under the guidance of men such as Ortega. Ramón was proof of such a rapprochement. He was one of the prophets of the new aesthetics, a truly revolutionary writer in the context not only of Spain but of all of Western Europe, yet he never became a part of any literary movement.

On this point Ramón was very definite: "I had not wished to found anything more than my own 'ism,' " he stated. "That slavery of those who enroll under a standard would have been very valuable for me, but I only wanted the solitary talent of every individual, and I wanted everyone to prosper on his own account."[8] This viewpoint precluded his having anyone close to him stylistically in his own generation. His relationship to those whom he followed, the early *modernistas* and the so-called Generation of 98, was basically

[5] Quoted in ibid., p. 144.
[6] Guillermo de Torre, Introduction to R. Gómez de la Serna, *Antología: Cincuenta años de literatura*, p. 18.
[7] Cardona, *Ramón*, p. 114.
[8] Quoted in Gaspar Gómez de la Serna, *Ramón (Obra y vida)*, p. 108.

one of revolt. He represented the opposite of the subjective outlook, of the Unamuno who saw Spain as a personal problem, and of the romantic overtones and lilting musicality of the early Valle-Inclanesque prose. His aesthetic approach was conceptual and objective, and, as Torre said, he did not view Spain as a problem but as a spectacle.[9]

Gómez de la Serna's atomization of reality and super-evaluation of the metaphor were strong influences on the next generation of writers, the young vanguardists who published their "ultraísta" manifesto in 1919. Guillermo de Torre, who was one of those young poets, says that Ramón's "influence in those moments was as obvious as his originality was vigorous and his work abundant."[10] By the time of their manifesto, Ramón had already been in direct contact with European vanguardist groups. He had spent some of the war years in Paris in the company of Picasso and Diego Rivera and the cubists who gathered in the Café de la Rotonde. He had been present in Switzerland at the birth of the Dada movement. And he and his group of friends had planned and executed the first Cubist exhibition in Spain in late 1914, with the showing of the paintings of Diego Rivera and María Gutiérrez Blanchard—one of the first overt acts of the vanguardist invasions into Spain. He was the guiding spirit—a beacon, Torre called him—of most of what was new and revolutionary in Spanish literature in the inter-war period.

Ramón was an irrepressible creative force, a "unipersonal" generation, a man always outside of the norm. No one has surpassed Reyes' metaphoric definition of this literary phenomenon: "If Spanish literature were (and it is not improbable) pine wood; if the knots in the pine were the natural effort to concentrate the fiber and transform it into pure ebony; if the general taste, on the other hand, were in reference to this literature as the saw is to the wood, then Gómez de la Serna would be one of those rebellious knots that refuse to run along the grain of the pine, making the artisan's saw break its teeth and screech with fury" (IV, 185).

[9] Torre, Introduction to R. Gómez de la Serna, *Antología*, p. 17.
[10] Torre, *La aventura estética de nuestra edad*, p. 113.

Ramón was an indomitable individualist who battled with language and with convention.

Both of these "battles," pursued with great success, are evident in his letters to Reyes. His penchant for flamboyant stationery was a colorful flaunting of convention. One finds in don Alfonso's files a letter in the form of an oversized pink rose decorated with sequins and bearing the motto "My Love," which Ramón describes as "ineffable." Competing with it for one's attention is a paper of a delicate blue shade, with a matching envelope sealed with a gold and silver butterfly. Shiny yellow paper is covered with writing in red ink, and suddenly staring up at one from a visiting card is a sketch of Ramón's head.

The first letter of the correspondence, undated as are most of his letters, but probably written in early 1915, is characteristic of his style of writing:

> Dear don Alfonso Reyes:
>
> (I owe to your name this solemnity) why don't you come to Pombo? Your smile, your delicate smile, has not been seen since you disappeared, no one has another the same or similar—It is a necessity after having heard it.
>
> On the 16th we are holding one of those banquets in Pombo. Do you want to attend? The 17th or 19th I leave for Paris and Florence. Do you want something from there?

Pombo is the subject of almost all of the early letters, "the Sacred Crypt of Pombo," inseparable now in literary history from Ramón himself, for it is there he formed his *tertulia*. He often used, in writing to Reyes, stationery bearing the letterhead of the "Sagrada Cripta de Pombo," adorned with a sketch in bright red of the gas lamp that lit the famous café, don Alfonso's and Ramón's most frequent meeting place.

"El Antiguo Café y Botillería de Pombo" represents the spirit of that epoch when, as Reyes has said, "literature flowed through the streets and the terraces of the café, and a good part of that which is called 'valuations' must have been lost amidst the chatting and the amenities of the *tertulia*" (VI, 407). Here, every Saturday night, Ramón presided over what was perhaps the most important *tertulia* of twentieth-century Spain, the one whose nature was most purely literary and artistic. What happened and what was said at Pombo influenced a broad spectrum of the cultural scene in the capital. It was, as Ortega observed, the only myth that had survived in the sordid reality of modern Spain, one that carried with it "a cheerful resonance and a chromatic splendor of farce."[11] In Pombo, Ramón communicated his ideas, maintained contact with his friends, and kept the *tertulia* in a constant state of effervescence with the verbal electricity of his speech.

Gómez de la Serna founded his *tertulia* in Pombo in the beginning of 1915, so that the recently arrived Reyes was one of the first *tertulianos*. He chose the locale because of the contrast its air of bourgeois solidity offered to the revolutionary theories of the young writers who were to congregate there and plan "subversive" literary movements. They constituted a defiant challenge to middle-class apathy. Waldo Frank, a perceptive visitor to Spain in the 1920's, has written, in his book *Virgin Spain*, his impression of the Spanish *tertulia*. It applies perfectly to Pombo's. He speaks first of the *tertulias* of the bureaucrats and continues: "But, beside them, at other tables, in the tertulias of other cafes, are other men who form the antiphony of their neighbors. These are the intellectuals. . . . They are the inevitable response—the stir against and within the sleep of Spain. They are the germs of dissolution. The burocrats hold Spain together—in sleep. The intellectuals plot and dream to burst Spain asunder—in a new waking."[12]

"You have wanted to infect with fantasy the very heart of the bourgeois,"[13] Ortega told the *pombianos*. And Reyes noted and delighted in the conspiratorial atmosphere: "The proclamations of Pombo always talk of the Iscariots, of the unfaithful, and the apostles: they recall the persecutory mania of the prophets. What tragedy is hidden in Pombo? Who has betrayed them?" (IV, 187) But Pombo was an eminently respectable café situated near the

---

[11] J. Ortega y Gasset, *Obras completas*, VI, 227.
[12] Waldo Frank, *Virgin Spain*, p. 254.
[13] J. Ortega y Gasset, *Obras completas*, VI, 227.

beginning of Carretas Street, an exceedingly popular central street that so enveloped Pombo in the nondescript bustle of everyday traffic as to render it all but invisible in the daylight hours. It was then frequented by small businessmen, old ladies, and discreet couples. "At night it is illuminated," said Reyes, "—a relic of olden times—with a deteriorated and somewhat dirty luxury of congealed mirrors, little marble tables, and benches of red velvet against the wall" (IV, 185). The setting seemed far from propitious for an avant-garde gathering, but Gómez de la Serna's genius imbued those decaying and undistinguished relics of another age with a completely unsuspected personality, and the middle-class café became "our fervent crypt."

Ramón would arrive at Pombo in the evening "firm and decided, plump, with his 'majo' sideburns and his wide face, his ruddy cheeks . . . and a wave of hair fallen over the right side of his forehead, and his big pipe."[14] One could write to him at Pombo, Reyes recounted, and send Christmas gifts to him there. Ramón distributed his books from Pombo. In 1918, for instance, he wrote Reyes: "Could you come on Saturday to Pombo so that I can give you the copy that belongs to you of the terrible book *Pombo*? It is so much of a ritual to give out that book right there that I would be upset not to see you." This first volume of *Pombo* is now in don Alfonso's library with the inscription: "To Alfonso Reyes for all the reasons that I give in the book and for many more." For *Pombo* contained yet another portrait of Reyes by one of his Spanish friends. Ramón wrote:

> Reyes has a placid and mature smile for everything. He possesses the secret of atmospheres, which is superior to the secret of styles and which is something that gives an inimitable subtlety. It always seems that his hand, as it gestures, depicts, with forefinger and thumb, Solomon's ring, the ring of serenity and persuasion. . . .
> Optimistic and healthy, with the quality of an antidote against venom, even far away from his country and trampled upon by many bloody accidents of fate, Reyes believes, for example, in things, and practices upon them an incantation of a sort of magic

[14] E. Correa Calderón, "Ramón en el recuerdo," *Insula* 18, no. 196 (1963): 3.

mysticism. Thus he told me one day, when I asked him for a letter opener to cut open a book: "I have created it for you," and he brought it out as if in fact he had just created it. That faith which Reyes has in certain unexpected faculties of the soul is worth its weight in gold.[15]

His impression of Reyes is surprisingly similar to that written by Juan Ramón Jiménez, who was also under the spell of the soothing quality of Reyes' presence and smile. Juan Ramón did not venture, though, into the realm of the occult, and it is precisely here that one sees what drew Ramón to Reyes. He felt that Reyes also had a mysterious affinity for and an understanding of things, and could therefore endow commonplace reality with a magical radiance. If he chose, Reyes could view the world around him with the same eyes as Ramón.

Pombo was also an organizing center for banquets, arranged by the commission "R.G. de la Serna, Ramón G. de la S., Ramón Gómez de la S., etc." Azorín, Ortega, and Díez-Canedo were so honored. At Canedo's banquet, Ramón recounted, "Alfonso Reyes, red like a cardinal, after an opulent dinner, spoke a few warm and emotional words in honor of Canedo, since all the concurrence asked it of him."[16] That same year Ramón offered to give a banquet in Reyes' honor. Don Alfonso refused and, consequently, was one of those censured in Ramón's invitation to one of the most successful of the Pombian banquets, that offered to don Nobody:

My dear friend: The last banquet of those that are to be given this year in the Sacred Crypt of Pombo will be dedicated to don Nobody.

Don Nobody, as his very name indicates, is no one; but not for this should it be thought that he is nothing. Let us put between exclamation points our opinion and we will see what don Nobody is worth: Don Nobody is not a nobody!

Among all those kinds of banquets that I have invented and solemnized: the banquet for Everyone, in alphabetical order; the banquet with a substitute for the banqueted one; the banquet to

---

15 R. Gómez de la Serna, *Pombo*, no page number.
16 R. Gómez de la Serna, *La Sagrada Cripta de Pombo*, p. 364.

myself, by a Commission consisting of myself; the banquet to the
illustrious dead man on the day of his centenary—unforgettable
banquet to Figaro!—the banquet to don Nobody was lacking and
I have been anxious for a long time to give a banquet against
Someone. . . .

A white cloth will occupy the place of don Nobody and we will
not even put a place setting, to better show how empty of solemnity
that space will be. . . .

We have another advantage in the organizing of this banquet,
and it is that don Nobody cannot refuse, moreover, this modest
dinner that we dedicate to him with such a good heart, sparing
ourselves thus that bitterness which our good and admired friends
sometimes leave in us when they sometimes refuse to accept the
sincere banquet that we offer them.

Ramón also issued various types of proclamations from Pombo
for which he requested his friends' collaboration. He wrote Reyes,
probably in 1915: "You, so prudent, so sensible, and such a friend
of the nuance: Can you write me five or six lines to publish alongside a proclamation which I am going to use right away as an
invitation to a banquet in Pombo? Something that tells of your
attitude when you half close your eye, seeing the perspectives,
something that in the mosaic will be your originality." And again,
in 1918: "I am going to put out a little proclamation and for it I
would like some lines of yours similar to those that are printed in
'Estampas de Madrid.' Do you have something unpublished, strong
and bold, of the same type as those women with rough voices? I
would like it short and sonorous." He refers to one of the best
pieces in *Cartones de Madrid*, "The Hoarse Women," in which
Reyes describes the water carriers of Madrid. Reyes acceded to his
request this time and sent him a passage entitled "Against the
Static Museum," a short, provocative piece sure to please Ramón
with its revolutionary attitude and its bizarre and thought-provok-
ing hypothesis, that of a museum which required the complete involvement of the spectator.

As Reyes' interests and activities expanded, his visits to Pombo
became more rare. Ramón was constantly reproaching him for

this desertion. Written on one of the visiting cards with a sketch of his own head in the center was:

> With the desire that if you desire it it should not rest with me not having invited you among the first of the first to our banquet of Pombo, thus I indicate to you that it is going to take place.
>
> It is only the notice I owe you if your spirit is in the mood to join with friends, in the religious peace of Pombo. (n.d.)

"But do not abandon us in Pombo," he wrote in 1920. "Come once in a while. Do not let it be only the obligatory things which oblige us, since for every official act committed, some extraofficial acts compensate for it and purify it." And in 1922 he wrote: "What is it that separates you from us? Why have you never come back since quite a while ago?" He did not, at least in the beginning, really resent Reyes' unfaithfulness, as one can see from the humor of his repeated rebukes: "Every time farther away from Pombo?" he asked. "I do not believe it. I tell your friends that you dedicate to Pombo every Saturday the prayer which you say kneeling on your bed before going to sleep" (n.d.).

In spite of all the accusations of desertion, Reyes was not banished from the second volume of *Pombo*, published in 1924. It even featured two pictures of Reyes, which Ramón had requested from him several times in his letters. Reyes commented upon this humorously in a book of reminiscences: "I have saved portraits of myself at three and six months. It seems to me that those are my true portraits and that the rest is decadence. I tend to offer them to newspapers when they request my effigy for their interviews, and I left one in the hands of Ramón Gómez de la Serna (along with another, sinner that I am, in a diplomatic uniform, with dress hat and rapier) for his Album of the Sacred Crypt of Pombo."[17]

Perhaps Reyes' baby picture was put in the album, but it is rather in the second edition of the book that we find the diplomatic portrait, accompanying a quite lengthy description of Reyes. Ramón had taken great pains with this, and he mentions it in no less than five letters to Reyes, saying, in the first one: "I have the

[17] Reyes, *Albores. Segundo libro de recuerdos*, p. 42.

silhouette begun, but the responsibility of each word overwhelms me and makes me go very slowly" (1920). Finally, in 1924, he wrote Reyes: "Saturday come to Pombo. The volume of Pombo that has your silhouette will be distributed without fail." The silhouette begins with a description of Reyes' way of life and appearance:

> He sat at the far side of an editor's desk, invented ingenious and worthy things to do to earn money, and lived in a faraway house, in a room that was cheerful but narrow like a closet, although from the windows, which looked out upon landscape in construction, Reyes gathered in, ideally, with his eyes, what was lacking to amplify his house. . . .
>
> Reyes, with his pear-like head and the smile in his eyes, always heard everything being said everywhere and knew how to give the wise answer, and even when he had no alternative but to be malevolent he was kind.
>
> How well he saw Madrid! He saw it as one sees on a winter day through recently washed windows when one is curled up at the very edge of the balcony.

His admiration was tinged, though, with spitefulness. Reyes is, he said, "like those little boys who want to seem much cleverer than they are. He already is clever enough, but he wants to be more so. . . . Alfonso Reyes is overly subtle. He is afraid not to be the first in the class. . . ." And he concludes: "Now, having become the minister of his country, he has forgotten us a little from the depths of his large official automobile."[18] Ramón must not have considered these comments too damaging, for he was anxious for Reyes to see the silhouette. The tone is most probably due to Ramón's chagrin when Reyes was no longer able to find the time for Pombo.

Ramón's *tertulia* seemed destined to last forever, for though Ramón would at times annouce its close, he invariably returned and opened it again. But Pombo did come to an end. Gómez de la Serna saw it approaching when he wrote Reyes in 1932:

> Pombo continues as on that night in which you left it but we

[18] R. Gómez de la Serna, *La Sagrada Cripta*, pp. 439–440.

no longer have words with which to give ourselves encouragement in the pure literary continuity. I give my silent perseverance and with difficulty I maintain a smiling face.

We prepare ourselves every day to understand better, not to lose the meaning of our ancient wake, but everything is lacking in the intellectual life of today.

His disillusionment did not destroy his faith in his friends, however. "I already know that you and I will be the last to weaken and fall and we will maintain the dialogue across the waves until the last palm tree dies," he continued in the same letter, clinging pathetically to hopes based more on the past than on the future. The past could not be recaptured. First Pombo itself—the site is now a luggage store—and then the man who made it famous disappeared, adding the note of finality to an epoch and an intellectual atmosphere that had long since been destroyed.

We can never know exactly what passed between Ramón and don Alfonso during the many nights of *tertulia*, but the sparks that passed between them can be readily imagined from a reading of their correspondence. Not only is the imagery a constant surprise and delight in these letters, but the correspondence shows a great deal of intimacy between the two men, who were, after all, but a year apart in age. The letter that don Alfonso wrote on his recovery from typhoid fever in 1916 and Ramón's response to it show clearly the two qualities they had in common: a love of the fantastic and an exceptional sense of humor.

Alfonso Reyes to Ramón Gómez de la Serna: greetings. Where had we left off? We left off in the moment in which you said to yourself: "It is useless; he does not want to come, let's leave him in peace. One more who flees: one less."

But don't you believe in typhoid fever? . . . Although I have thought of you, I have preferred not to give you notice of my life during my convalescence; I don't like to go out in the streets without having shaved, nor to have to go along saying why I have gotten thin. —Yesterday, accidentally, a brother of mine who is embarking for America, with the secret desire to discover some mine, started to pack his suitcase in my presence and let fall, by chance, a certain pocket novel. And I remembered, seeing the cover, our conversations about chessboards, in that fugitive night at Pombo which did not want to be—in spite of your bad habits— a Saturday night. I looked at myself in the mirror, and since I verified that I have recovered my figure, I decided to announce my return. I return to you because we owe it to our friendship. I cannot think that you—who look for the scorch of fire in every contact—are resolved to let me slip along the surface of your friendship without having left—I no longer say a weak scratch—even the complacent saliva of a snail. It is necessary that we "suffer" each other a little, before the inescapable separation. (It is not that I propose to go and die for my country, no. It is not that imperative duties call me elsewhere. It is that to remain has not been my destiny. And since I am now getting settled, I expect from one moment to the next the thunderbolt that will throw me up in the air again. My life is a series of absurd experiences; I have never needed vices. Even the most natural objects have always become excessively refined on my approach. I must have some mission that I have forgotten.)

And I thought: Diego Rivera—that traitor who, deep down, cannot tolerate me because he is lazy and I, a good "snob," diligent —is to blame for your imagining that I am a type of Doctor of Philosophy and Letters. It would not matter to me in another; but in you it almost irritates me. Perhaps my last desertion finally convinced you that your suspicions and hopes were unfounded, and that—unpardonably—there was not hidden behind me, as you would have wished, any other person. Less "improbable" than your doctor, you did not dare to make the unexpected incision in my thigh, to see if thus you could get out my soul. I am very happy with my mask, but I do not resign myself to the failure of our relations: let it be said for the dignity of both of us.

I am going to remind you of an old story, a story by Stevenson— the most penetrating he has written, profound, theologically absolute: around it a thousand philosophies could be constructed: but my admirable, my unforgettable Stevenson (whose traces I have followed step by step in the little town of Bourron, near Fontainebleau, where he used to spend the summer) has had the bravado, the brazenness, to recount it as a simple fact, without digressions or symbolic frivolity, with the loyal nudity of the material and without the muddied fog of symbolism: "The Strange Case of Doctor Jekyll and Mr. Hyde." Do you remember it? In me there is a Jekyll who does philology and a Hyde who writes with vari-colored ink; another who admires both of them, one who laughs at all of them together, and another—finally?—who justifies all of them and afterwards tranquilly goes to sleep. —No, let us not talk of hypocrisy: ready-made names for things prevent under-standing and evaluating them. It has nothing to do with that, but with something like a case of double or multiple fecundation. One body has taken charge of several souls that were born at the same time. The body is a good administrator, and, for weeks on end—at times for years—it alternates its service. It is for some-thing that I have not been able to be a tall man, even though I felt the impetus to project myself some centimeters higher: because I am bent over with the weight of the invisible that I carry: imag-ine that I am like Aeneas on escaping from Troy, with his father, his wife, and his son on his shoulders. Don't pay any attention, then, to the fact that etc. etc. etc. . . .

Supposing all that came before, do you want to give yourself the trouble to tell me when, where, and how we can lose an afternoon taking a stroll? Or, if you are not seduced by my electric fondness for movement and action, we could sit down wherever you liked. . . .

Receive an embrace (in my country, as you have written some-where with approval, men embrace each other on greeting) from your inconstant friends

AA.RR. (May 18, 1916)

Reyes tries in this letter, with considerable success, to prove to Ramón that he also has a bizarre side to his personality that should appeal to the baroque affinities of his friend. He was aware that it was this facet of his personality that united him with Ramón. For though the predominant note here is, of course, a humorous one, this does not exclude the conjecture that don Alfonso felt there was some underlying truth in his self-analysis. Juan Ramón Jiménez had coincided with this self-evaluation when he talked of Reyes' seven personalities. "the oblique, the round, the straight, the pointed, the squared, the horizontal, the vertical."[19] And Reyes returned at other times in his writing to this manipulation of the multiple personality of AA. RR.

Ramón's answer from Segovia was in his usual, very personal style:

> Dear friend Reyes: You saw in me that great attention which you deserved from me and which was the fruit, insistent, not at all punctilious, and you needed to write me that letter that you carried in your wallet; doesn't it seem to you that that is slight loyalty? I am sufficient unto myself and satisfy myself. Myself, I needed that letter, I would have needed it always, all my life, and in that far-off province to which we are definitively exiled I would have sometimes thought along the poplar walk, "Oh, that Reyes, that Reyes owed me something, he owed me something! That Reyes, so different from the masses and from the kings!"
>
> Sometimes one meets true, authentic Honorées de Balzacs, Di[c]kens[es] with much more genius, Anatoles Frances with an identical and valuable smile, Gourmonts even corrected and augmented. Why should we not be as categorical with our friendships as we are with those men whose value we adjust—or which publicity shamefully adjusts for us—when generally they are irremediably strangers to us, they are our enemies, our disdainers, those who keep us atrociously forgotten? I want to act with great decision in my life. You, friend Reyes, whether you move away from me or come toward me, are one of those men who have an indubitable and prime worth although publicity does not accompany you enough. I have kept you present during all your absence and I will keep you present during all your presence. . . .
>
> Next Saturday at ten forty-five I will be in Pombo, there we will see each other, and if it is [illegible word] we will arrange to get together some other day in the week.
>
> My stay in this stony Segovia has made me postpone the time of our meetings. (n.d.)

To Ramón, don Alfonso is at various moments in the correspond-

---

[19] Juan Ramón Jiménez, *Españoles de tres mundos*, p. 181.

ence "the jester" and "dear and admired and too ironic Alfonso."
Gómez de la Serna had found a kindred soul and felt free to let his
fantasy rove unhindered throughout his letters. A note he sent to
Pío, the porter at the Mexican Legation, served as a pretext for
fabricating the story that this was the "old servant Pío, who saw
you born and who took you through the public gardens in Mexico.
(With impunity, he could take you again now because you have
known how to conserve that which only you and I have conserved:
a complete state of infancy)" (n.d.). The latter part of this note is
indeed true, for both of them took a childlike delight in the simple
incongruities of everyday life and the small jokes ignored or unap-
preciated by more "serious" people. Ramón gleefully wrote a letter
in which he told Reyes that he owed him ten words of gratitude
and preceded to list them: "one, two, three," et cetera. Another
time he claimed Mexican blood because of the existence of a rich
and mysterious relative by the name of Cienfuegos, in search of
whom he was planning an imaginary voyage to America.

His letters reveal the attention he gave to the insignificant and
the minute: "In my room one hears only the scratching of the
pen and the terrible ripping noise of the sheets from my pad as they
are torn from the precise place of their pinpoint holes" (October
7, 1919). Such working conditions might not always be the case,
however, for Reyes wrote years later, tongue in cheek, that Gómez
de la Serna turned on the radio for inspiration, " and made use of
the objective precipitations of the commercials" (XIV, 299).
Ramón's letters are also full of expressions that recall his "greguerías": "September, the ruby-colored month, the most like a precious
stone in our annual life" (n.d.). Referring to his habit of writing
without putting any accents on the words, he said: "I do not write
more today because I am afraid that I may twist the accents that
none of my words have" (n.d.). Particularly characteristic, not
only of his style of writing, but of his way of life, are the following
phrases with which he had again tried to convince don Alfonso to
come to Pombo: "One has to see at least once a week the night of
the streets. The beds, the towns, the consolation of the houses,
everything in them takes on a greater importance and on the other

nights when one does not go out one sleeps upon the model of the night" (n.d.).

His love of the night—especially of walking the streets at night —is one of the reasons why Reyes saw Ramón as the sublimation of the *golfo madrileño*: "Child of your people, intellectual *golfo* of the capital city: I see you sneak out beneath the suspicious cap of your irony, jumping along the 'Carolus' of the paved street, with your writing knife in your hand. Only you know where the heart of Madrid is bleeding, drop by drop" (IV, 191). The *golfo* is the lazy but quick-witted vagabond of the streets. Gómez de la Serna's bohemianism, his sardonic wit, and his unaffected generosity fit well with this description.

In his much praised analysis of Ramón, Reyes further stated:

Madrileños are called cats. He is this in many ways . . . even in his love for his corner—a love always compatible with the nocturnal prowl—and in his being so well wrapped up and voluptuously enveloped within himself and within his small and very cluttered study.

His study is famous: all kinds of "junk" furnish it, hang from its walls, climb up to the ceiling. Pictures, and hangings, chandeliers, African sculptures, large paper dolls without eyes, a museum of broken dolls, kitchen and magical objects. A tubular chimney, an orphan found in the depths of January nights, stands erect in a corner, like a bronze warrior. There is no freakish object that is not represented there, alongside of many beautiful things, so that the majesty of an Italian head contrasts with the stupidity of an odd shoe. A minute image of the Rastro, bricabrac of a very out-of-date style (the epoch of Eugène Sue) and in every way previous to the microbial theories of Pasteur.

The corner is worthy of the cat, and the cat finds in it the objectification of his soul. Even if you open the door and the window, it is a closed and intractable room. And let it be clear, in all this, that Ramón is a man of enchanting and spontaneous joviality and courtesy. But that whole atmosphere in which he lives—just like the language in which his books are written—results in an antihygienic excess of individualism. It is the point farthest from Greece, without leaving the Mediterranean. (IV, 184)

Reyes was fascinated and, at the same time, slightly repelled by the overwhelming baroqueness of Gómez de la Serna's physical and mental environment. Ensconced amid the chaotic ruins of past worlds and a fantastic conglomeration of new ones, sealed off from any intrusion from the outer, "sane" universe, Ramón was not tempted toward classical clarity.

It is not hard to find examples to show the contrast between Reyes' approach to literary creation and that of Ramón. Quoted earlier, for instance, was Reyes' description of Ramón "jumping along the 'Carolus' of the paved street." Years later Reyes carefully explained the historical origins of this metaphor as referring to a certain type of paving done in the times of Charles III, and when Ramón read it, he wrote: "Your explanation of the 'Carolus' . . . amused me because the best that that witticism of yours has is that it had no explanation" (November 9, 1942). Here is a basic difference in their character as expressed in their methods of composition. Reyes meditated upon and had explanations for what he wrote and did. Gómez de la Serna never tried to decipher or explain an artistic creation.

There are few writers as "primitive," in a certain sense, as Ramón, who in reality did nothing but say what came from within himself, what the zigzagging of his imagination suggested to him. The creative impulse in Ramón was uncontrollable and, moreover, Ramón possessed no controls. He wrote on impulse and from intuition. This explains in part why Reyes said of his work that it was "the point farthest from Greece, without leaving the Mediterranean." Reyes, on the other hand, could be described as the point nearest to Greece, outside of Greece itself.

He wrote of Ramón: "Of course, in the 'traditional' sense of the word he is not a writer: he lacks the inner structure and the cohesion. He is all instinct, understood in the good sense of the word. His incursions into culture are voluble and personal. He never explains an idea, but rather suffers it, has spasms beneath it, and leaves—from his torture—a mark on the paper" (IV, 187–188). It is only natural that in a critical analysis of Gómez de la Serna's work don Alfonso would point to the lack of cohesion, for this is what was most in conflict with his own love of clarity and order. Even those of don Alfonso's essays that have a rambling structure —and this includes the majority of them—seem extremely organized if compared with the disjointed quality of Gómez de la Serna's prose. It is, in many cases, a chain of "greguerías," that is to say, of unusual associations between normally distant objects. Ramón was as disinterested in logic as Unamuno. His is not the clarity originating in the discipline and order with which questions are presented, but the sudden brilliance of the lightning flash. For this reason the "greguería" is brief, and Ramón's style resembles a burst of sparks rather than a flame. Reyes pointed out quite correctly that Ramón could not develop a plot:

> His perfect works do not last more than seven lines. Line number eight is the critical point of disintegration. Afterwards, the machine either resists or stops.
>
> Thus conditioned, Gómez de la Serna is the master of a weapon that is like a needle, and he is capable of crucifying all the insects with it; only it cannot serve him as a chisel to carve statues. (IV, 189)

Not all in the styles of Ramón and Reyes were contrasts. Reyes' Madrid sketches were in some ways very similar to the descriptions of that city written by her most faithful chronicler, Ramón. Undoubtedly this is one of the reasons why Ramón was so enthusiastic about *Cartones de Madrid*. He wrote Reyes in 1917: "Your 'Cartones de Madrid' pleased me infinitely. As soon as I received them I went out to a café and there face to face with the consecration of the coffee, milk, and sugar they were the gospel of a good afternoon of those that are not repeated."

For the ordinary observer, for the unimaginative writer, the spectacle of Madrid was a usual one, but for Reyes, by virtue of being a stranger, and for Ramón, by virtue of his native inventiveness, objects and places had a magic significance. From coinciding attitudes of dazzlement it was logical to expect some stylistic similarity, and Reyes' abnormal state of sensitivity, which focused his attention on minute details, gave his sketches that instantaneous, sketch-like quality that brought him close to the methods and viewpoint of Ramón.

Ramón always expressed in a very personal fashion his opinion of Reyes' writings. In reference to a series of essays on Bordeaux, Ramón wrote: "Ever since I found it suddenly in Portugal of all places and among some old notes I have brought with me to work upon, I have thought to write you on this old paper from a hotel in Bordeaux of before the war. I want to thank you on this paper as if I were an old Bordelais for those impressions of Bordeaux that were so good. Congratulations" (1919).

Ramón was especially delighted with the portrait Reyes did of him: "Today on reading in print, again, your silhouette of me I feel that gratitude grows in me like the milk in the kettle that the cook has left forgotten on the lit stove. In my abandonment and in my solitude, it grows, grows" (1922?). He was equally eloquent about Reyes' work in general when he wrote him in 1927:

> My dear and magnificent Reyes:
>
> I have been wanting to write you for a long time but my recent settling in Madrid has kept me very busy. After my flights throughout the world this newly rooted wish to remain in Madrid has kept me putting out anchor until now.
>
> Your latest books have brought me the most rarified conversations from the king of kings who is Reyes. If after all he returns among us—it is necessary to be here—the hydrographic system of the Spanish word again will see the great volume of its open channel flowing in Sunday festival.
>
> But we ourselves must perform the act of throwing water into the Manzanares and setting it in motion and the growth and broadening of the verbal river has to be done in our presence if it is to be vital. . . .
>
> Pombo wishes to rejoice again at having you once more in its company.
>
> With my congratulations on your latest books, I remain your admirer from the very first moment who embraces you, Ramón.

The image of the flowing waters is one that could hardly be improved upon to conjure up an idea of the creative output of both

Reyes and Ramón. The two writers were very productive and used the hours of daylight and darkness indiscriminately in their compulsive need to put their thoughts on paper. Reyes quoted Francisco Icaza as saying of Ramón: "He is a man who says all that occurs to him, writes all that he says, publishes all that he writes, and gives away all that he publishes" (IV, 183). Ramón had had his first book printed in 1905, while still an adolescent, and it was in 1915 that *El Rastro* came out, his first book to appear under a publisher's name. He was just beginning to achieve fame at the time of Reyes' arrival in Spain. His name began to be known through his newspaper articles, and then, in 1917, he published three important books, *Greguerías*, *El circo* (The circus), and *Senos* (Breasts), and the critics began to pay attention. It seems that with almost every letter in this period Ramón announced the appearance of a new book. And, in addition to this, of course, there were his contributions in newspapers and magazines. Like Reyes at this time, he earned his living through journalistic literature.

Ramón, a creative torrent, published in all more than one hundred books, under the spell of what he called "plumiferous" frenzy, from the Spanish word for pen, *pluma*. Reyes, who described himself as suffering from "tintophilia," a disease analogous to hemophilia where not blood but ink (*tinta*) flows, does not quite keep pace with Ramón's enormous capacity for verbal invention, but nineteen volumes of his complete works have already appeared and the end is not yet in sight. Perhaps what Reyes has said to explain his "tintophilia" can also be applied to Ramón: "My writing is the same as my living. I write as part of my natural economy."[20] Salinas wrote of Ramón in the same terms: "He is the type of writer par excellence, of the man who writes, who in writing finds the normal and indispensable function of his spiritual life."[21]

A few years after Reyes left Madrid—and Pombo and Ramón—Ramón made his first trip to the New World, the fulfillment of a desire he had expressed to Reyes years earlier, saying: "I hope

[20] Reyes, *Ancorajes*, p. 19.
[21] Quoted in R. Gómez de la Serna, *Automoribundia*, p. 774.

some day to go there and to remember you with all the praise that wells up in my spirit" (1922?). Ramón passed through Río de Janeiro, where Reyes was then living, and a warm reunion between the two friends took place. On his arrival in Buenos Aires, Ramón wrote him:

Thank you again for your attentions in Río, which I was able to observe thanks to your intervention as a subtle connoisseur of every city you inhabit (many times you were my guide even in Madrid). . . .

I am going to give lectures in many provinces in Argentina and I am going to approach Chile and Montevideo with the same obligation.

This enchants me. I have found what a great amphitheater it is and how full it is of new lyricism.

I speak a lot of you and everyone here remembers you as an indispensable companion. (June 20, 1931)

And a short while later he writes: "I am now very much adapted to this atmosphere, enchanted with the American phenomenon, pleased to see arriving those waves of horizon that break on this light" (n.d.).

His enthusiasm about America was due in part to the fact that it was then that he met and married a young Argentine writer, Luisa Sofovich. It was on the couple's return to Spain that Ramón wrote to Reyes about the change which had overcome Pombo. In that same letter he says:

I live in as austere surroundings as ever and I do not know what the future will be. I would leave again for America if America would offer me again her bosom. I do not know Mexico and you already know that that is one of my visionary predilections of always. If something comfortable and good could be prepared there, I would go to see old friends and dream of landscapes. . . .

Let us have more proofs of your lesson in style, print more confidences, let us have your aspirins for our heroic penitence. (1932)

A trip to Mexico did not come about, but Ramón returned to

Buenos Aires for the Book Fair of 1933, sending Reyes a telegram
as he passed through Río and writing him on his return to Spain:

> I am glad to have gotten your pardon for having passed incog-
> nito through that picture-postcard port.
> But I have been an interminable visitor of your subtle artist's
> study for many years.
> Here the intellectual life continues in spite of all the occur-
> rences. Thus is Spain throughout the centuries.
> Our Madrid is harmony, mythic conscience, hope without ap-
> prehension. Come! (1934?)

He was not to be able to keep for long his faith and optimism in
the eternal Spain. Only two years later, in September, 1936,
shocked by the violence of the Civil War, he again crossed the
ocean and settled permanently in Buenos Aires. En route he wrote
Reyes a letter still alive with the horror of what he had seen.

> Through a miracle of luck I have been able to escape Madrid
> and I am now on my way there in the Belle Isle, which will arrive
> in Río the 10th or 11th of September.
> Then I will tell you the accidents of this life or death trip if I
> have the pleasure of seeing you as I pass through. I am going to
> establish myself in Buenos Aires and live that peace that is now
> breathed only in America, where in spite of all the predictions I
> think it is going to be very lasting.
> My sensation of life at this moment is that of someone resur-
> rected and I am going as if to see life for the first time.
> I do not think that many of our friends remain after the ruth-
> less selection made by both sides, and those who remain will float
> in life with their spirit broken because you cannot imagine—
> even having passed through the Mexican revolution—how that is.
> (September, 1936)

He arrived in America optimistic about the future. Like Ortega
he remembered with pleasure the success of his previous visits, but,
again like Ortega, he found the times and his situation to be different now. He felt alone and unsure, and his money was fast running
out. In 1937 he and Reyes exchanged letters about the possibility

of newspaper contributions in Mexico. They are depressing letters. He writes:

> This is the great city of silence and of surrounding indifference. A good place to work but a bad place to publish work.
>
> In a moment of clear light I have decided to write you this letter since I do not see you, since I do not run into you.
>
> Is there in Mexico some newspaper or magazine of good friends in which to undertake a series of contributions? The links should be remade.
>
> An easy shore to arrive at, this, it is like a shore of quicksand and one sinks as one walks.
>
> Here you find me with the table covered with paper and with a fearless pen. I would invite you to spend some time far from all the world in this corner in order to see how to foresee the future, the futures. (1937)

His next letter repeats the question about Mexican contributions and ends: "I scarcely go out, I do not see anyone for weeks and fortnights on end, I only write and wait. Wait for what? I wait." He isolated himself more and more. Torre, also a Buenos Aires resident by then, writes: "Those who knew him and heard him in Madrid, in Paris, in Naples, in Lisbon, in any of the cities where he lived, will find it difficult to imagine how distant and invisible he lives now in the great city that surrounds him."[22] He had to work even more than in Madrid to earn a living, he was tired, and the times were not favorable for his beliefs and his ideals.

Reyes was in Buenos Aires when he arrived, having been sent back again as ambassador to Argentina in July, 1936, and they did see each other at many of the embassy gatherings. So it was natural that he should turn to Reyes for help in finding newspapers in Mexico to which he might send articles. But as this was slow in coming, he began to believe it might be due to extraliterary reasons. In his next letter to Reyes, still in 1937, he comments on this:

> You already know that I am a liberal, a believer in democracy,

---

[22] Torre, Introduction to R. Gómez de la Serna, *Antología*, p. 31.

but an enemy of communism and of permanent violence. Take care with the leftist sentiments ("lo comunistoide")! For this reason I am separated now from many people who pass over one with ease and even drag one, without one being aware of it, toward the communist menace, toward the contagion.

Mexico is a great democracy and for this reason I am with you and for this reason I thought that I could write in the democratic newspapers there. It cannot be? Well, patience. That cannot alter my intimate affections and my intimate beliefs.

Moreover, art and intelligence are above all this, they have their indestructible future and the victory will be definitely theirs because among other things they take control and put their stamp on all the victories.

Reyes, meanwhile, had been trying to set up some arrangement for Ramón, but without success. He found that his letters to newspaper editors were being ignored. He was touched and upset by Ramón's declaration:

> Please, Ramón, do not feel the necessity to reveal to me your credo and to explain to me your criterion in relation to the things that happen, since I understand everything perfectly; and also I beg you not to relate the inattention of my friends with this matter, nor suppose for an instant that in Mexico there has been any express negative to my request; simply, they have not paid any attention to me because they are lazy and because, evidently, I chose a bad route.
>
> Do not fear either that the fact that others do not understand you affects in the least my admiration and affection for you. And do not think that I could fall under contaminations foreign to the line which, even if I did not know how to draw it for myself, would be drawn for me by those who have the right to do so in Mexico. (April 16, 1937)

Ramon's constant faith in Reyes is manifest in his answer: "You must pardon me this confidential whim since I am so absolutely the same man of those times—neither my position nor my poverty has changed—that I dare to treat you like one of those times because

I know that there is something invariable in you above all things"
(1937).

It seemed that Reyes' close friend Genaro Estrada might be able
to help in the Mexican matter and Reyes immediately wrote to him
—one of the many letters he wrote in his friend's behalf: "If you
would like to help him from Mexico, you could do it very well by
getting some solvent newspaper to ask for and pay him for frequent
articles, so many per month. I have written various letters along
these lines to Manuel Sierra, since Ramón was interested in 'El
Universal.' But Manuel never answers me and our poor friend has
begun to imagine that there is some predisposition against him in
Mexico. You will well understand the state of mind in which he
finds himself" (April 16, 1937).

Actually, as Reyes admitted to Ramón years later, it was himself against whom the Mexican newspapers were predisposed: "You
should know that, on my return, and for no less than three years,
the newspapers not only closed their doors to me but attacked me
every day, moved by stupid 'nationalistic' motives, to make me pay
for a grave sin, that of dedicating my efforts to finding a place for
the many Spaniards, companions in letters, whom the political
currents had carried to Mexico" (1942).

It was hard for Ramón to live in the present and to keep his
faith in the future during these difficult years, when everything
was politicized and everyone had to be of one band or the other.
He was a man who had always put his profession above all things
and tried to keep himself completely untouched by any extra-
artistic influences. He had written don Alfonso in 1916: "The
greatest act of dignity we can accomplish is that of recognizing, of
elevating, of fixing the pure spirit above all the rest, separating it
truly, ostensibly, irrefutably from the rest, basing ourselves, for
this, on interior, immovable proofs." He placed primary importance on the inalienable independence of the writer. He had remained faithful personally and in his writing to a belief in art for
art's sake and would have found this a simple task had the world
been organized as he would have liked. Torre comments on this

point: "His ideal world is a world in which nothing happens . . . so that public attention can freely converge upon his literature, publishing a book each month and having available a morning and an evening paper where his variations would appear without interruptions."[23] But this was far from the case in June, 1938, when he wrote Reyes:

> I am still sticking to my opinions. I want to see and know up to what point an independent writer can exist, one who mixes his opinions, mixed in one way or the other according to his conviction of his duty, since the truth is that I believe it is not worthwhile to live, it is not pleasant nor fitting to live, if one does not have this independence, being a writer.
>
> Life here is ever more difficult and the values of the world of our tongue and some of the others having been put in the balance, nothing and nobody answers. Only mercenary soldiers from one and the other side like each other, as long as they are decidedly sectarian.
>
> I know that this has always been the case, but there remained a margin in life for the inspired ones, for the moonstruck who made their moonschemes—pardon me for wanting to join those two words which are so fond of one another—but now, nothing, nothing.

And it was true that in an epoch of literature of commitment the pure artist had little chance to interest the public. If Gómez de la Serna had remained completely apolitical, abiding by his belief in the writer's superior freedom of spirit, such a stand would have been completely defensible, but when he visited Madrid in 1949 he isolated himself from many of his old companions by making statements in favor of Franco. His definition of himself as an enemy of violence is perhaps the best explanation that can be given for this. Reyes understood it thus, calling him in 1937 " a spirit frankly democratic and open to the legitimate love of the people, but driven away by the violence that his sensibility cannot tolerate." He adds: "This tragedy is that of many Spanish intellec-

---

[23] Torre, "Picasso y Ramón: paralelismos y divergencias," *Hispania* 45 (December 1962): 610.

tuals."[24] As Ramón had perceived years earlier, there was no malice in Reyes, who did his best to help Ramón adjust to life in America, just as he did for those Spanish companions who came to Mexico.

On Reyes' return to Mexico, Ramón wrote in farewell: "My future books will go there to find you, and your old admirer and friend will always think of you in his solitary and intellectual hours" (1937–1938). Ramón was to think of Mexico with nostalgia throughout the years, for, although he had never visited it and never did, so many companions of his youth were there. "Writing to Mexico," he told Reyes in one of his letters, "is like writing to a Madrid that is in another place but that has the spirit of Alarcón and Lope" (n.d.). He saw Mexico in those years as a happier land, perhaps in part because he imagined Reyes' life as a happier one than his own. He wrote in 1938: "I do not know why it seems to me that after all that has happened we have become closer and that you are creating literary things with the clarity and subtlety of the good moments. . . . I imagine you happy in your clear and moving Mexico, where the joy of life is still true."

The same feeling pervades his next letter, of 1939:

Many thanks for the sending of your new book, in which I have reread with delight many things that I had known but that, because of their definitiveness, will always be admissible.

I follow Mexican life from some of its magazines and it gives one literary optimism to see how intellectualism is alive there in these times. I imagine you at the side of Canedo, Salazar, Jarnés, Ontañón, and other friends, and I beg you to give my greetings to all of them.

I continue my sinuous and difficult life, precisely because I am faithful to a straightforward independence and a faith that every day takes the circumstances less into account. Just as you left me I continue: a sorry sight and this in spite of the fact that I throw seeds toward all the horizons. Nothing affirms itself, nothing has continuity, nothing has the slightest solidity.

[24] Unpublished letter to Genaro Estrada, April 16, 1937.

My intimate happiness continues, however, and I am an optimist.

In these days I see much of José Ortega y Gasset, who it seems is going to stay here a while. I also have been with don Ramón [Menéndez Pidal], who is now going directly to Spain.

I imagine you dedicated to the simple life of a writer and patriot, full also of intimate satisfactions, and thus I send many greetings to your wife and son. (November, 1939)

Reyes recognized the attenuated sadness that pervaded Ramón's words:

It grieves me, although it does not surprise me, to find sorrow between the lines of your letter of November last. The truth is that we are passing through the worst moment of our life.

Yes, here we are doing what is possible in order that intellectual life may breathe, but don't think that we accomplish it without struggle and sacrifice. We are only sustained, like yourself, by an unbreakable faith.

I did not know that don Ramón was there nor that he had decided to return to Spain. Perhaps it is too late for me to send him my greetings. I beg you to do so if he is still there.

An embrace, full of admiration and affection, for José Ortega y Gasset, from whom I am anxious to receive news. (December 6, 1939)

There are fewer letters in the 1940's and 1950's, though don Alfonso, prompted by a rereading of Gómez de la Serna's old letters, wrote him during this period:

Time has passed, much water has gone under the bridge: I read you wherever I find you and there comes to mind memories of our old and good Madrid friendship and of those days when I dedicated to you that little essay collected in my *Simpatías y diferencias*.

When we were together in Buenos Aires, there were many clouds on the horizon, and I think that they made me more gloomy and even more stupid than usual.

.   .   .   .

Time has passed and the waters have calmed. I begin to live in my memories. I examine a handful of your old letters. I feel the nostalgia of our good relationship of old. Let us not let the grass grow any more on the paths. Send me a word, let me know that you also feel yourself my friend, and know that I always admire and have affection for you.

The reply he received was no less affectionate and nostalgic:

What has happened to us is that there is not time to write each other when there is so much to write.

.   .   .   .

Magnificent your house and its nooks for meditation and verification.

I have to write now, to be able to live in days of so much inflation, more than 30 articles a month, and I want them all to be inspired. Can you imagine that a good opportunity to publish came up for me in Mexico and, with great sorrow, I could not do it.

The days that go by are more arduous for me than those of before, but they are not for me so unhappy.

I am going to stay until I die in the peace of America.

Wishing you very happy days with your wife, your son, and all your family, do not doubt that you are appreciated as in those first days in Madrid by your admirer who embraces you.

There is no doubt that memories of happiness shared in the past were the bond that kept them close to each other until the end. Gómez de la Serna's last note to Reyes, thanking him for books and reprints and wishing him happiness in the New Year, was written but a few days before don Alfonso's death.

Mexico and Spain

DON ALFONSO ONCE WROTE to a friend, and not altogether in jest, that he was convinced that "the only serious contact between Mexico and Spain, after Hernán Cortés, and if one excepts the bullfighter Rodolfo Gaona, . . . [had] been established by . . . [him], living ten years in Madrid."[1] He did exaggerate, but not as much as one would think. Many Spanish Americans had passed through Madrid, many had lived there, and some had established connections with literary groups, but very few had penetrated into the circle of serious and dedicated writers. Reyes' friends had been dazzled by the brilliance and bohemianism of Rubén Darío and had admired the erudition of the Mexican scholar Francisco A. de Icaza. But Reyes represented something unique in their experience with Latin Americans: a free and open spirit who was at the same time a figure of refinement and culture, a man of dignity and in-

[1] Letter to Amado Alonso, March 6, 1932.

tegrity. He was different from them but not adverse, stimulating but not antagonistic; they could consider him one of themselves.

Because of the bonds of sympathy that soon united him to the Spanish intellectuals, he was able to help dispel certain of their prejudices concerning the Latin American. Rivas Cherif called him "the most wise, most understanding and European of all those who came, with the century, to give their reply to the Spanish conquistadors, winning us, not by undermining the ground at our feet, not by attacking hard and at the head, but, agile fencers, by touching our hearts."[2] Eugenio d'Ors said that Reyes' greatest accomplishment in Spain was that of disproving, by his own example, the legend of the prevalence of excessive stylistic flourishes in Spanish American writing: "Alfonso Reyes is the one who has wrung the neck of Exuberance and has left clean of its mythical image the ideal map of our America."[3] And, as it was in this instance, so it was in the case of other of the myths about Spanish America against which Reyes waged a constant war. "It is up to the American writers who live here," he wrote, ". . . to rectify, for the Spanish reader, the fable of America" (IV, 339).

Reyes was eminently successful in this task, for he shared with Unamuno the role of cultural ambassador for Latin America long before he re-entered the diplomatic service. Pursuing the same goal of popular cultural dissemination that had been of deep concern to him since his days in the Athenaeum of Youth in Mexico, he fomented mutual comprehension between the two hemispheres both in his newspaper work and in his later diplomatic capacity. Typical of his efforts and of the informal yet informative journalism he practiced with such success is the essay in which, with refreshing candor, he ponders "Sobre una epidemia retórica" (On a Rhetorical Epidemic):

> There is nothing more discredited here than sermons on Hispanoamericanism, than campaigns to "tighten the intercontinental ties," than the Days of the Race, than the interchange of rhetorical

[2] Cipriano Rivas Cherif, "México, lago y volcán," *España* 9, no. 40 (1923): 8.
[3] Eugenio d'Ors, *Nuevo glosario*, I, 911.

streams of confetti from one side of the Atlantic to the other. And
it is natural: from time to time, twenty republics discharge upon
Spain a broadside of adjectives. Spain, whose days of imperial
grandeur are over, suffers in silence. We court her with such
clumsiness! We wear ourselves out calling her Mother, and the
Spain of today is not our Mother, nor can she stand to have us anymore in her lap. The Spain of today is something like our first
cousin and she likes us better as companions for her graceful new
infancy than as official beaux with a flower in the buttonhole and
a ridiculous hat and tailcoat.

The discredit of Americanism in Spain is due to two complementary causes: the ignorance of the emissaries from America and
the ignorance of the official Americanists in charge of receiving
them. . . .

An important Madrid paper pointed out a few days ago the
almost inexplicable uselessness of the Americanist centers in
Spain. And a sardonic writer, a compatriot of ours, commenting
on it, gave me this formula: "The Americanists, with five very
honorable exceptions, are completely ignorant of American matters." (And the magic is in not discovering who the five very
honorable exceptions are.)

. . . And we have not said, in reply to all of this, the only thing
that should be said: that America is very different from Spain,
but that it is, on the earth, the place that is most like Spain; that
where everyone talks now in French or in English, only we have
kept on speaking Spanish; that both of us, those here and those
there, have very little patience, and that having an ocean between
us is a very good idea; that fraternity is a natural thing, and that
it can even become very annoying, but that it is always inevitable,
for which reason it is better to treat with and to know each other
than to threaten each other from afar; that true fraternity excludes
continual protestations of mutual love, and that just as we can say
that America was not independent while it felt the necessity to
accuse Spain, we can also affirm that America will not be the true
sister of Spain while one or the other feels obliged to swear fraternity; . . . and that one should act more and talk less, leaving
good words for the construction of Hell.

The Spain of today is of a moving sobriety. Its dealings are
rapid, schematic. The American recently arrived in this world

feels suddenly the unease of Wells's character in *Mr. Britling Sees It Through*: A Yankee who visits England for the first time. To the recent arrival it seems that the adjectival modes of address are briefer here than in his own land; that they have done away with many solemnities; that there is something rough and masculine in these customs, something that in leisure hours becomes uncomfortable, but that in working hours is of a comforting and knowledgeable convenience; and that, finally, he still needs to learn from Europe a superior and rigorous art: the art of simple elegance, the mathematical art of the straight line, the art of saying "yes" or "no" at once, the art of the naked life. The Spaniard reaches out his hand—somewhat calloused—and the American propagandist, instead of greeting him frankly, pirouettes, throws his hat in the air, kicks up his heels, and then lets go with a discourse!

No: let us do away with these verbal campaigns, and let us begin, in agreement and as close together as possible, the unified campaign of life. (IV, 348–351)

By speaking frankly and sensibly, he opened the way for a more realistic approach to Hispanoamericanism.

Reyes' cultural ambassadorship was not a one-sided affair. As well as awakening Spain to a more realistic view of Latin America, he also was an eager disseminator of the authentic values of Hispanic culture in America. When he returned to Mexico for a short while in 1924, he was full of optimism about the Spanish situation, and of a kind of Hispanic idealism that he wished to impart to his countrymen. The reaction was not cordial, and was just the beginning of the many attacks he was to suffer for his loyalty to *his* Spain and, in fact, for his humanistic interests in general. In an intensive and revealing letter to Amado Alonso, famed scholar who was also part of the Center of Historic Studies, he related:

When I returned from Spain, everyone laughed at me because I assured them that Spain was worth more in every way than our America, because I assured them that great things were going to take place there, etc. etc. The Spanish colony in Mexico City was at the point of making a hostile demonstration against me . . . because in my declarations as a recent arrival I spoke of another

Spain, different from the official one, and assured them that there
were more than enough people in Spain who would want the advanced laws of Mexico. (March 6, 1932)

Certainly this was true of Valle-Inclán, who had angered the same
groups in Mexico as Reyes had.

In this 1932 letter to Alonso, Reyes expressed his solidarity with
the Republic: "I consider myself the prophet of the new Spain in
America, and almost one of those responsible and one of the
authors of the revolution." He repeated frequently the phrase "the
new Spain"; its creators were his friends, and many were to form
a part of the Republican government. As a believer in a regenerated
Mexico, he could easily understand and be understood by the
Spanish reformers. He referred with pride to his position: "Luck
has given me the high honor of incarnating, for the new Spain, the
first friendship of the new Mexico, although without doubt the
most modest. I will yield this honor to no one" (II, 43).

When the Civil War broke out in Spain, imperiling the Republic,
Reyes continued to be its staunch defender, and, as the hopeless-
ness of the cause became apparent, his offers of aid were generous
and immediate. The earlier chapters show how he offered Ortega
his home, how anxious he was to bring the Jiménezes to Mexico,
and how diligent were his efforts to help the poverty-stricken
Gómez de la Serna find new newspaper connections. He also
solicited aid on behalf of Valle-Inclán's widow. Reyes saw very
soon, though, that the problem was too immense for his personal
efforts alone. He had written as much to Jiménez in 1937, saying,
"I had already felt the necessity of helping the dispersed Spanish
intellectuals."

This led him to a correspondence with the President of Mexico,
Lázaro Cárdenas, and culminated in the founding in July of 1938,
by the Mexican government, of La Casa de España, whose name
was later changed, at Reyes' suggestion, to El Colegio de México. It
seems that the Spanish colony in Mexico City that had received
Reyes with hostility earlier, and was now supporting Franco, was

causing difficulties because it also had a Casa de España. But this was a minor problem.

At the end of 1938 Reyes himself returned to live in Mexico, after twenty-five years in Europe and South America. He built himself a magnificent library to live in—he described his house as a library with additions—and settled down to what he called an "unending honeymoon" with his books, which, for the first time, he was able to gather together in one place. The room that contained them, and where he worked and slept, was a welcoming and comfortable one, spacious and sunlit, with six skylights, and surrounded by a second-floor gallery, one end of which formed the balcony where don Alfonso had his work table, always piled high with papers. From this vantage point he would warmly greet his visitors. Friends, old and new, came from near and far to the Alfonsine Chapel, as it was baptized by Díez-Canedo.

Reyes finally had the time to complete projects long suspended, some since 1918 and 1919 in Madrid. He began to organize and publish his complete works. "Chance has put me in charge of a gentleman," he told Guillermo de Torre during one visit, "who is called by my name. I have to take care of his affairs, I have to collect matters that refer to him, pleasing or unpleasing, for God will choose his own. . . . I think I have the right to take inventory of my life."[4] Reyes had set up his tent in Mexico, as Juan Ramón would have said, after his years of wandering. He soon found, though, that it was no longer the clear valley he had described nostalgically in *Visión de Anáhuac*. A year after his return he wrote in despair his "Palinode of Dust," in which he asks wonderingly "Is this the most transparent region of the air? What have you done then with my high metaphysical valley? Why is it blurred, why is it yellowing?"[5] And one of his Mexican friends indirectly confirmed the change by saying, "I have often had the feeling, as I made my way to the Colegio de México, that the transparency of the air in our Valley

[4] Quoted in Guillermo de Torre, *Tres conceptos de literatura hispanoamericana*, p. 78.
[5] Alfonso Reyes, *Ancorajes*, p. 29.

of Mexico is a phenomenon that exists only because Alfonso Reyes will have it so."[6]

The first official position given him on his arrival in Mexico was the presidency of the Colegio de México, which he retained until his death twenty years later. He never lost his original personal interest in the aims of the Colegio. "I did not want them to suffer what I had suffered, those who one day shared there with me their scanty resources," he had written to Ortega in 1947, referring to the hardships of his early years in Spain under circumstances similar to those of the Spanish refugees. "I arrived in Spain," he wrote in the introduction to his *Tertulia de Madrid,* "leaving behind grim horizons. My Spanish friends alleviated my sorrows and helped me to persist in my true vocation."[7] The atmosphere of Madrid had given him the opportunity to follow his own interests in the way he chose, for it was an atmosphere of freedom. Don Alfonso recognized this as a decisive factor: "My Madrid epoch corresponded, with rare and providential exactitude, to my desire for emancipation. I wanted to be who I was, and not someone forced to follow other people's wishes. Thanks to Madrid, I achieved it."[8]

He also gained something else from his association with the Spanish writers and his life in Madrid. There was in the Spanish spirit a certain sobriety, a directness, a force toward severity and self-discipline, that had a decided influence on his attitude toward his profession. He attempted to describe the change in his character and in his outlook in this passage: "I am acquiring something of iron inside, and since in great part I owe it to Spain—not, you should note, to the literary academies: to my writer friends, to the street, to the people, to the towns, to the live rock of the soil, to the pure electricity of the air—I thank Spain for it."[9]

The model for the Colegio was itself a Spanish one. Reyes created

[6] Wilberto Cantón in "Our Alfonso Reyes," *Books Abroad* 19, no. 2 (1945): 122.

[7] Reyes, *Tertulia de Madrid,* p. 10.

[8] Reyes, "Historia documental de mis libros," *Universidad de México* 9, no. 7 (1955): 16.

[9] Ibid., 10, no. 5 (1956): 17.

the Colegio de México in the image of his beloved Center for Historical Studies in Madrid—he so described it to Menéndez Pidal. He must have felt very nostalgic at times. Walter Starkie writes that "Reyes' tertulia in the Colegio de México, owing to the presence of the Spanish writers, recalled the ancient tertulias of the Calle de Alcalá, but from a tertulia it had been sublimated into a symposium in which Alfonso Reyes played the part of Socrates."[10]

The Colegio became, under his direction, a private non-profit corporation dedicated to humanistic studies, a home and a haven for the investigative and creative talents of the intellectual elite who would promote the development of the human sciences in Mexico. "Its function," Reyes wrote, "is to invite to Mexico and make available to all the culture centers of the country the Spanish scholars, professors, and writers of note who thereby constitute its staff of 'Resident Members.' . . . At the same time it endeavors to secure the aid of the most distinguished Mexican intellectual leaders, who are thus placed in contact and collaboration with the Spaniards."[11] It sponsors lectures and seminars, has published many important studies, is the home of several journals, and now gives courses leading to advanced degrees. Its aims and interests have developed over the years. There are no rigid, preconceived plans to be carried out, as both Reyes and José Gaos, one of the founding members, were careful to point out. Flexibility and adaptability are one of the secrets of its success, its evolution, and its permanence. Another was the eminence of its original collaborators, some of the most highly esteemed men of letters and men of science of Spain.

Reyes' guiding hand, his sagacity, his tact, and his equilibrium were, of course, no small factor in the renown which the Colegio de México was to achieve and maintain. These are the qualities that had aroused the admiration of his Spanish friends in the early years, and that Gaos again had occasion to note in relation to

[10] Walter Starkie, "A Memoir of Alfonso Reyes," *Texas Quarterly* 2, no. 1 (1959): 77.
[11] Reyes, "The 'Casa de España en México,' " *Books Abroad* 13, no. 4 (1939): 415.

Reyes' presidency of the Colegio. He talks of his "imperturbably comprehensive and conciliatory attitude—principally with the Spaniards, frequently so touchy, so inopportune and impertinent, so rough: how well he knew us," he adds, "and he always succeeded in dominating us, that is to say, in calming us, in orienting us, in guiding us, without it seeming so: because in Spain he had learned to esteem us for our virtues, of which he had experienced the good deeds, and, thanks to them, to pardon us our defects."[12] The example Gaos gives of Reyes' tact is an amusing one. One day in the Colegio he received a commission of students who requested urgently that he buy them expensive metal files for their notes. His response was immediate. Everyone in the Center for Historical Studies in Madrid, he told them, from Ramón Menéndez Pidal on down, kept their notes in shoe boxes, without this at all impairing their accuracy and usefulness. The group dropped its request.

This good sense, good will, *and* good humor were sorely taxed during the early years of the Colegio, when, as Reyes wrote Ortega, he had never been more abused in his life, by extremists of both sides. Therefore, it is all the more noteworthy that the Colegio still stands today as a living memorial to Reyes' love and understanding for Spain *and* Mexico, to his lifelong mission of promoting intellectual and spiritual ties between the two continents, and to his belief in the future of America. It is one of his greatest achievements.

It seems fitting to cite here a passage from Reyes' introduction to an unusual bibliography published in 1947. It listed the work in America of the exiled Spanish intellectuals. Reyes saw the significance of this work in the light of his own idea of America: "Every day and in every tone we repeat that the mission of America—whose very birth was illuminated by the lights of Utopia and the desire to create a dwelling place for a more just and happy humanity—has for its supreme destiny that of serving as an asylum and a new field for the fecund seeds educated in the soil that the tempests of the world have devastated. . . . It is true that

---

[12] José Gaos, "Alfonso Reyes y el Colegio de México," "Boletín Capilla Alfonsina" no. 7 (31 March 1968): 19.

America turns out to be a propitious land; it is true that it opens itself, generously, toward hope" (VIII, 111).

His views on America had been reshaped by his stay in Spain, an experience similar to that of several other Spanish American essayists who had spent some time in Europe.[13] It can be described as having fomented his natural universalist tendencies. It did not cause him to push aside his Mexicanism, as had so often been said. It did not turn him into a Spaniard, but into an Hispanic. Here, for instance, is the testimony of one of his Spanish colleagues: "In Spain . . . he was looked upon from his arrival as a Spaniard, although he was careful at all times to let us know that he was a Mexican, which ended up convincing us that there was another and better way to be a Spaniard."[14] And this is exactly the spirit of what Reyes said of himself in his letter to Amado Alonso:

> My national sentiment passes through the sieve of Mexico, where it leaves a few grains of gold in the straining (of Indian gold, my maternal portion of "mestizaje") and it continues flowing toward the Spanish bottom. Do I make myself clear? . . . I consider myself a Spaniard with nuance. My decided propensity toward gentleness and agreeable things is not very Castilian, it seems a contamination from the French, and perhaps it is a personal elaboration of the Mexican. But what Spaniard is not so with his own distinct nuance? So that, for me, being Mexican comes to mean possessing a legitimate title of Spaniard.

He reveals similar sentiments in a letter to Díez-Canedo: "When I turn my eyes to my land I see it and I understand it as such a natural prolongation of Spain! Going to Spain was for me entering more into Mexico. The two loves are fused within me, and nothing will be able to separate them" (January 15, 1932).

The natural corollary of his personal experience, of his penetration into the essence of Mexico through the experience of Spain, is his belief that the foundations of his being, and that of every Spanish American, were Hispanic. It was in Spain that he was to

[13] Martin Stabb (*In Quest of Identity*, p. 74) mentions the European experience of José Vasconcelos and Octavio Paz, among others.

[14] Federico de Onís, "Alfonso Reyes," *Sur* 18, no. 186 (1950): 21.

look for and find the roots of his own culture, taking cognizance of the significance of the Hispanic and the Mexican elements as they applied to himself, and of the "simpatías" and "diferencias" that were essential to his way of being. For Reyes was to see in Hispanism, if not the basis, at least the transmitter of those ideas that were responsible for his personal cultural formation and that of Spanish America as a whole. The Hispanic traditions were his link with the fundamental values of Latin culture. The Mexican spirit, Reyes said, "is in the color that the Latin water, just as it arrived to us, acquired here, in our house, as it flowed during three centuries licking the red clay of our earth" (XI, 161).

His broad humanistic outlook was a most needed tonic in the excessively chauvinistic atmosphere of the Mexico to which he returned. He spoke out against any limit to intellectual curiosity in the name of misguided nationalism: "To think that only that which expresses and systematically accentuates its exterior aspect of Mexicanism is Mexican is a true puerility," he wrote. "Whatever I may do belongs to my land to the same degree that I belong to it." And finally: "Nothing can be foreign to us but that which we are ignorant of."[15]

Spain had given Reyes a great gift—liberty and independence. It permitted him to see Mexico and Mexicanism in perspective. It freed him from what he once called his "Mexican wounds." The identification he felt with Spain and the Hispanic world as a whole permitted him to project his Mexicanism on a universal scale of values. Do I not have the right, he once asked, to cast upon the Mexican landscape the light of Vergil or of Goethe? He is not an international writer, but, in the terms of Juan Ramón Jiménez, a universal one, that is, one who has deep roots in his native land, yet in his work projects outward. Reyes understood this well. He wrote: "The profound roots, unconscious and involuntary, are in my Mexican being: it is a fact and not a virtue. . . . The universal heritage is mine by right of love and by a dedication to study and work, the only authentic qualification."[16]

[15] Reyes, *La X en la frente*, pp. 62, 61, 57.
[16] Reyes, *Parentalia*, p. 17.

His Spanish friendships set the pattern for the whole of his life. They are the most telling proof of a statement he was to make in later years that aptly describes his way of being: "My home is the earth. I never felt profoundly foreign in any country, though always somewhat a shipwrecked soul of the planet. . . . I am the brother of many men, and I am on intimate terms with people of various countries. Wherever I was I felt myself bound with true ties."[17]

[17] Ibid., p. 16.

BIBLIOGRAPHY

Adams, Mildred. "First Lady." *New York Times Book Review*, 2 October 1966, pp. 38, 40, 42.

Alonso, Amado. "Alfonso Reyes." *Sur* 6, no. 23 (1936): 120–123.

Aub, Max. "Retrato de Unamuno, para uso de principiantes." *Ínsula* 19, no. 216–217 (1964): 4, 14

Azorín. "Azorín habla de la personalidad literaria de Alfonso Reyes." In *Páginas sobre Alfonso Reyes*. 2 vols. Edited by Alfonso Rangel Guerra and José Ángel Rendón. Monterrey: Universidad de Nuevo León, 1955–1957.

Barrios, Roberto. Interview with Valle-Inclán for *El Universal* (Mexico City), reprinted in *Repertorio Americano* 3, no. 13 (28 November 1921).

Blanco Aguinaga, Carlos. *El Unamuno contemplativo*. Mexico City: El Colegio de México, 1959.

Cardona, Rodolfo. *Ramón. A Study of Gómez de la Serna and His Works*. New York: Eliseo Torres and Sons, 1957.

Cela, Camilo José. *Cuatro figuras del 98 y otros retratos y ensayos españoles*. Barcelona: Editorial Aedos, 1961.

Chacón y Calvo, José María. *Ensayos sentimentales*. San José de Costa Rica: Biblioteca Repertorio Americano, 1923.

Correa Calderón, E. "Ramón en el recuerdo." *Ínsula* 18, no. 196 (1963): 3.

Díaz-Plaja, Guillermo. *Las estéticas de Valle-Inclán*. Madrid: Editorial Gredos, 1965.

"Digesto sobre Alfonso Reyes." P.E.N. Club de México, Volante no. 14 (31 May 1924).

Durán, Manuel. "Actualidad de *Tirano Banderas*." *Mundo Nuevo*, no. 10 (April 1967): 49–54.

Esplá, Carlos. "Vida y nostalgia de Unamuno en el destierro." *La Torre* 9, no. 35–36 (1961): 117–145.

Ferreter Mora, José. *Ortega y Gasset. An Outline of his Philosophy*. London: Bowers and Bowers, 1956.

Fichter, William L., ed. *Publicaciones periodísticas de don Ramón del Valle-Inclán anteriores a 1895.* Mexico City: El Colegio de Mexico, 1952.

Frank, Waldo, *Virgin Spain.* New York: Boni and Liveright, 1926.

Gaos, José. "Alfonso Reyes y el Colegio de México." "Boletín Capilla Alfonsina" no. 7, 31 March 1968: 18–23.

———. "Carta abierta a Alfonso Reyes." *El Nacional* (Mexico City), 21 September 1947.

Garasa, Delfín Leocadio. "Los empeños teatrales de Unamuno." *Ínsula* 19, no. 216–217 (1964): 23.

García Blanco, Manuel. *América y Unamuno.* Madrid: Editorial Gredos, 1964.

———. "Don Miguel y la Universidad." *Cuadernos de la Cátedra de Miguel de Unamuno* 13 (1963): 13–32.

Gillespie, Gerald, and Anthony Zahareas. "Valle-Ínclán." *Kenyon Review* 29, no. 5 (1967): 610–613.

Gómez de la Serna, Gaspar. *Ramón (Obra y vida).* Madrid: Taurus Ediciones, 1963.

Gómez de la Serna, Ramón. *Automoribundia (1888–1948).* Buenos Aires: Editorial Sudamericana, 1948.

———. *Don Ramón María del Valle-Inclán.* Buenos Aires: Espasa-Calpe Argentina, 1944.

———. *Pombo.* Madrid: Imprenta, Mesón de Paños 8, 1918.

———. *Retratos contemporáneos.* Buenos Aires: Editorial Sudamericana, 1941.

———. *La Sagrada Cripta de Pombo.* Madrid: Imprenta G. Hernandez y Galo Sáenz, n.d. [1924]. [This was called vol. 2 of *Pombo.*]

———. *Total de greguerías.* Madrid: Aguilar, 1955.

Gullón, Ricardo. *Autobiografías de Unamuno.* Madrid: Editorial Gredos, 1964.

———. *Conversaciones con Juan Ramón Jiménez.* Madrid: Taurus Ediciones, 1958.

———. *De Goya al arte abstracto.* Río Piedras, Puerto Rico: Editorial Universitaria, 1963.

———. *Direcciones del modernismo.* Madrid: Editorial Gredos, 1963.

———. *Estudios sobre Juan Ramón Jiménez.* Buenos Aires: Editorial Losada, 1960.

———. Introduction to Juan Ramón Jiménez, *Three Hundred Poems, 1903–1953.* Translated by Eloïse Roach. Austin: University of Texas Press, n.d. [1962].

———. "La novela personal de don Miguel de Unamuno." *La Torre* 9, no. 35–36 (1961): 93–115.

————. "Técnicas de Valle-Inclán." *Papeles de Sons Armadans* 127 (October 1966): 21–86.

————. *Última lección de Unamuno.* Santander: Cantalapiedra, 1964.

————. *El último Juan Ramón.* Madrid: Ediciones Alfaguara, 1968.

Guzmán, Martín Luis. *Obras completas.* 2 vols. Mexico City: Compañía General de Ediciones, 1961, 1963.

Henríquez Ureña, Pedro. *Obra crítica.* Mexico City: Fondo de Cultura Económica, 1960.

Hernández Luna, Juan, ed. *Conferencias del Ateneo de la Juventud.* Mexico City: Centro de Estudios Filosóficos, Universidad Nacional Autónoma de México, 1962.

Huxley, Aldous. "Meditation on El Greco." In *Collected Essays.* New York: Bantam Books, 1960.

Iglesias, Ignacio. "Valle-Inclán, de nuevo." *Mundo Nuevo,* no. 5 (November 1966): 76–78.

Jiménez, Juan Ramón. *La corriente infinita.* Edited by Francisco Garfias. Madrid: Aguilar, 1961.

————. *Cuadernos de Juan Ramón Jiménez.* Edited by Francisco Garfias. Madrid: Taurus Ediciones, 1960.

————. *Españoles de tres mundos.* Edited by Ricardo Gullón. Madrid: Afrodisio Aguado, 1960.

————. *El trabajo gustoso.* Edited by Francisco Garfias. Mexico City: Aguilar, 1961.

Jiménez-Fraud, Alberto. "The 'Residencia de Estudiantes.' " Translated by Robert Williams. *Texas Quarterly* 4, no. 1 (1961): 48–54.

Machado, Antonio. *Poesías completas.* Buenos Aires: Editorial Losada, 1958.

Madrid, Francisco. *La vida altiva de Valle-Inclán.* Buenos Aires: Poseidón, 1943.

Marías, Julián. *Ortega. Circunstancia y vocación.* Madrid: Revista de Occidente, 1960.

————. "La voz de Unamuno y el problema de España." *La Torre* 9, no. 35–36 (1961): 147–156.

Martínez, José Luis, ed. *El ensayo mexicano moderna.* 2 vols. Mexico City: Fondo de Cultura Económica, 1958.

Mejía Sánchez, Ernesto. "Más sobre Unamuno y Reyes." *Boletín de la Biblioteca Nacional* 15, no. 3–4 (1964): 7–23.

Millán, María del Carmen. "La generación del Ateneo y el ensayo mexicano." *Nueva Revista de Filología Hispánica* 15, no. 3–4 (1961): 625–636.

Olson, Paul R. *Circle of Paradox: Time and Essence in the Poetry of Juan Ramón Jiménez.* Baltimore: The Johns Hopkins Press, 1967.

Onís, Federico de. "Alfonso Reyes." *Sur* 18, no. 186 (1950): 17–22.

———. "Introducción." *La Torre* 9, no. 35–36 (1961): 13–20.

Ors, Eugenio d'. *Nuevo glosario.* 3 vols. Madrid: Aguilar, 1947.

Ortega y Gasset, Eduardo. *Monodiálogos de Unamuno.* New York: Ediciones Ibérica, 1958.

Ortega y Gasset, José. *La deshumanización del arte. Ideas sobre la novela.* Madrid: Revista de Occidente, 1925.

———. *El espectador.* Madrid: Biblioteca Nueva, 1950.

———. *Obras completas.* 11 vols. Madrid: Revista de Occidente, 1958–1969.

"Our Alfonso Reyes." A symposium by Waldo Frank, Albert Guerard, Muna Lee, Ramón Sender, Tomás Navarra, Rafael Heliodoro Valle, Alberto Rembao, Antonio Castro Leal, José Luis Martínez, Wilberto Cantón. *Books Abroad* 19, no. 2 (1945): 111–124.

Pérez de Ayala, Ramón. "Los muertos del año." *La Prensa* (Buenos Aires), 28 February 1937, section 2.

Reyes, Alfonso. *Albores. Segundo libro de recuerdos.* Mexico City: El Cerro de la Silla, 1960.

———. *Ancorajes.* Mexico City: Tezontle, 1951.

———. *Burlas veras. Primer ciento.* Mexico City: Tezontle, 1957.

———. "Carta de Alfonso Reyes." *La Torre* 5, no. 19–20 (1957): 17–18.

———. "The 'Casa de España en México.' " *Books Abroad* 13 (Autumn 1939): 414–417.

———. *Cortesía.* Mexico City: Cultura, 1948.

———. "Historia documental de mis libros." *Universidad de México* 9, no. 7 (1955): 1–2, 10–16; 9, no. 8 (1955): 7–10; 9, no. 9 (1955): 1–2, 10–13; 10, no. 5 (1956): 16–18; 11, no. 6 (1957): 22–24; 11, no. 7 (1957): 11–12.

———. *Mallarmé entre nosotros.* Mexico City: Tezontle, 1955.

———. *Marginalia, Segunda serie.* Mexico City: Tezontle, 1954.

———. "Mis relaciones con Unamuno." *Cuadernos de la Cátedra de Miguel de Unamuno* 6 (1955): 5–8.

———. *Obras completas.* 19 vols. Mexico City: Fondo de Cultura Económica, 1955–1968.

———. *Oración del 9 de febrero.* Mexico City: Ediciones Era, 1963.

———. *Parentalia. Primer capítulo de mis recuerdos.* Los Presentes, no. 5. Mexico City: Imprenta de Juan Pablos, 1954.

———. *The Position of America and Other Essays.* Translated by Harriet de Onís, foreword by Federico de Onís. New York: Alfred A. Knopf, 1950.

———. *Quince presencias. 1915–1954.* Mexico City: Obregón, 1955.

————. *Tertulia de Madrid.* Colección Austral, No. 901. Buenos Aires: Espasa-Calpe Argentina, 1949.

————. "Treno para José Ortega y Gasset." *Cuadernos Americanos* 85, no. 1 (1956): 65–67.

————. "La 'tzantza' de Valle-Inclán." "Biblioteca Alfonsina" no. 6–7 (June–July 1959): 1–2.

————. *La X en la frente.* Mexico City: Porrúa y Obregón, 1952.

Río, Angel del. *Historia de la literatura española.* 2 vols. 2d ed., rev. New York: Holt, Rinehart and Winston, 1963.

Río, Angel del, and M. J. Benardete, eds. *El concepto contemporáneo de España, Antología de ensayos.* Buenos Aires: Editorial Losada, 1946.

Rivas Cherif, Cipriano. "La comedia bárbara de Valle-Inclán." *España* 10, no. 409 (1924): 8.

————. "México, lago y volcán," *España* 9, no. 401 (1923): 8.

Robb, James Willis. *Patterns of Image and Structure in the Essays of Alfonso Reyes.* Washington, D.C.: The Catholic University of America Press, 1958.

Rubia Barcia, José. *A Biobibliography and Iconography of Valle-Inclán.* University of California Publications in Modern Philology, vol. 59. Berkeley: University of California Press, 1960.

————. "The Esperpento: a New Novelistic Dimension." In *Valle-Inclan Centennial Studies.* Edited by Ricardo Gullón. Austin: The University of Texas, 1968.

Rubia Barcia, José, and M. A. Zeitlin, eds. *Unamuno. Creator and Creation.* Berkeley: University of California Press, 1967.

Salcedo, Emilio. *Vida de Don Miguel.* Salamanca: Ediciones Anaya, 1964.

Salinas, Pedro. "Significación del esperpento o Valle-Inclán, hijo pródigo del 98." *Atenea* 164 (October–December 1966): 101–125.

Sánchez-Barbudo, Antonio. *La segunda época de Juan Ramón Jiménez.* Madrid: Editorial Gredos, 1962.

"El silencio por Mallarmé." *Revista de Occidente* 2, no. 5 (1923): 238–256.

Speratti Piñero, Emma Susana. *La elaboración artística en Tirano Banderas.* Mexico City: El Colegio de Mexico, 1957.

————. "Valle-Inclán y México." *Historia mexicana* 8, no. 29 (1958): 60–80.

Stabb, Martin S. *In Quest of Identity.* Chapel Hill: The University of North Carolina Press, 1967.

Starkie, Walter. "A Memoir of Alfonso Reyes." *Texas Quarterly* 2, no. 1 (1959): 67–77.

"Testimonios inéditos de maestros, compañeros, discípulos y amigos

acerca de la persona, la obra y la significación de Alfonso Reyes."
La Gaceta 6, no. 65 (1960): 4–5.

Torre, Guillermo de. *La aventura estética de nuestra edad.* Barcelona:
Editorial Seix Barral, 1962.

———. *La difícil universalidad española.* Madrid: Editorial Gredos,
1965.

———. Introduction to Ramón Gómez de la Serna, *Antología: Cincuenta años de literatura.* Buenos Aires: Editoriales Losada, Espasa-Calpe
Argentina, Poseidón, Emecé, Sudamericana, 1955.

———. *Las metamórfosis de Proteo.* Buenos Aires: Editorial Losada,
1956.

———. "Picasso y Ramón: paralelismos y divergencias." *Hispania* 45,
(December 1962): 597–611.

———. *Tres conceptos de literatura hispanoamericana.* Buenos Aires:
Editorial Losada, 1963.

———. "Unamuno crítico de la literatura hispanoamericana." *La
Torre* 9, no. 35–36 (1961): 537–561.

———. "Unamuno, escritor de cartas." *Insula* 19, no. 216–217 (1964):
9.

Unamuno, Miguel de. *De esto y de aquello.* 4 vols. Edited by Manuel
García Blanco. Buenos Aires: Editorial Sudamericana, 1950–1954.

———. *Del sentimiento trágico de la vida.* Colección Austral. Madrid:
Espasa-Calpe, 1967.

———. *Ensayos.* 2 vols. Madrid: Aguilar, 1945.

———. *Obras completas.* 15 vols. Madrid: Afrodisio Aguado, 1958–
1964.

———. "El Unamuno censurado." *La Torre* 9, no. 35–36 (1961): 23–54.

Uría-Santos, Rosa María. "El Ateneo de la Juventud: Su influencia en
la vida intelectual de México." Ph.D. dissertation, University of
Florida, 1965.

Valle-Inclán, Ramón del. "¡Nos vemos!" *Repertorio Americano* 4, no.
17 (17 July 1922).

"Why Spain Deports Unamuno." *Literary Digest* (New York) 81 (21
June 1924): 17.

INDEX